AutoCAD 3D

John W. Gibb

MIS:
PRESS

A Subsidiary of
Henry Holt and Co., Inc.

First Edition—1996

Printed in the United States of America.

Library of Congress Cataloging-in-Publication Data

Gibb, John W.
    AutoCAD 3D / John W. Gibb.
        p.   cm.
    ISBN 1-55828-434-6
    1. Computer graphics. 2. AutoCAD (Computer file) 3. Three-dimensional display systems. I. Title.
    T385.G5215   1995   95-439-58
    620'.0042'02855369—dc20   CIP

10 9 8 7 6 5 4 3 2 1

Associate Publisher: *Paul Farrell*   **Copy Edit Manager**: *Shari Chappell*
Managing Editor: *Cary Sullivan*   **Production Editor:** *Anne Incao*
Acquisitions Editor: *Jono Hardjowirogo*   **Technical Editor:** *Jeff Pilcher*
Development Editors: *Laura Lewin/Andrew Neusner*   **Copy Editor:** *Gwynne Jackson*

Acknowledgments

I would like to thank my girlfriend, Margaret, and her son, Brian, for their patience during another lost summer. Without their support, this book would not have been written. Thanks must be extended to my mother and father for their sharing of their haven of sanity during the pressures of deadlines, conferences, and business trips. My technical editor, Jeff Pilcher, deserves special mention for his contributions above and beyond the call of duty. Thank you to J. C. Malitzke and Don McIntyre at Moraine Valley for support and ideas that made this a better book. Thanks must also go out to my editors and publisher who, with their usual professional and painless process, gave me the opportunity to write this book. A special thanks to Bob Verdun, the owner, and to my fellow employees at Computerized Facility Integration, Inc., for their patience when that glassy-eyed look would appear on my face on Monday morning after a long weekend of writing.

I would like to thank the following companies and institutions for their generous contribution of drawings and ideas for the practices and examples in this book:

Amco Engineering Company, Schiller Park, IL.

CFI, Inc., Chicago, IL.

Interlake Material Handling Division, Lisle, IL.

Moraine Valley ATC, Palos Hills, IL.

Paladin, Midlothian, IL.

CONTENTS

PREFACE..**xiii**

CHAPTER ONE: Display...**1**

What is 2D Viewing and How Does It Relate to 3D Viewing? 2
Visual Clues to Your 3D Position in Space 2
Viewing in the XY Plane 4
Viewing from the XY Plane...6
Control Your Display with the VPOINT Command...7
    The VPOINT Rotate Option 7
    The VPOINT Vector Option...8
    The VPOINT Tripod Option 10
    VPOINT Command Summary 17
    Dynamic View (DVIEW) Command in Perspective....................................17
    The Select objects: Prompt 18
    The Hide Option..19
    The Camera Option 19
    The Target Option..23
    The Distance Option 24
    The Off option 25
    The Points Option..25
    The Pan Option..27
    The Zoom Option...27
    The Twist Option..28
    The Clip Option 29
    The Undo and Exit Options 32
    The Specify a Point Option...32

DVIEW Command Summary 33
Chapter Exercise 33
In Conclusion 34

CHAPTER TWO: Display II 35

Plan View in 3D 35
PLAN Command Menu Locations 39
The UCS Command for Viewing...39
    Practice Procedure for Using Saved Named UCS Coordinates 41
    UCS Command Menu Locations 42
Using UCSFOLLOW to View Your Geometry 44
2D Viewing in 3 Dimensions 45
The PAN Command in the Third Dimension..45
    The PAN Command Menu Locations 47
    The ZOOM Command in the Third Dimension.......................................48
    The ZOOM Command Menu Locations 48
The DDVIEW Command in 3D 50
    Creating Views for Designing..52
    The DDVIEW Command Menu Locations 52
    The DDVIEW Command Summary...54
The VPORTS Command in 3D 54
    Viewports to Assist Your Design...54
    Swapping Views Between Two Viewports 56
    The VPORTS Command Menu Locations...56
    The VPORTS Command Summary 58
Chapter Exercise 58
In Conclusion 58

CHAPTER THREE: Tools for 3D Design..59

Tools...59
    Elevation 60
    The ELEVATION Command Menu Locations...61
    Thickness 61
    The THICKNESS Command Menu Locations 64
    Point Filters 64
    The Point Filters Command Menu Locations 66
    Coordinate Systems...67

Geometric Calculator 68
Object Snaps, Grid/Snap, and Ortho Mode in the 3D Environment 71
The User Coordinate System 71
3D Wireframe Drawing Commands..80
The 3D Polyline 82
Practice Procedure for the 3Dpoly Command 82
In Conclusion 83

CHAPTER FOUR: Wireframe Construction **85**

Creating Geometry Using 3D Primitives 85
The 3D Box AI_BOX Command 86
The Pyramid AI_PYRAMID Command 87
Creating a Wedge with the AI_WEDGE Command.......................................89
The 3D Dome AI_DOME Command 90
Creating a 3D Sphere with the AI_SPHERE Command 91
The 3D Cone Using AI_CONE 91
The 3D Torus Using the AI_TORUS Command 92
The 3D Dish Created by the AI_DISH Command 94
The 3D Surface Primitives Command Menu Locations................................94
Wireframe Construction Techniques...94
Simple 2D Drawing Commands 95
Using the UCS to Create an Object in 3D 97
Using the UCS in Iso View...98
Using the UCSFOLLOW Method 101
Using 3D Surface Primitives to Create a Wireframe Object 102
Chapter Exercise...108
In Conclusion 109

CHAPTER FIVE: Wireframe Editing...**111**

Tools 112
Object Projection Using PROJMODE...115
Object Snaps...119
Align Objects in 3D Using the ALIGN Command 120
The ALIGN Command Menu Locations 123
Rotate Objects Using the ROTATE3D Command 123
The ROTATE3D Command Menu Locations...129
Creating a Duplicate Object with the MIRROR3D Command....................129

The MIRROR3D Command Menu Locations 138
Three-Dimensional Arrays Using the 3DARRAY Command 139
The 3DARRAY Command Menu Locations 144
In Conclusion 144

CHAPTER SIX: 3D Surfaces 145

Hidden Line Removal 145
The HIDE Command Menu Location 147
Placing Surfaces with the 3DFACE Command 147
The 3DFACE Command Menu Location 151
Using the EDGE Command to Hide 3D Face Edges 152
The EDGE Command Menu Location 154
Controlling the Visibility of a Face Edge with DDMODIFY 155
The DDMODIFY Command Menu Location 156
Creating a Polymesh Surface Using the 3DMESH Command 157
The 3DMESH Command Menu Location...159
Produce a Polygon Mesh Using the PFACE Command 160
The PFACE Command Menu Location..160
3D Primitive Object Surface Commands 160
The 3D Primitive Objects Command Menu Location 162
Variables for Controlling Surfaces and Surface Display 163
The SPLFRAME System Variable...163
The SURFTYPE System Variable 164
The SURFU and SURFV System Variables..166
The SURFTAB1 and SURFTAB2 System Variables.............................167
The 3D Surface System Variables Menu Location..................................168
The REVSURF Command..168
The REVSURF Command Menu Locations 171
The TABSURF Command...171
The TABSURF Command Menu Locations 174
The RULESURF Command...174
The RULESURF Command Menu Locations...178
The EDGESURF Command...179
The EDGESURF Command Menu Locations...180
Using the SOLID Command 181
The SOLID Command Menu Location...182
Editing Surfaces 183
Surface Editing Using Basic Editing Tools 183

The PEDIT Command for Editing Meshes..184
The PEDIT Command Menu Location 187
Chapter Exercise 188
In Conclusion 189

CHAPTER SEVEN: Solid Geometry...191

Creating a Region 191
The DELOBJ System Variable 193
The DELOBJ System Variable Menu Location...............................194
Variables for Controlling a Solid Model's Display 195
Control Tessellation Lines with the ISOLINES Variable.........................195
Control the Mesh Density of Renderings with the FACETRES Variable....197
Control Silhouette Edges with the DISPSILH Variable 198
Solids Display Variables Summary...199
Solid Model's Display Variables Menu Location...................................200
Creating Geometry Using Solids Primitives 200
The BOX Command...201
The SPHERE Command 204
The CYLINDER Command 205
The CONE Command..206
The WEDGE Command 209
The TORUS Command..211
Solid Primitives Menu Location 214
Chapter Exercise..215
In Conclusion 215

CHAPTER EIGHT: Solids Editing Commands 217

Region Editing..218
The SUBTRACT Command...218
The UNION Command..219
The INTERSECT Command...221
The SUBTRACT, UNION, and INTERSECTION Commands
Menu Locations...223
The MASSPROP Command 224
The MASSPROP Menu Command Locations...................................226
The EXTRUDE Command...227
The EXTRUDE Menu Command Locations 231

Regions in Review 232
Solids Editing..232
  The FILLET Command...233
  The CHAMFER Command 234
  The MASSPROP Command 236
  The SUBTRACT Command 237
  The UNION Command 239
  The INTERSECT Command 240
  The SLICE Command...242
  The SECTION Command 258
  The INTERFERE Command 260
  The AMECONVERT Command......................................262
  The SLICE, SECTION, INTERFERE, and
    AMECONVERT Commands Menu Locations 263
In Conclusion..264

CHAPTER NINE: Managing Modeling Issues 265

Expectations of Managers and Users 266
When and What to Model...268
  Architectural Models 268
  Manufacturing Models..270
  Engineering Model..273
  When and What to Model Wrap-Up 275
Staging Model Elements..275
  Libraries of Assemblies 275
  Visual Organization of the Model 276
Dimensioning in 3D..276
  3D Dimensioning in Model Space...........................276
  3D Dimensioning in Paperspace 279
Export File Formats 281
  CAD Output Formats...281
  Image Output File Formats 286
  Solids Output File Format.....................................289
  Surfaces Output File Formats 291
  Export Commands Menu Locations 293
  Export File Formats Wrap-Up 294
Hardware Requirements..294
Software Availability 296

Prototypes..297
In Conclusion...297

CHAPTER TEN: Rendering..299

Setting up for Rendering 299
    Video Setup...303
    Hardware Requirements 305
Rendering Commands and Tools 306
    The RENDER Command..306
    Render Preferences 313
    Render Statistics 314
    Lights..315
    Scenes...331
    Rendering Commands and Tools Menu Locations 333
Chapter Exercise 334
In Conclusion 335

CHAPTER ELEVEN: Rendering Materials...............................337

Controlling Materials 337
    The Materials Library 338
    Materials Properties..349
    Attaching Materials to Objects...355
    Render Materials Commands Menu Locations 362
    Assigning a Material to a Part..362
    Assigning Multiple Materials to Multiple Objects......................364
In Conclusion 366

CHAPTER TWELVE: 3D Prototypes and Toolbars Equal Productivity 367

3D Prototype 367
    Set Up User Coordinate Systems...368
    Set Up Views...371
    Set Up Viewports 373
    Set Up for Rendering 377
Customizing 3D Toolbars...382
    Creating and Editing Toolbars..382
    Meru Hierarchy 382

Productivity Routines 383
In Conclusion 403

GLOSSARY **405**

INDEX **409**

PREFACE

A book of this nature is hard to focus. The presented material requires that you start with an intermediate knowledge of 2D AutoCAD drafting while covering beginning to advanced concepts in 3D. Modeling in 3D and rendering are complex subjects that require many steps of preparatory work before starting a procedure. This book approaches these complex subjects by starting simply and building upon the work. Many of the practice procedures build upon earlier procedures and many chapters build upon earlier chapters. When you cannot complete a series of procedures, you need to save the drawing and settings to a temporary file so you can pick up where you left off at a later date. Never save the practice drawing unless the procedure tells you to do so.

This book is broken into sections. They are wireframe/surfaces, solids, rendering, and productivity through prototypes and toolbars. The wireframe/surfaces and solids sections are broken into three categories: viewing, drawing, and modifying. Each section and category has tools, tips, and techniques intermingled with the commands and the practice procedures.

Most procedures give commands and system variables as keyboard input. The toolbar and menu locations are given at the end of each section. This approach was taken because it is important that you know the name of the command or system variable that you are using (the menu or toolbar selections do not always reflect the name accurately). Several support files are included on the companion disk. Chapter 12 takes you through the creation of many of the buttons and toolbars that are covered in the book. The more advanced user, who is comfortable with the Release 13 toolbars and menu structure, can attach the menu called 3DWORLD using the MENULOAD command to have access to the toolbar buttons during the practice procedures. All of the toolbar buttons on the 3DWORLD menu call the commands and system variables just as if you were typing them at the keyboard.

You can automate the menu loading by adding these two lines to ACAD.LSP or your menu .MNL file.

```
(command ".menuunload" "3dworld")
(command ".menuload" "3dworld")
```

The companion disk to this book contains the drawing files needed for the practice procedures, menus, prototype drawings, bitmaps for the menus, and support routines. The support routines are handy, time-saving routines that allow you to perform the same commands automatically that you normally would have to do by hand. They have been debugged and are stable, but no warranty is implied. They are to be used at your own risk. Most of the routines deal with manipulating viewing, so they should never corrupt any data.

Preparation for using the companion disk's support files is easy. Create a sub-directory called 3DWORLD (this named is recommended because the procedures refer to this directory by name) and add the directory path to your AutoCAD support directory line in the Preferences dialogue box. The support files are contained in a self extracting file called 3DWORLD.EXE. Copy the file into the directory you created and run it. All of the support files are extracted into the directory. You need to make the 3DPROTO drawing supplied on the disk the default prototype drawing for your work sessions.

Chapter 12 walks you through the creation of a 3D prototype drawing based on the mechanical discipline. The resulting prototype drawing is available on the companion disk as 3DSEEDX.DWG. The file is there for your convenience to compare with your prototype drawing when you have completed the practice procedures. The full menu you create in Chapter 12 is also available as 3DWORLDX.MNS for comparison.

The images in this book are gray scale images. Every effort was made to make the color images of the renderings as clear as possible by labeling the image when needed or by explaining the results.

This book was created using AutoCAD R13c3 for Windows on the Windows 95 platform. AutoCAD R13c3 was not written for the Windows 95 platform and some captured images appear without a toolbar header as a result. This is not the fault of Autodesk but of the authors desire to run the software even on an unsupported platform. Autodesk will have an official version of Release 13 for the Windows 95 platform by the time this book is released.

CHAPTER ONE

Display

When moving around in 2 dimensions (2D), the ZOOM, PAN, VIEW, and VIEWPORTS commands are used. Those commands are still used in 3 dimensions (3D) and they will be reviewed in Chapter 2. Three additional commands designed for 3D viewing are present in AutoCAD. Those commands are DVIEW, VPOINT, and PLAN. In this chapter, you are introduced to the 3D viewing commands DVIEW and VPOINT, and given the opportunity to practice using them.

Of the three major categories of working (drawing, editing, and viewing) in 3D space, the viewing category of commands seems to give the most trouble to a novice 3D user. This is a little surprising, since we all live in a 3D world and we interact with it everyday. The problem seems to be one of intuition. We have all moved around in 3D space since birth. The action we take to see or touch something is automatic from a very early age. We do not have to think about it, we just do it. In CAD, you must think about how you are going to move to another spot to better see your object. It is not a natural process that you just do. The commands to alter your view are not hard to learn, but the process of having to think of where you want to be seems unnatural at first. Here you are given the chance to practice the following commands in 3D space:

- Viewpoint
- DVIEW

What is 2D Viewing and How Does It Relate to 3D Viewing?

When you work in 2D, you are always viewing your object from directly above. This view is called the *plan view*; the PLAN command and how it is used in 3D viewing is covered in Chapter 2. Viewing an object in your 2D drawing is much like positioning a camera directly above the object and seeing the object through the camera's lens. The ZOOM command manipulates the camera to a position closer or farther away from your geometry (located *in* the XY plane). The PAN command allows you to move your camera in any direction *in* the XY plane while staying exactly the same distance away from the geometry. The VIEW command allows you to save or restore the camera's position by name. The VPORTS command allows you to save and restore different multi-viewport configurations that can contain different views. You should be familiar with each of these commands and how they work before trying to apply them in 3D space. Chapter 2 briefly reviews the 2D viewing commands and how they work in conjunction with the 3D viewing commands.

Visual Clues to Your 3D Position in Space

2

Autodesk has given you the User Coordinate System (UCS) to work in 3D space. The details for using the coordinate system are discussed later in this chapter. Part of the user coordinate system is the UCS icon, which gives a visual clue to your position as you move around in 3D space. The icon (shown in Figure 1.1) is redundant in 2D space because you know that the positive X axis is to the right and the positive Y axis is pointing up.

FIGURE 1.1 UCS Icon.

The icon seems to bother many users, especially in dense drawings, so they turn it off and forget about it. The icon is important and should remain on when working in 3D space. The command that controls the display of the icon is called UCSICON. The command has several options, including:

- On—view the icon on screen.
- Off—no view of the icon on screen.
- All—apply changes to the icon in all viewports on screen.
- Noorigin—do not show the icon at the currently defined coordinate system's origin (0,0,0).
- Origin—show the icon at the currently-defined coordinate system's origin (0,0,0).

When starting to learn 3D and how to manipulate the space, you should have the UCSICON command options set to on and origin. Take the time to turn on your icon now if it is not already on.

Practice Procedure for Enabling the UCS Icon:

1. In any drawing, type **UCSICON** and press **Enter** to activate the command.
2. Type **on** and press **Enter**.
3. Press **Enter** to activate the UCSICON command again.
4. Type **or** and press **Enter**.

This procedure insures that the icon will be on and it will indicate the 0,0,0 position when possible.

The icon setting is stored in each drawing. It is best to have it set on your prototype drawing.

When the 0,0,0 location is too close to a screen boundary, the icon will move to the lower-left corner of the screen and the + in the icon will disappear. There must be room on the screen for the whole icon to display or it will move to the lower-left corner.

Other clues to your position in 3D space are present in the UCS icon. They are as follows:

- When a + appears in the lower junction of the two arrows, the icon is on the 0,0,0 coordinates of the current user coordinate system.

- When the lower junction forms a box, you are above the object looking down at it.

- When a W appears above the lower junction area, the current user coordinate system is the World Coordinate System (explained later in this chapter).

- When the icon changes from the one shown in Figure 1.1 to a broken pencil (shown in Figure 1.2), you are in a position where the icon can not be represented. This is usually a side view to the current UCS.

FIGURE 1.2 UCS broken pencil icon.

4   Viewing in the XY Plane

The XY plane plays an important part in learning to manipulate your camera's view in 3D space. With the 2D viewing commands, you had to supply a point or a factor to move your camera around. In 3D viewing, you must know the angle *in* the XY plane and the angle *from* the XY plane to place your camera with accuracy. You must be aware of the target position (your object) and the source position (your camera) you desire. Figure 1.3 shows an object from plan view *in* the XY plane.

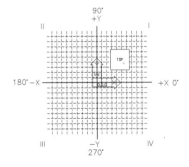

FIGURE 1.3 Object *in* the XY plane.

From the plan view, you can tell that this is the outline of a square. The angles *from* the XY plane mean nothing in 2D viewing. When you want to see the square in 3D, you need to know both the angle *in* and *from* the XY plane that the camera will be sitting at when aimed at the square. For the purposes of this discussion, the square is located at the 0,0 location. When calculating the angle, you should always consider the object to be at 0,0 and calculate the angle based on that premise.

NOTE This is because the viewing commands work off of the angle and/or vector, not the spatial position. The object is always considered to be at the center of the view when the command calculates the new camera position.

It is easier to place names (in English) on the object that represents the orientation of the object. The front of the object faces the -Y axis *in* the XY plane. The right side faces the +X axis in the XY plane. Figure 1.4 shows the "square" as it really exists in 3D space. It is not a square but a cube. The faces have been labeled to give you a feel for the orientation of the cube on the XY plane. You are looking at the cube from an angle of 315 degrees *in* the XY plane and an angle of 33 degrees *from* the XY plane.

5

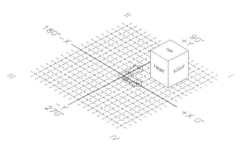

FIGURE 1.4 Cube *in* the XY plane.

To see the cube from the front side, you must position your camera right on the -Y axis (270 degrees *in* the XY plane) and at 0 degrees *from* the XY plane (or at 0 in the Z axis). Figure 1.5 shows the front of the cube when viewed from that position.

FIGURE 1.5 Cube front in the XY plane.

To see any of the side faces of the cube, you must specify the angle from 0 degrees (as if the object was located at 0,0 on the plane) for viewing. Viewing the left front of the cube would mean positioning the camera at approximately 225 degrees from the +X axis. Viewing the back side would mean positioning the camera at 90 degrees from the +X axis. These degrees for positioning are the degrees *in* the XY plane. To get above or below the object you must specify the degrees *from* the XY plane.

Remember, all degrees *in* the XY plane are calculated with zero being the +X axis and moving in a counter-clockwise fashion.

NOTE

Use the HIDE command in future practices to obtain the view of the cube similar to those shown in the figures in this chapter.

TIP

Viewing from the XY Plane

6

The degrees *from* the XY plane are the units up or down on the Z axis. The object is theoretically at the center of 0,0,0. Once you have positioned your camera pointing toward the object's face *in* the XY plane, you need to position the camera above, even with, or below the object. This is easy to envision when you look at the cube at 0 degrees *from* the XY plane. Figure 1.6 shows the cube from Figure 1.5 with the degrees from the XZ plane mapped out.

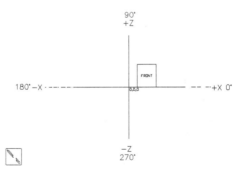

FIGURE 1.6 Cube front view with degrees *from* the XZ plane mapped.

You can look at the object from above by giving a degree between 1 and 179. The closer you come to 90 degrees, the closer you are to directly above the object. The degrees from 181 to 359 show you the object from below and the closer you get to 270 degrees, the closer you get to looking directly up at the object from below. A standard ISO view is considered to be between 31 to 35 degrees *from* the XY plane (above the object).

Both the VPOINT and the DVIEW commands allow you to dynamically place your camera without accuracy. This is very handy for everyday production, and both the VPOINT command and the DVIEW command allow you to specify an exact angle *in* and *from* the XY plane for accuracy.

Control Your Display with the VPOINT Command

The VPOINT command is the quickest and easiest 3D viewing command to learn. It has several options that allow you to position the camera in relation to the object in the drawing. It also has the advantage of two accuracy options that the DVIEW command does not have. Options to the VPOINT command are:

- Rotate—allows you to specify angles *in* and *from* the XY plane for accuracy.
- Vector—allows you to specify the camera's exact location using X,Y,Z coordinates.
- Tripod—allows you to dynamically position your camera in all three axes at once using a target icon.

THE VPOINT ROTATE OPTION

The Rotate option asks you for the angle *in* the XY plane (the angle is based on the +X axis or 0 degrees) and the angle *from* the XY plane.

To view the cube's left front from above, use the VPOINT command with the rotate option.

Practice Procedure for Using the VPOINT Command's Rotate Option

1. Open the *Cube3D* drawing in your *3Dworld* directory.
2. Type **VPOINT** and press **Enter** or select it from the menu system.

3. Type **r** and press **Enter**.

4. Type the angle *in* the XY plane (**225**) and press **Enter**.

5. Type the angle *from* the XY plane (**33**) and press **Enter**.

The result should look similar to Figure 1.7. This option makes moving the camera into position anywhere in 3D space simple. You must think of the target object as being the center of the XY plane and determine your angles from that position. First determine the angle *in* the XY plane and then determine the angle *from* the XY plane.

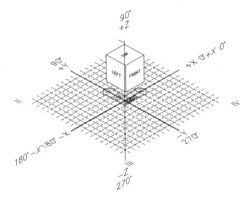

FIGURE 1.7 Cube viewed from the left front and above.

TIP

Keep your angle *from* the XY plane between +90 and -90 degrees. You can use degrees higher than 90, but the result is to flip (or turn you around) to the other side of the object. The result of the above practice procedure using 135 degrees *from* the XY plane is a view looking at the cube from the above right rear of the cube.

THE VPOINT VECTOR OPTION

The VPOINT command allows you to position your camera by explicit coordinate vectors. You can type in the X,Y,Z coordinate vectors and the VPOINT command will position the camera along the vectors so that all the objects are in view. This method of positioning assumes that your geometry is at 0,0,0 (even though it probably isn't) and that you calculate the direction vector of the camera from the geometry. Figure 1.8 shows the cube on the imaginary X, Y, and Z planes for calculating the vectors. (Don't let the term *vector* throw you, it just means the direction calculated between two points.)

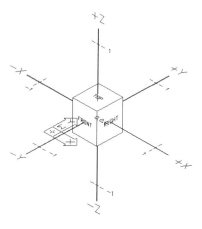

FIGURE 1.8 Cube viewed from the right front and above.

The planes are marked with just one unit because that is all you need for the option, even though you can use decimals and integers larger than 1. Remember that you are giving direction, not distance, to the object (although using a distance other than 1 can effect the view). The view shown is 1,-1,1. This way of thinking is usually too alien for the average user; most users don't like this option. Try positioning your camera to view the left rear of the cube from underneath.

9

Practice Procedure for Vector Positioning Using VPOINT

1. In the *Cube3D* drawing, type **VPOINT** and press **Enter**.

2. Type in the X,Y,Z vectors for the camera's position. (The answer is listed below.)

Another reason many users stay away from this option is that the field of movement of the camera is difficult to calculate unless you limit yourself to the major axis (XYZ) and the minor axis (the axis halfway between the major axis).

NOTE

The answer to the above practice is -1,1,-1. The vector -1, for the X axis, is measured from the theorical 0 of X (at the center of the object) along the X axis, for a distance of -1.

The VPOINT Tripod Option

The VPOINT option called Tripod is a free form option. You do not have to know the exact angle, distance, or coordinates to place your camera. Instead, you are given a target that represents 3D space with which to position your camera. You must select a point on the target, and AutoCAD will position your camera relative to the object based on the selected point. Figure 1.9 shows the tripod option target. The target and tripod temporarily replace your geometry on the screen for the selection purpose.

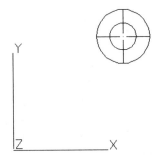

FIGURE 1.9 VPOINT tripod target.

The tripod option has two visual clues to help in your camera placement: the target, a visual representation of the XYZ plane, and the tripod showing the X,Y,Z on the ends. The tripod helps you in your visualization of what you will see in 3D space. In Figure 1.9 you are directly over the object (plan view). The tripod shows that the +X axis is pointing to the right, the +Y axis is pointing straight toward the top, and the +Z axis is pointing straight up at you (so it can not be seen).

The tripod is the computer representation of the right-hand rule. If you hold your right hand in front of you, looking at the palm, and bend your middle, fourth and fifth fingers toward you; you have a representation of the XYZ axes formed by your hand. Your thumb points toward the positive X axis, your index finger points towards the positive Y axis, and the other three fingers are pointing toward the positive Z axis. You are in plan view looking at your hand. When an object is placed in your hand, you can twist your hand around (twisting the object around at the same time) and see different views of the object. Figure 1.10 shows how your hand would look in relation to the Cartesian plane.

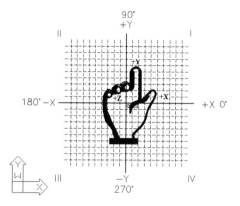

FIGURE 1.10 Right hand rule and the Cartesian plane.

As you move your mouse around the target axis, the tripod spins around, showing you the relation of your camera view to your object on the XYZ plane.

The target itself is broken into two distinct visual clues for positioning. The lines represent the XY plane. When you imagine your object at the junction of the two lines, the target would look something like Figure 1.11 if it had the object on it and was labeled.

11

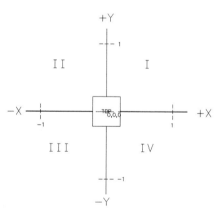

FIGURE 1.11 Axis target with imaginary object and labels.

The circles represent the Z axis above and below the XY plane. The inside circle is the area above the XY plane and the outside circle represents the area below the XY plane. The closer you move your cursor to the junction of the lines, the closer to plan view (90 degrees *from* the XY plane) above your geometry you position the camera. The closer you move the cursor to the inside circle, the closer to a side view you get (0 degrees *from* the XY plane). When you select closer to the outside circle, you are positioning the camera directly underneath your geometry (-90 degrees *from* the XY plane). Figure 1.12 shows the labels for the circles *from* the XY plane.

FIGURE 1.12 Axis Circle labels *from* the XY plane.

Using the Axis target option is simple if you follow the same steps you use with the Rotate option. First, determine the approximate angle *from* the XY plane you want to position the camera in. A view of the object from left rear would be from the second quadrant at approximately 135 degrees (the quadrants are labeled in Figure 1.11). Second, determine how high above or below the object you want to be. An ISO view is approximately 33 degrees above the object. Move the crosshair into the second quadrant of the target inside the inside circle (approximately 1/3 distance away from the inside circle towards the lines junction) and pick a point. The resulting view of your object is an ISO view of the left rear of your object. Practice this option in the procedure below.

Practice Procedure for the Axis Option of the VPOINT Command

1. In the *Cube3D* drawing, type **VPOINT** and press **Enter** to activate the VPOINT command.
2. Press **Enter** to activate the Axis target option.
3. Select a point on the target that will result in the view shown in Figure 1.13. (The answer is shown below in Figure 1.14.)

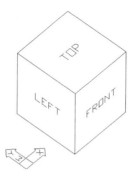

FIGURE 1.13 Axis target practice results zoomed in close.

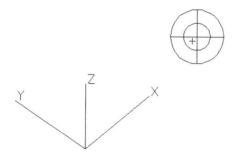

FIGURE 1.14 Answer to Axis target practice procedure.

The only negative aspect of the VPOINT command option is the lack of seeing your geometry as you maneuver your camera into position. This takes a certain amount of imagination on your part. The DVIEW command, discussed later in this chapter, has the ability to view your object as you maneuver your camera.

VPOINT Command Menu Locations

Currently, there is no toolbar location for the VPOINT command options. They are located under the _View_ pull-down menu item _3D Viewpoint_ shown in Figure 1.15. A detailed explanation of how to add a command button to your toolbar is in Chapter 12, "3D Prototypes and Toolbars Equal Productivity."

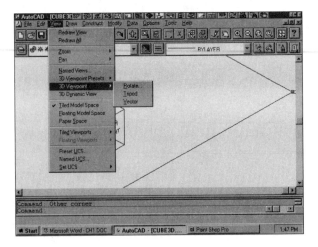

FIGURE 1.15 3D Viewpoint menu item.

Autodesk has given you a convenient way of using the Rotate option on the menu items. Rather than typing in the angles for the *in* XY plane and *from* XY plane, you can use a dialogue box to select the angles. The *Viewpoints Preset* dialogue box located under the *View / 3D Viewpoint / Rotate...* menu item gives you access to the dialogue box shown in Figure 1.16.

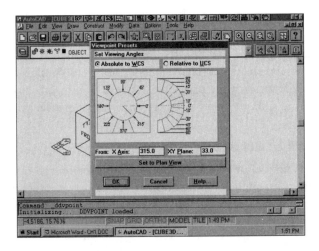

FIGURE 1.16 Viewpoint Presets dialogue box.

The left side of the dialogue box controls the angle *in* the XY plane, while the right side of the dialogue box controls the *from* the XY plane portion of the Rotate option. You can select a point inside one of the wedge shapes to set the angle to exactly that angle or you can pick a point outside the wedge shape (but inside the center) to set the angle, to approximately the angle indicated inside the nearest wedge. The right side of the dialogue box represents the Z axis as represented by a semi-circle reaching from 90 degrees above the XY plane to 90 degrees below the plane. It is easiest to think of the top of the icon as the north pole and the bottom of the icon as the south pole. You are looking from the side of the globe. Try doing the Rotate practice procedure again using the dialogue box.

Practice Procedure for Using the VPOINT Command's Rotate Dialogue Box Option

1.   Open the *Cube3D* drawing in your *3Dworld* directory.

2.   Select the *View menu* pull-down.

3.   Select the *3D Viewpoint* menu item.

4.   Select the *Rotate...* menu item.

5.   Select the wedge marked **225** in the left section of the icon.

6.   Select in the inner circle next to the 30 degree wedge in the right section of the icon.

7.   The degree number in the lower left field should say 225, and the number in the lower right field should say about 33 degrees. You can select either field and edit it to the correct number.

8.   Select the **OK** button.

The result should be the same as the one shown in Figure 1.7 from the earlier Rotate option practice procedure. This method has an advantage of seeing the XY plane represented by degrees on the left icon and the Z axis on the right icon. The disadvantage is that you must move through 3 menu picks to activate the dialogue box (you could type DDVPOINT at the command line).

N O T E

Autodesk has labeled the lower left field in the dialogue box as *From: X Axis:*. This is the same as saying "*in* the XY plane." The right field is labeled *XY Plane* and that is the same as "*from* XY plane."

AutoCAD has many preset viewpoints already defined on the pull-down menu, and the same definitions are in a toolbar. These menu item picks correspond both from the object's points of view (front, top, back, etc.) and to the Cartesian plane when it is labeled as shown in Figure 1.17. The menu and the corresponding toolbar are shown in Figure 1.18.

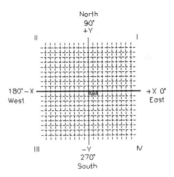

FIGURE 1.17 Cartesian plane with menu labels shown.

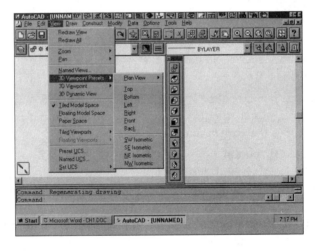

FIGURE 1.18 3D Viewpoints Presets on menu pull-down and toolbar.

The menu and toolbar items are using the VPOINT Rotate option to quickly position your camera at the preset view. The isometric views are at the standard 35 degrees *from* the XY plane.

NOTE

You can activate the VPOINT command toolbar by selecting the pull-down menu series _Tools_ / _Toolbars_ / _View_.

VPOINT Command Summary

This command's options make it easy to position your view of your geometry quickly, accurately, and easily. The Rotate option makes accurate positioning easy, while the Tripod option allows you to position quickly but not as accurately. The only real disadvantage to the command is the lack of viewing your geometry as you position it. A firm grasp of the way the command options work effectively nullifies this inconvenience.

Dynamic View (DVIEW) Command in Perspective

The DVIEW command options allow the viewing of the geometry as you position it, but it can be disorienting with geometry that is similar-looking on all sides. The benefits from the command are in the form of better control over the display of your geometry. With this command you can twist the view of your geometry along the viewing axis, or clip off the view of your geometry from the front or rear. The command has many more options than the VPOINT command, including:

- Select objects—allows you to select specific objects to include in the DVIEW command, or you can press **Enter** to activate a special feature.
- Hide—hidden line removal of unplottable lines on selected objects.
- Camera—specifies a new camera position rotated about the target.
- Target—specifies a new position for the target by rotating it about the camera.
- Distance—moves the camera in or out along the line of sight, activating the perspective mode.
- Points—locates the camera and target position by using XYZ coordinates.
- Pan—shifts the object without changing the magnification.

- Zoom—adjusts the camera lens length similar to the ZOOM command by scale when not in perspective mode, and the lens length when in perspective mode.

- Twist—twists or tilts the view along the line of sight.

- Clip—chops off the front or back of the view, like an invisible wall.

- Off—turns off the perspective view turned on by Distance.

- Undo—reverses the effect of the last DVIEW operation.

- <eXit>—exits the DVIEW command.

- specify a point—allows you to dynamically adjust the camera view.

THE SELECT OBJECTS: PROMPT

This option allows you to select specific objects to include in the DVIEW command, or you can press **Enter** to activate a special feature, the built-in "object" (a house).

A house will appear when you press the **Enter** key with nothing in the selection set. A house is used because everyone knows the orientation of a house and it is easy to position your camera relative to the house. When you exit the DVIEW command after using this feature, your object is in the same relative position as the house was. Figure 1.19 shows the house object.

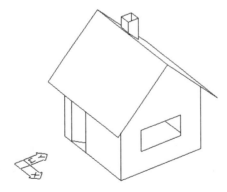

FIGURE 1.19 Internal house object used by the DVIEW command.

Notice how the house has a front door and the window is on the right side. The chimney and roof make it easy to tell if you are above or below the house. Take the time to experiment with the feature. The general rules are:

1. Enter a drawing (Cube3D is good) or draw a 3D object

2. Type **DVIEW** and press **Enter**.

3. Press **Enter** at the `Select object:` prompt to activate the house.

4. Type **ca** and press **Enter** to activate the Camera option.

5. Move your cursor around until you get the view you want and select the point.

6. Press **Enter** to exit the DVIEW command.

THE HIDE OPTION

This option will remove hidden lines from the objects selected. It is much quicker than the HIDE command used for normal viewing. You control the objects you choose to work with in the DVIEW command, so you can select just enough objects to tell what your view looks like and then use this Hide option to check the results after moving your camera around.

In the case of a cube, it is hard to tell which cube face you are looking at unless you include the face text in your selection.

TIP

19

THE CAMERA OPTION

This option has three methods of working. You can dynamically move your cursor around on all axis at one time, you can type in angles similar to the Rotate option of the VPOINT command, or you can combine the first two methods by locking down one of the two angles (typing it in) and then dynamically selecting the other angle by selecting a point on the screen. All three methods are presented here.

The typing of the angles method is similar to the Rotate option of the VPOINT command, but it uses a slightly different set of angles and it wants them in the opposite order from the Rotate option. After issuing the DVIEW command, selecting the objects to view, and typing CA to activate the Camera option, the `Toggle angle in/Enter angle from XY plane <90.0000>:` prompt appears. This is the equivalent to the `Enter angle from XY plane <33>:` prompt of the VPOINT command's Rotate option.

N O T E   The reason for this backward approach is that once you enter the angle above or below the XY plane, you can then dynamically move around your view (and pick a point *in* the XY plane for view placement) or type the angle at the `Toggle angle from/Enter angle in XY plane from X axis <90.0000>:` prompt.

The angles you are allowed to enter are slightly different from the angles in the Rotate option of the VPOINT command. There you could use from 0 through 360 degrees for both *in* the XY plane and *from* the XY plane. The Camera option only allows you the range of -90 to +90 degrees *from* the XY plane and the range of -180 to +180 degrees *in* the XY plane. These angles are illustrated in Figure 1.20.

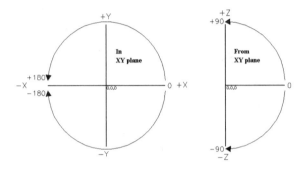

FIGURE 1.20 Angles used by the typing method.

Practice two different views of the cube using the methods of the Camera option. Show the back of the cube from a side view and show the bottom left front view.

Practice Procedure for Viewing Using the Typing Method of the Camera Option

Rear view first.

1. In the *Cube3D* drawing, type **DVIEW** and press **Enter**.
2. Select the cube and its text.
3. Type **ca** and press **Enter**.
4. Type the correct angle for the *from* XY plane.
5. Type the correct angle for the *in* XY plane.

Now do the same for the bottom left front view. The results are shown in Figures 1.21 and 1.22. The answers to steps four and five for both views are supplied below.

FIGURE 1.21 Practice results for rear view.

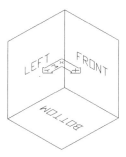

FIGURE 1.22 Practice results for bottom left front view.

N O T E

The rear view is 0 and 90. The bottom left front view is –33 and –135.

The dynamic method of the Camera option allows you to interactively move your object around in 3D space. You can see the object twist and turn as you move your cursor on the screen. This method is very handy for quick changes of view. It does take a little getting used to, however, because there does not seem to be any logical reason the object moves as it does. This is not the case. The screen is blocked off by AutoCAD into quadrants and a horizon. The horizon runs horizontally through the middle of the screen. When your cursor is above the horizon, you are above your object. When your cursor moves below the horizon, you are below your object looking up at it. The quadrants are mapped in a particular order. Figure 1.23 shows how AutoCAD maps your screen when using the Camera dynamic option.

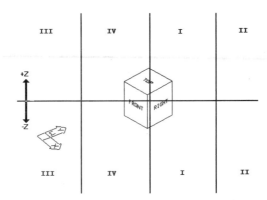

FIGURE 1.23 The DVIEW Camera option screen mapping.

The layout of the screen shows that you can use your knowledge of angles *in* and *from* the XY plane in a more intuitive way, when you remember that the quadrants start in the middle of the screen. Many users do not care about the quadrant but use the option because of its WYSIWYG (What You See Is What You Get) quality. Practice the Camera option of the DVIEW command .

Practice Procedure for Viewing Using the Dynamic Method of the Camera Option

Rear view first.

1. In the *Cube3D* drawing, type **DVIEW** and press **Enter**.
2. Select the cube and its text.
3. Type **ca** and press **Enter**.
4. Select a point on the screen that will get you the view shown in **Figure 1.24**.

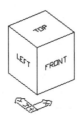

FIGURE 1.24 The DVIEW Camera option practice result.

The selection point you need to select to get the result shown in Figure 1.24 is shown in Figure 1.25.

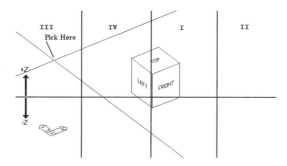

FIGURE 1.25 The DVIEW Camera option practice procedure selection point.

The Camera option is the equivalent of moving your camera around the object.

THE TARGET OPTION

This option has the same three methods of working as the Camera option. The only difference is that the target appears to be moving instead of the camera. The result is that the dynamic method of the target's option works in a different fashion from the Camera option's dynamic method. Figure 1.26 shows the screen mapping of the Target option.

23

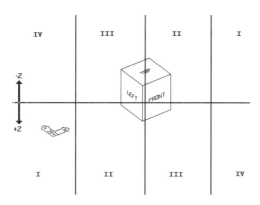

FIGURE 1.26 The DVIEW Target option screen mapping.

TIP

You should use the Camera or the Target option exclusively from each other. This is because they behave differently in the dynamic method (the method you use the most with this option) and remembering both methods is more effort than it is worth.

THE DISTANCE OPTION

This option moves the camera in or out along the line of sight. Unlike the Zoom option discussed later in the chapter, this option places you in a perspective view which causes objects farther away to appear smaller. The perspective view of the Distance option is represented on your screen by a change in the UCS icon, shown in Figure 1.27.

FIGURE 1.27 The DVIEW Distance perspective icon.

NOTE

You are not allowed to draw (create points), modify objects (use points), or use display commands (use points) while in the perspective view. This view is for your final display (plotting). To remove the perspective view, you use the Off option in the DVIEW command.

24

TIP

You can save a perspective view as a named view and restore it at any time.

After selecting the Distance option, a slider bar appears across the top of the screen. This slider bar helps you judge how far you are moving your camera from the object. Figure 1.28 shows the slider bar with the 3D cube in the Distance option.

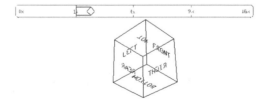

FIGURE 1.28 The slider bar of the Distance option.

THE OFF OPTION

Turns off the perspective view that the Distance option turns on. When the option is used, the UCS icon returns to normal. Try practicing the Distance option in the *Cube3D* drawing.

Practice Procedure for Using the Distance Option and the Off Option

1. In the *Cube3D* drawing, type **DVIEW** and press **Enter**.
2. Select all of the cube and text.
3. Type **d** and press **Enter** to activate the Distance option.
4. Adjust the cube closer or farther away to your choice using the slider bar and your eye. (Notice that the UCS icon appears after you select the point and it has changed to a rectangular box in the lower left corner.)
5. Type **h** and press **Enter** to hide the wireframe of the cube. (The UCS icon temporarily disappears.)
6. Type **o** and press **Enter** to turn off the Distance option.
7. Press **Enter** to exit the DVIEW command.

25

THE POINTS OPTION

This option locates the camera and target position by using XYZ coordinates. You can use absolute coordinates, relative coordinates, polar coordinates, object snaps to existing geometry, or pick a point at random for both the target and the camera position. The Points option is handy for positioning a view at an exact target and camera angle. Many people use it for the final view when inserting a building into a scene. The process is to take a picture of the area where the building is to be built and set up the view of the finished building using the same camera and target positions. When the building is rendered, the rendered image can be inserted into the picture with no seam.

The Points option takes a point for the target and a point or a direction and magnitude for the camera. Direction and magnitude are used by other CAD systems, and Autodesk has made the camera in the DVIEW Points option able to accept this format. *Magnitude* is how much the object will roll over under the camera, and *direction* is the direction the front of the object is facing. Few users take advantage of this option because, unless you are used to working with it, it can be hard to use. Try the Points option with points for both the camera and target.

Practice Procedure for the Points Option of the DVIEW Command

1. In the *Cube3D* drawing, type **DVIEW** and press **Enter**.
2. Select all of the cube and text.
3. Type **po** and press **Enter** to activate the Points option.
4. Select a point near the bottom center of the cube for the target position.
5. Type **@1,1,1** and press **Enter** to position the camera.
6. Type **h** and press **Enter** to activate the Hide option.
7. Press **Enter** to exit the DVIEW command.

Figure 1.29 shows the result.

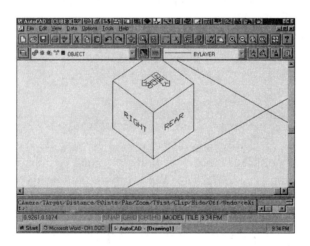

FIGURE 1.29 The result of using the Points option.

NOTE

You can use object snaps, grid/snap, or any of the coordinate systems for the target and camera points. The absolute coordinate system should be used carefully for the camera point because your object—the target—is usually not at 0,0,0, so you could get unexpected results. Relative or polar coordinates are better to use.

THE PAN OPTION

This option shifts the object without changing the magnification, same as the Pan command. You select a "base" point (from point) and then drag the object over to a "to" point. This option is handy for centering your object without changing any of your previous settings. Try the Pan option.

Practice Procedure for the Pan Option of the DVIEW Command

1. In the *Cube3D* drawing, type **DVIEW** and press **Enter**.
2. Select all of the cube and text.
3. Type **pa** and press **Enter** to activate the Pan option.
4. Select a point near the bottom center of the cube for the target position.
5. Select a point near the center of the screen.
6. Type **h** and press **Enter** to activate the Hide option.
7. Press **Enter** to exit the DVIEW command.

The Pan option can be used as often as you need it.

THE ZOOM OPTION

This option adjusts the camera lens length, similar to the ZOOM command. A slider bar is provided at the top of the screen for reference as you zoom in or out. Unlike the Distance option, the Zoom option does not place you into perspective view. Figure 1.30 shows the 3D cube in the Zoom option.

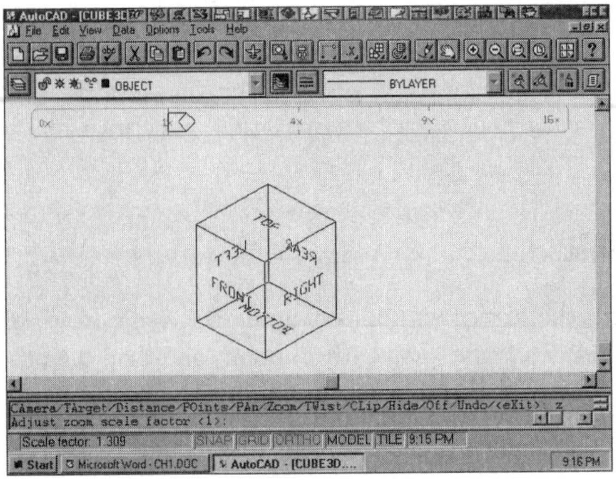

FIGURE 1.30 The 3D cube in the Zoom option.

Try the Zoom option of the DVIEW command.

Practice Procedure for the Zoom Option of the DVIEW Command

1. In the *Cube3D* drawing, type **DVIEW** and press **Enter**.

2. Select all of the cube and text.

3. Type **z** and press **Enter** to activate the Zoom option.

4. Adjust the zoom in or out by moving your cursor left or right on the slider at the top of the screen. Select a point on the slider bar once the cube is positioned as you desire.

5. Type **h** and press **Enter** to activate the Hide option.

6. Press **Enter** to exit the DVIEW command.

THE TWIST OPTION

This option twists or tilts the view along the line of sight (the axis between you and your object). It is like holding the object in your hand, looking along your arm, and turning the object left or right using your wrist only. Figure 1.31 shows the 3D cube after being twisted with the Twist option.

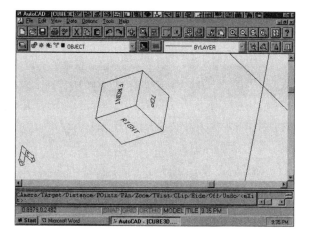

FIGURE 1.31 The 3D cube in the Twist option.

Try the Twist option of the DVIEW command.

Practice Procedure for the Twist Option of the DVIEW Command

1. In the *Cube3D* drawing, type **DVIEW** and press **Enter**.
2. Select all of the cube and text.
3. Type **tw** and press **Enter** to activate the Twist option.
4. Select a point near the side or top of the screen.
5. Type **h** and press **Enter** to activate the Hide option.
6. Press **Enter** to exit the DVIEW command.

THE CLIP OPTION

This option chops off the front or back of the view, like an invisible wall. The Off option turns off any clips being applied. The Back option puts an invisible wall between you and the objects in the rear of the scene. The Front option puts an invisible wall that you peer over to see the objects behind it. The objects in front of the wall are hidden. By using both the Front and Back options of the Clip option, you can effectively hide surrounding objects, making it easier to edit objects in a dense file where all of the geometry is on the same layer. Figure 1.32

shows a sample drawing, while the Back clip is applied to the same drawing in Figure 1.33, and the Front clip is added in Figure 1.34.

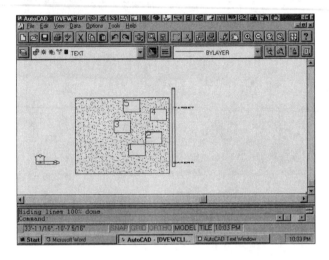

FIGURE 1.32 Sample drawing for the Clip option.

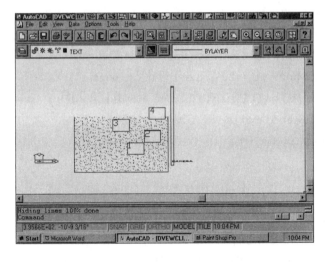

FIGURE 1.33 Sample drawing with the Back option applied.

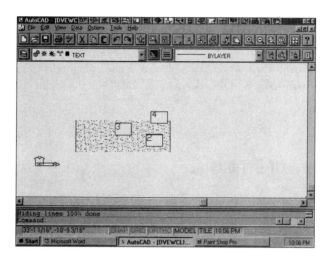

FIGURE 1.34 Sample drawing with the Front option added.

Practice Procedure for Using the Clip Option

1. In the *DVEWCLIP* drawing, type **DVIEW** and press **Enter**.

2. Select all of the geometry.

3. Type **cl** and press **Enter** to enter into the Clip option.

4. Type **b** and press **Enter** to use the Back option.

5. Move the slider bar to the left to about the middle of the second section from the right side and select a point (the marker number three should be the last marker showing on the screen).

6. Type **cl** and press **Enter** to activate the Clip option.

7. Type **f** and press **Enter** to use the Front option.

8. Move the slider bar to the left to the middle of the slider bar and select a point (the marker number three should now be the only marker showing on the screen).

9. Type **h** and press **Enter** to activate the Hide option.

10. Press **Enter** to exit the DVIEW command.

The visual aspect of positioning the invisible wall in the front or back makes it easy to see what is happening as you position the walls using the slider bar.

Be patient when moving the slider bar. Pause occasionally to get your bearings. The more objects in the selections set, the slower the screen update.

TIP

THE UNDO AND EXIT OPTIONS

The Undo option reverses the effect of the last DVIEW operation. The Exit option exits the DVIEW command.

Use the **Exit** option or press **Enter** to exit DVIEW. Canceling will return you to your original view.

TIP

THE SPECIFY A POINT OPTION

This option is the default of the command. It allows you to dynamically adjust the camera view in several ways. You can select a target point and the command prompts you to enter a direction and magnitude. This is a dynamic version of the Points option. The Points option allows you to enter a direction and magnitude for the camera but it does not drag the object around on the cursor as you move it. This option is handy for quickly positioning your geometry without accuracy. Try the Specify a Point option.

Practice Procedure for the Specify a Point Option of the DVIEW Command

1. In the *Cube3D* drawing, use the VPOINT Rotate option to place the cube in plan view by making the angle *in* the XY plane 0 and the angle *from* the XY plane 90.
2. Type **DVIEW** and press **Enter** to activate the DVIEW command.
3. Select all of the cube and text.
4. Select a point near the middle of the bottom of the cube.
5. Position the cube as shown in Figure 1.35 and select a point.

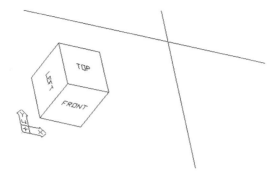

FIGURE 1.35 Result of the select a point option.

6. Type **h** and press **Enter** to activate the Hide option.

7. Press **Enter** to exit the DVIEW command.

NOTE

In the last procedure, you used the VPOINT Rotate option to maneuver the cube into a plan view. There is a PLAN command covered in Chapter 2 that can be used to quickly do the same thing. The direction used was approximately 50 and the magnitude was approximately 50.

33

DVIEW Command Summary

This command's options (like the VPOINT options) make it easy to position your view of your geometry quickly, accurately, and easily. The DVIEW command has the advantage of allowing you to see any geometry you select as you position the camera. The options of this command allow a greater range of control of the positioning of your camera. Options like Twist and Clip allow you to control the view of your geometry in ways no other display command can duplicate. Many users use the VPOINT command to do simple viewing and the DVIEW command to do more complex viewing. The principles of viewing in 3D space remain the same for both commands.

Chapter Exercise

Use either the **DVIEW** or the **VPOINT** command to line up the monitor in the MONITOR drawing, as shown in figure 1.36.

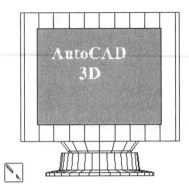

FIGURE 1.36 Desired result of chapter exercise.

In Conclusion

In this chapter, you learned how to interpret the visual clues the UCSICON gives as to your whereabouts in 3D space. You learned that there are two basic parts to viewing in three dimensions, *in* the XY plane and *from* the XY plane. These basic parts can be applied to any of the options in the DVIEW or VPOINT commands. Each option of the DVIEW and VPOINT commands were explored and practiced. In the next chapter, you are introduced to more of the relationship between 2D viewing commands and 3D space. You are given the opportunity to practice using the VIEW and VPORTS commands in 3D space. The use of the User Coordinate System (UCS) in viewing is covered, and the PLAN command is explored.

CHAPTER TWO

Display II

In this chapter, you are introduced to the PLAN command and the various ways of using the 2D display commands in 3D space. The technique for using the User Coordinate System (UCS) as a display tool is also covered.

The 3D display commands covered in the last chapter are used to set up your view with accuracy or to quickly get a view approximately where you want it in 3D space. The commands in this chapter allow you to refine the 3D view using the 2D display commands. The 2D viewing commands are not covered in depth as it is expected that you already have the basic experience with them from designing in 2D space. The PLAN command is a 3D display command that is used to put you in a 2D view of your geometry based on the current UCS setting. This means that the UCS can be skewed to any position, and the PLAN command always places you above the UCS XY plane.

Plan View in 3D

The PLAN view command places you above your geometry. Imagine your geometry as in the center of a globe of the world. The plan view is the view you get if you were standing on the north pole looking down at the geometry. This illustration is why the basic coordinate system in AutoCAD is called the World Coordinate System (WCS). It is necessary to understand the coordinate systems inside AutoCAD to view, draw, and edit in 3D space, because they effect everything you do. The User Coordinate System (UCS) is covered later in this chapter. The PLAN command has the option of placing you above your geometry based on the WCS or above the UCS. The WCS is easiest to use because it never changes. The resulting view you get is always the same; you can think of it as your home base. The WCS is the coordinate system that AutoCAD uses internally and you cannot change it.

The PLAN command has three options for controlling the view:

- <Current UCS>—this option places your camera above the current UCS.
- UCS—this option places your camera above a saved UCS name.
- World—this option places your camera above the WCS.

Try using the World option (the WCS) of the PLAN command.

Practice Procedure for the World Option of the PLAN Command

1. Open the *Wedge* drawing in the *3Dworld* directory.
2. Type **plan** and press **Enter**.
3. Type **w** and press **Enter**.
4. Type **hide** and press **Enter**.

The resulting view, shown in Figure 2.1, is a plan view based on the WCS.

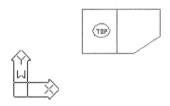

FIGURE 2.1 Practice procedure result.

This is the view you get every time you use the World option of the PLAN command. Since the WCS never changes, the view never changes. However, the User Coordinate System (UCS) is completely changeable. You can control it and set it to any position you want. The UCS command, covered later in this chapter, allows you to set, store, and restore the UCS to any position. You can think of the UCS as being the sheet of paper you are drawing on inside AutoCAD. By changing the UCS, you can tilt that sheet of electronic paper any direction in the 3D world. Figure 2.2 shows, in an isometric view, the plan view camera looking down at the wedge on the electronic sheet of paper (represented by a title border).

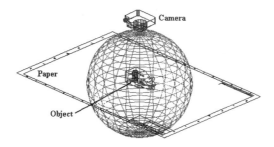

FIGURE 2.2 Plan view and your paper.

The UCS icon is the same as the paper (title border). By changing the pitch and angle of the UCS, you change the pitch and angle of the paper you are drawing on. Since AutoCAD always draws perpendicular to the UCS—even if your view isn't in the plan view—you can use plan view for your UCS and feel like you are drawing that elevation from above. The PLAN command allows you to do this. Try using the PLAN view command with the UCS option.

This procedure has several steps for changing the UCS. The UCS material is not covered until the next section.

NOTE

Practice Procedure for the Current UCS Option of the PLAN Command

1. In the *Wedge* drawing in the *3Dworld* directory, type **ucs** and press **Enter**.
2. Type **r** and press **Enter** to restore a saved UCS view.
3. Type **right** and press **Enter** to restore the right UCS view.
4. Type **plan** and press **Enter**.
5. Press **Enter** to accept the default of *<Current UCS>*.
6. Type **hide** and press **Enter**.

The result looks like Figure 2.3. The PLAN command placed your camera at the north pole of the globe as it related to the sheet of electronic paper represented by the UCS icon. The UCS icon appears in the lower left corner with no **W** in it, telling you that you are in a user-defined view.

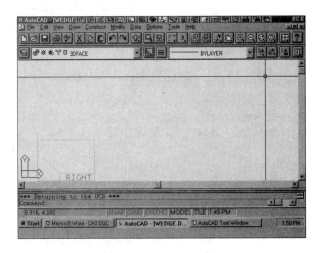

FIGURE 2.3 Plan view in a user-defined view.

N O T E

In step four, the UCS icon jumped to the front of the wedge. The reason for this was covered in the UCSICON section of Chapter 1. The UCSICON is set to On and Origin in the wedge drawing.

The UCS option of the PLAN command allows you to place your view in plan view as it relates to a saved UCS. Saving a UCS is covered in the next section on the UCS command. The wedge drawing has several saved UCS positions based on the different views of the wedge. Try restoring the right plan view as you did in the last procedure, but use the UCS option instead of the Current UCS option.

Practice Procedure for the Current UCS Option of the PLAN Command

1. In the *Wedge* drawing in the *3Dworld* directory, type **plan** and press **Enter**.

2. Type **ucs** and press **Enter** to activate the UCS option.

3. Type **right** at the ?/Name of UCS: prompt and press **Enter**.

4. Type **hide** and press **Enter**.

The view looks like the view shown in Figure 2.3.

TIP

This method of using saved named UCS positions can increase your production speed. Chapter 12 covers many of these types of tricks and techniques that can be set up in your prototype drawings.

PLAN Command Menu Locations

The PLAN command options are located on the *Plan View* menu item on the *3D Viewpoint Presets* menu item under the *View pull-down* menu, as shown in Figure 2.4.

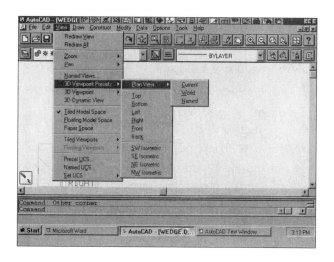

FIGURE 2.4 Plan view menu items.

39

There is no toolbar for the PLAN command options. The customizing section in Chapter 12 covers creating you own toolbars.

The UCS Command for Viewing

The User Coordinate System command is designed to aid you during drawing, editing, and viewing. In this section, you are introduced to the UCS command for viewing purposes. The command moves the electronic sheet of drawing paper around according to several different options. The options include:

- Origin—moves the UCS origin to any point selected.
- Zaxis—allows you to tilt the Z axis at an angle relative to the XY plane.
- 3point—positions the UCS around a user selected origin point, X vector (direction) point, and Y vector (direction) point.
- Object—changes the UCS to the objects Entity Coordinate System.
- View—changes the UCS parallel to the current view.
- X—allows you to rotate the UCS about the X axis.
- Y—allows you to rotate the UCS about the Y axis.
- Z—allows you to rotate the UCS about the Z axis.
- Prev—changes the UCS to the previous UCS setting.
- Restore—allows you to restore a saved, named UCS coordinate.
- Save—allows you to save and name a UCS coordinate.
- Del—allows you to delete a saved, named UCS coordinate.
- ?—gives you a list of saved, named UCS coordinates.
- <World>—sets the UCS to WCS.

Since the PLAN command can be set to the current UCS or a saved, named UCS, you can use the UCS to set up quick plan views for drawing and editing. Working in plan view to your geometry is not always desirable, but many times it is necessary. An example is the wedge and 3Dcube drawings used in Chapters 1 and 2. The text on those drawings was placed by creating a named UCS coordinate for each face of the object. Then the text was placed on the object with the corresponding UCS name. Moving objects or drawing objects from an isometric view can sometimes result in unpredictable results. By being in plan view to the UCS of the face of the object, the problem is eliminated. The steps for using UCS and PLAN to control viewing are as follows:

1. Create a UCS named coordinate system
2. Save the named coordinate system.
3. Use the UCS command to restore the desired saved named coordinate.
4. Use the PLAN command's Current UCS option to position yourself in plan view.

NOTE

The process for creating saved named UCS coordinate systems and restoring them is covered in Chapter 4.

Try using the already-created UCS saved names in the wedge drawing.

PRACTICE PROCEDURE FOR USING SAVED NAMED UCS COORDINATES

1. In the *Wedge* drawing in the *3Dworld* directory, type **ucs** and press **Enter** to activate the UCS command.

2. Type **r** and press **Enter** to activate the Restore option of the command.

3. Type **front** and press **Enter** to restore the saved named coordinate called front.

4. Type **plan** and press the **Enter** key to activate the PLAN command.

5. Press **Enter** to accept the default of *<Current UCS>*.

6. Type **hide** and press **Enter**.

The result should look like Figure 2.5.

41

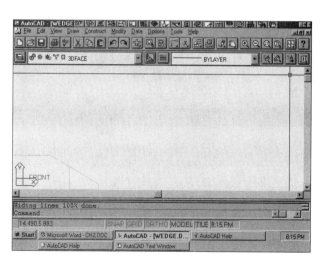

FIGURE 2.5 View using UCS saved named view front and PLAN command.

The UCS and PLAN commands change your view and the position of the electronic sheet of paper you are drawing on. This is unlike the VPOINT and DVIEW commands covered in Chapter 1 that only change your *view* of the geometry and not the *position* of the electronic sheet of paper.

UCS COMMAND MENU LOCATIONS

The UCS command and the various options are defined in many places in AutoCAD. The UCS toolbar is permanently attached to the Standard toolbar as a flyout menu. The exact same toolbar can be activated as a floating pallet by selecting the *UCS* menu item from the *Toolbars* menu item on the *Tools* menu pull-down. The pick sequence is *Tools/Toolbars/UCS* and the result is shown, with the toolbar flyout activated from the *Standard* toolbar, in Figure 2.6.

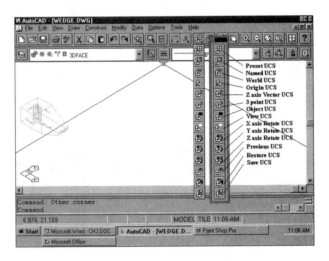

FIGURE 2.6 UCS Toolbars.

The *Set UCS* menu item under the *View* menu pull-down contains all of the UCS options listed earlier in this chapter. The options are shown in Figure 2.7.

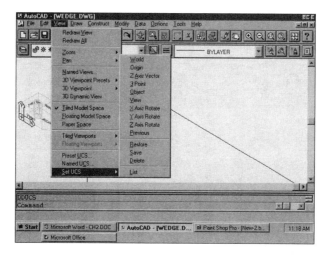

FIGURE 2.7 Set UCS menu options.

There are two other options in the pull-down menu for accessing the UCS options. The first is the *Preset UCS...* menu item, which allows you to select from several previously set UCS settings in a dialogue box shown in Figure 2.8. These options used by this dialogue box are discussed in depth in Chapter 3. The dialogue box is just a visual shortcut for the USC X, Y, or Z options.

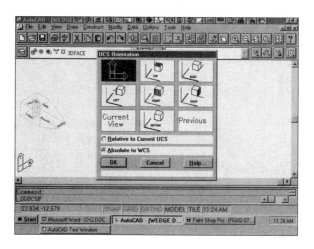

FIGURE 2.8 Preset UCS dialogue box.

The second is the *Named UCS...* menu item which allows you to select from saved named UCS coordinates in a dialogue box, shown in Figure 2.9.

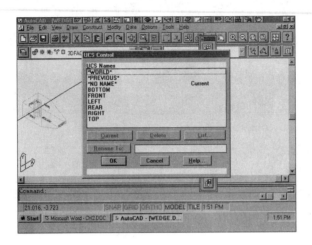

FIGURE 2.9 Named UCS dialogue box.

Using UCSFOLLOW to View Your Geometry

44

UCSFOLLOW is a system variable that is set to either 0 (off) or 1 (on). When set to on, changing the UCS will result in a plan view of the change automatically. You do not have to use the PLAN command when it is set on. This feature, when used in conjunction with the saved named UCS coordinates, can speed up production significantly. Try the feature in the wedge drawing.

Practice Procedure for Using the UCSFOLLOW System Variable

1. In the *Wedge* drawing in the *3Dworld* directory, type **ucsfollow** and press **Enter** to activate the command.

2. Type **1** to turn on the feature.

3. Type **UCS** and press **Enter** to activate the UCS command.

4. Type **r** and press **Enter** to restore a named coordinate.

5. Type **rear** and press **Enter** to restore the rear view.

6. Type **hide** and press **Enter**.

The rear of the wedge should appear in plan view. You can try more UCS named coordinates as you wish by substituting the name of the saved UCS coordinate in step 5. To see all the named coordinates available in the UCS command for the wedge drawing, type a question mark (?) and press **Enter** at step 5. Read the prompts and respond accordingly.

NOTE

Turn off the UCSFOLLOW variable when you are done experimenting by typing **UCSFOLLOW** and setting it to zero.

2D Viewing in 3 Dimensions

All 2D viewing commands work in 3D views. They behave exactly the same way as in 2D. Several 2D viewing commands are view-dependent (like PAN and ZOOM), so they behave the same as always but they act upon the current view. Others, like the VIEW and VPORTS command, are not view dependent, so they force the view to the settings you saved.

The PAN Command in the Third Dimension

The PAN command does not magnify your view in any way. In the plan view in 2D, it allows you to select a point and drag the view to another selected point. This is also true in the third dimension. The difference is that the command treats the current view as if it were the plan view in 2D. The view can be an ISO view or any other view not a true 2D plan view and the command does not care. The PAN command will allow you to select a point and drag the view to another point, no matter what the current view looks like. Try the PAN command in the third dimension. The first part of the procedure is to make sure that you get to the correct view before using the PAN command.

Practice Procedure for Using the PAN Command in 3D

1. In the *Wedge* drawing in the *3Dworld* directory, type **vpoint** and press **Enter** to activate the VPOINT command.

2. Type **r** and press **Enter** to activate the Rotate option of the VPOINT command.

3. Type **315** and press **Enter** at the Enter angle in XY plane from X axis <315>: prompt.

4. Type **35** and press **Enter** at the `Enter angle from XY plane <35>:` prompt.

5. Type **pan** and press **Enter** at the command line prompt.

6. Select a point on the screen near the point P1 shown in Figure 2.10.

7. Select a point on the screen near the point P2 shown in Figure 2.10.

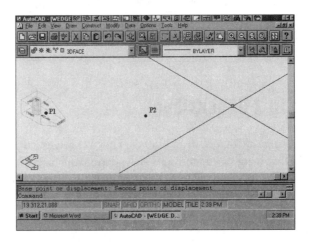

FIGURE 2.10 Practice procedure selection points.

The result should look similar to Figure 2.11. The command behaved exactly as it would in plan view, but it was in an ISO view when doing the work.

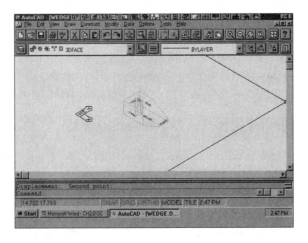

FIGURE 2.11 Result of practice procedure for PAN command in 3D.

THE PAN COMMAND MENU LOCATIONS

The pick sequence for using the pull-down menu to access the PAN command is *View* / *Pan.* Several standard options are provided on the menu as shown in Figure 2.12.

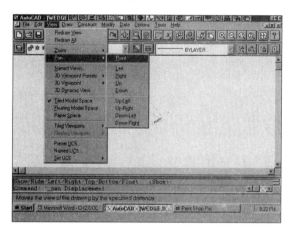

FIGURE 2.12 The PAN command options on the pull-down menu.

The PAN toolbar is permanently attached to the *Standard* toolbar as a flyout menu. The exact same toolbar can be activated as a floating pallet by typing **TOOLBAR** and **ACAD.PAN** and then accepting the <show> option. The result is shown, with the toolbar flyout activated from the *Standard* toolbar, in Figure 2.13.

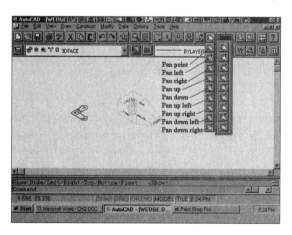

FIGURE 2.13 The PAN command options on the toolbar.

THE ZOOM COMMAND IN THE THIRD DIMENSION

The ZOOM command options behave exactly the same in 3 dimensions as they do in 2D. They work on the current view regardless of the view's orientation. You can zoom closer or farther away. The Previous option works by stepping you back one view. The Scale option works based on your limits or the current screen size, depending on whether or not you use the x after the scale factor. The Extents, Center, Dynamic, and Left options work without any difference. This command allows you to refine your current view in 3D space by using the same options you use in 2D space. Try using the ZOOM command in 3D space.

Practice Procedure for the Using the ZOOM Command in 3D

1. In the *Wedge* drawing in the *3Dworld* directory, position yourself in an ISO view.
2. Type **z** and press **Enter** to activate the ZOOM command.
3. Type **w** and press **Enter** to activate the Window option of the ZOOM command.
4. Select a window around the wedge part.
5. Press **Enter** to activate the ZOOM command again.
6. Type **p** and press **Enter** to activate the Previous option of the ZOOM command.

THE ZOOM COMMAND MENU LOCATIONS

The pick sequence for using the pull-down menu to access the ZOOM command is *View/Zoom*. Several standard options are provided on the menu as shown in Figure 2.14.

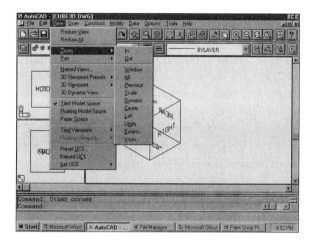

FIGURE 2.14 The ZOOM command on the pull-down menu.

The ZOOM command has several toolbar locations. The ZOOM toolbar is permanently attached to the *Standard* toolbar as a flyout menu. The exact same toolbar can be activated as a floating pallet by typing **TOOLBAR** and **ACAD.ZOOM** and then accepting the <show> option. The result is shown, with the toolbar flyout activated from the *Standard* toolbar, in Figure 2.15.

49

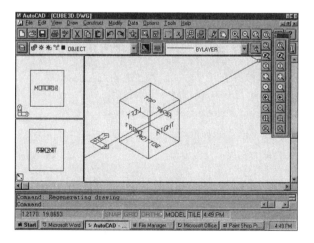

FIGURE 2.15 The ZOOM command options on the toolbar.

The DDVIEW Command in 3D

The Dynamic Dialogue VIEW command allows you to save and restore both 2D and 3D views. The Release 13 menu item *3D Viewpoint Presets* under the *View* pull-down menu has many standard views defined. The problem with these predefined views is that they never seem to be exactly where you want them. It is easier to use the stored predefined views on this menu to setup your own standard views. Views that show the top, bottom, right, left, rear, and front of your geometry should be created. These views are then available to you at any time for quick access to the side of your geometry you wish to work on or view. Try using a stored view.

Practice Procedure for Using Stored Views in 3D

1. In the *Wedge* drawing in the *3Dworld* directory, type **ddview** and press **Enter** to activate the view dialogue box, shown in Figure 2.16.

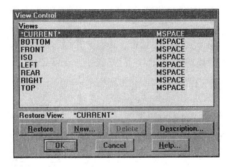

FIGURE 2.16 The DDVIEW dialogue box.

2. Select the **ISO** view from the list of views.
3. Select the **Restore** button.
4. Select the **OK** button.

The view can be a view in 3D space. You must save the view before you can restore it from the list. The procedure for creating saved views is as follows:

1. Position your camera in the view you wish.
2. Call the DDVIEW command.
3. Inside the *View Control* dialogue box, select the **New...** button.

4. Inside the *Define New View* dialogue box, shown in Figure 2.17, type the name by which you wish the viewed saved in the New Name: edit box.

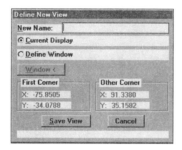

FIGURE 2.17 The Define New View dialogue box.

5. Make sure the *Current Display* radio button is selected.

6. Select the *Save View* button.

The new named view will appear in the list in the *View Control* dialogue box. Since your current view is the one you just named, you do not have to restore it at this time. This is one simple way of creating your views. You can use the standard predefined views on the menu to help setup your own standard views. Try that method in the practice procedure.

Practice Procedure for Storing Views in 3D

1. In the *Cube3D* drawing in the *3Dworld* directory, use the *View/3D Vpoint Presets/Front* option to place the cube in front view.

2. Adjust the cube to the center of the screen and size it using the ZOOM and/or PAN commands.

3. Type **ddview** and press **Enter** to activate the view dialogue box.

4. Select the *New*... button.

5. Type the name **front** in the New Name: view edit box.

6. Select the Save view button.

7. Select the **OK** button to exit the view dialogue box.

Repeat this method for all of the standard views listed on the *3D Vpoint Preset* menu. The results should look like Figure 2.18.

51

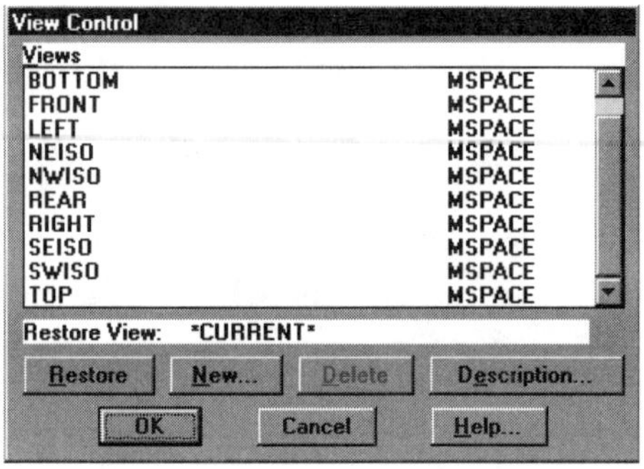

FIGURE 2.18 The View Control dialogue box with your standard views.

CREATING VIEWS FOR DESIGNING

The customized standard views you create become the basis for your working views. They can then be used to quickly move to the desired view of your geometry. The geometry is centered and you have only to use your PAN or ZOOM command to refine the view. Your standard views can be used to develop more detailed custom views. A detailed custom view is desired when you find yourself using a standard view and then having to refine it the same way most of the time. It makes sense to give the view a saved name; then you can quickly access it. These kinds of views are used less often than the standard views and they can become a nuisance because it is hard to remember a lot of custom view names. It is a good idea to limit your use of customized views to, generally, less than six. The standard views are used more often and reflect the faces of your geometry, making them easier to remember.

THE DDVIEW COMMAND MENU LOCATIONS

The DDVIEW command is defined in many places in AutoCAD. The DDVIEW command is located on the VIEW toolbar, which is permanently attached to the Standard toolbar as a flyout menu. The exact same toolbar can be activated as a floating palette by selecting the *View* menu item from the *Toolbars* menu item on the *Tools* menu pull-down. The pick sequence is *Tools/Toolbars/View* and the result is shown, with the toolbar flyout activated from the *Standard* toolbar, in Figure 2.19. The DDVIEW command button is the top button on the *View* toolbar; the button is shown in Figure 2.20.

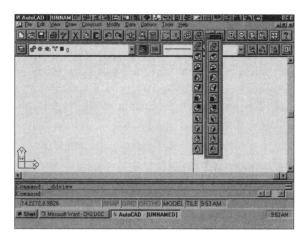

FIGURE 2.19 The View toolbar.

FIGURE 2.20 The DDVIEW command button on the View toolbar.

The DDVIEW command is also located on the _View_ pull-down menu by selecting the _Named Views..._ menu item. The menu is shown in Figure 2.21.

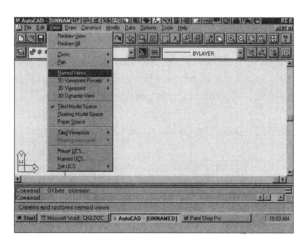

FIGURE 2.21 The DDVIEW command menu item on the View pull-down menu.

THE DDVIEW COMMAND SUMMARY

The ability to save a named view and later to retrieve it with the DDVIEW command benefits you, allowing you to increase your production speed, by quickly moving to predefined 3D views. The key to using the command lies in determining your basic standard views for your project and setting them up in your prototype drawing. This technique is discussed in Chapter 12.

The VPORTS Command in 3D

Viewports are used frequently in the 2D design of large objects to allow the user to span the distance from one end of the object to the other, or to align objects on separate ends of a large object. This technique is a convenience and occasionally a necessity in 2D design, but viewports are essential to 3D design.

VIEWPORTS TO ASSIST YOUR DESIGN

You can not always work in one view at a time in 3D space. That costs much in design time and can lead to errors. Objects that look snapped correctly in one view can actually be snapped to the wrong object. Seeing the objects in several views at once helps to eliminate those kinds of errors. You can design 3D objects faster when you combine the multiple viewports with design tools like point filters and the UCS command (discussed in the next chapter) and 2D viewing commands such as the DDVIEW command discussed earlier in this chapter. A typical viewport setup is two small viewports on the left of the screen and a large viewport on the right of the screen. The two small viewports contain the top and a side view of your object, while the large viewport would contain an isometric view of the object. Try making a typical 3D viewport configuration.

Practice Procedure for Creating Customized 3D Viewports

1. In the *Cube3D* drawing in the *3Dworld* directory, type **vports** and press **Enter** to activate the VPORTS command.
2. Type **si** and press **Enter** to set the viewports to a single viewport.
3. Press **Enter** to activate the VPORTS command again.
4. Type **2** and press **Enter**.
5. Press **Enter** to accept the default option of *Vertical*.

6. Select a point in the left viewport and repeat steps 3 through 5.

7. Press **Enter** to activate the VPORTS command again.

8. Type **j** and press **Enter** to activate the *Join* option of the VPORTS command.

9. Select the far right viewport and the middle viewport to join together (the order does not matter).

10. Select the far left viewport and repeat steps 3 and 4.

11. Type **h** and press **Enter** to activate the *Horizontal* option.

12. Place a top view in the upper left viewport, a front view in the lower left viewport, and an isometric view in the right viewport by using the methods you learned in the previous chapter.

13. Use the *Save* option of the VPORTS command to saved a named viewport (call it **3R**).

The above steps in the practice procedure, while seeming a bit long, are standard steps used in the creation of viewports. The setting up of the viewports is the same in the 2D design environment as in the 3D environment. The difference is the view you place in each viewport. The result of the practice should look similar to Figure 2.22.

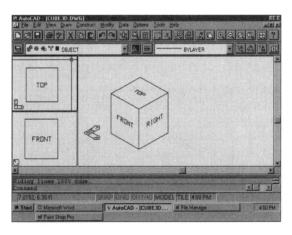

FIGURE 2.22 VPORTS practice procedure results.

By saving named views and using them with saved named viewport configurations, you use two simple 2D design viewing commands to maximum benefit in the 3D design world. The combinations are virtually limitless when combined with the ability to change a view or viewport interactively at any time.

Swapping Views Between Two Viewports

AutoCAD does not give you the ability to swap the views between two viewports. Many programmers have written AutoLISP routines to allow this functionality. The AutoLISP routine SWAPVP.LSP included on the disk with this book is a simple routine that allows you to swap views between two viewports. When the viewports are the same size, the views size will not change. When the two viewports are different sizes, the larger view changes size in the smaller view. This is not a problem because you can always use the ZOOM command to correct the size of the view. Try using the SWAPVP AutoLISP routine on the saved named viewport configuration you just created in the last practice procedure (3R, if you named it as suggested).

Practice Procedure for Using the SWAPVP Routine to Swap Views in Viewports

1. In the *Cube3D* drawing in the *3Dworld* directory, load the routine by typing **(load "swapvp")** and pressing **Enter**. This assumes that you have the *3Dworld* directory on the search path as instructed at the beginning of the book.

2. In any viewport configuration (3R) that has two or more viewports, type **swapvp** and press **Enter**.

3. Select a point in the desired viewport at the Select first viewport: prompt. If the selected viewport is not the current viewport, you will need to select a second point as the first one activated the viewport as current.

4. Select a point in the desired viewport at the Select other viewport: prompt. You will need to select a second point as the first one activated the viewport as current.

The routine allows you to have two unnamed views in the viewports and switch them without naming them. It is an interactive command that automates several steps you would have to take to swap the views.

The VPORTS Command Menu Locations

There is not a toolbar for the VPORTS command. You can create your own following the steps in the "Customizing 3D Toolbars" section of Chapter 12.

The VPORTS command and its options are located on the *View* pull-down menu under the *Tiled viewports* menu item, as shown in Figure 2.23.

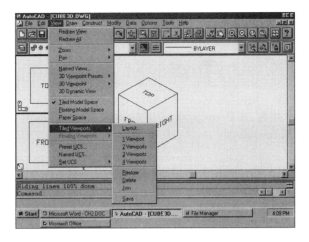

FIGURE 2.23 VPORTS menu items.

The *Layout...* menu item activates a dialogue box shown in Figure 2.24, which allows you to select from several predefined viewport configurations. These configurations are generic with no special views saved in them. They are useful as a shortcut for creating your own custom viewports that have saved named views in them. Many users also use them as they are without any additional work.

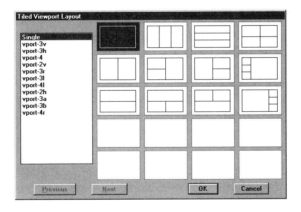

FIGURE 2.24 Tiled Viewport Layout dialogue box.

The rest of the menu items on the *Tiled Viewports* menu are the regular options used by the VPORTS command to save, restore, join, and create different viewport configurations.

THE VPORTS COMMAND SUMMARY

The object of using the VPORTS command in 3D design is to make it faster and easier to view, draw, and edit your objects. The command by itself is powerful because of its ability to save and restore viewport configurations. The key to using the command lies in determining your basic standard viewports for your project and setting them up in your prototype drawing. This technique is discussed in Chapter 12 later in this book.

NOTE

AutoCAD has two commands for refreshing all viewports currently displayed. They are the REGENALL and the REDRAWALL commands. They perform just as their corresponding commands, REGEN and REDRAW, for all of the current viewports.

Chapter Exercise

Open the *Wedge* drawing in the *3Dworld* directory and add a three viewport configuration and a four viewport configuration. Both configurations should have an ISO view, a top view, and a side view in three of the viewports. The fourth viewport configuration should be an extra side view that is opposite of the other side view.

In Conclusion

In this chapter, you have had the opportunity to practice with the PLAN command and the UCS command as a viewing tool. You reviewed the 2D viewing commands in the 3D environment and practiced using them. Each of the commands covered in this and the preceding chapter are good for manipulating the views in your drawing. The real power comes from using them in conjunction. Plan how to set up complex viewing environments that allow you quick access to your desired views. Chapter 12, "3D Prototype and Toolbars Equal Productivity," examines many of the complex combinations you can create in your prototype drawing to enhance your viewing in 3D space. In the next chapter, you are introduced to the commands that allow you to create wireframe 3D geometry. Many of the same commands are also used in the creation of 3D solids.

CHAPTER THREE

Tools for 3D Design

You develop your own style of working in 3D as you are introduced to the many tools and commands. Some tools or commands are better suited to a given task than others. Do not fall into the trap of thinking that since some commands or tools feel comfortable, they are all you need to do your work. Many of the commands and tools presented in this chapter and in the book are used only occasionally in average production. It is important that you are exposed to all of them, so you have choices in selecting your production style.

The various tools and the User Coordinate System presented in this chapter are necessary tools for drawing in the third dimension, whether you are drawing wireframe constructions, AME solids (no longer supported in Release 13), or ACIS solids. They are presented as part of this wireframe drawing chapter because they are necessary to the drawing process of all 3D design.

Tools

Every tool presented in this section, with the exception of Elevation and Thickness, have uses in the 2D design world. The techniques for using the tools in 3D space are the same as the techniques in 2D space, except that you are using them on objects that are extruded into 3D space. Some tools are better suited to working with the User Coordinate System (UCS) set to the working plane. Others can work independent of the UCS. Tools like point filters and the calculator are ignored by many users even in 2D design. In 3D design, they become almost mandatory tools that you need every day.

ELEVATION

This command is a tool for setting up your drawing platform. You can think of elevation as the platform, or sheet of electronic paper that you stand (draw) upon. Elevation is set to zero when your platform is on the ground. When your platform is on the third floor of a building, it has an elevation of approximately thirty feet. Move the platform to the basement and it has an elevation of minus ten feet. The Cube3D drawing, used in Chapters 1 and 2, uses an elevation of 4.4388 for the top surface of the cube. The bottom surface of the cube has an elevation of zero.

Elevation is dependent upon the current UCS. The ELEVATION command sets your working surface relative to the current UCS. When your current UCS is the same as the World Coordinate System (WCS), the effect of setting the elevation is to make your drawing platform higher or lower relative to the WCS. When you change your UCS (discussed later in this chapter), the drawing platform is set relative to the new current UCS setting. This makes it confusing when you query an object that you placed at an elevation of five and it is actually setting at an elevation of seven. The AutoCAD LIST command reports the position of the object in XYZ space relative to the current UCS. When an object is created in a UCS that is not the WCS and you list out its information in a different UCS (or the WCS), the resulting information will appear wrong. The information appears correct only when you do the listing of the information while in the UCS in which the object was created. Try using the ELEVATION command.

Practice Procedure for Using the ELEVATION Command

1. In a new drawing, type **elevation** and press **Enter** to activate the command.
2. Type **2** and press **Enter** to set the elevation at two.
3. Draw a circle with a radius of 1 at the grid intersection of 2,2.
4. Type **elevation** and press **Enter** to activate the command.
5. Type **4** and press **Enter**.

6. Draw a circle with a radius of 1 at the grid intersection of 2,2.

7. Use the VPOINT command to view your objects 315 *in* the XY plane and 35 *from* the XY plane.

The results should look like Figure 3.1.

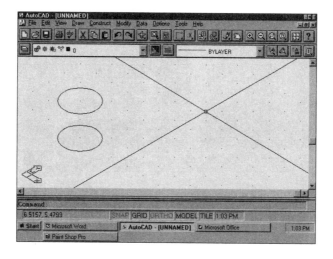

FIGURE 3.1 Practice procedure result.

THE ELEVATION COMMAND MENU LOCATIONS

This command is not present in any menu location as shipped with Release 13. See the "Customizing 3D Toolbars" section in Chapter 12 for instructions on adding this command to your own toolbar or an existing toolbar.

THICKNESS

The simplest way to think of thickness is to think of the wall of a room. The wall has a thickness measured from the floor to the ceiling. The floor and ceiling are two different elevations, so thickness is the distance between two different elevations. Any primitive object in AutoCAD can have thickness assigned to it. The default thickness of an object is zero. Many users take a simple floor plan and create a crude 3D projection of the plan by assigning a thickness to the lines in the floor plan. Figure 3.2 shows a before and after example of this technique.

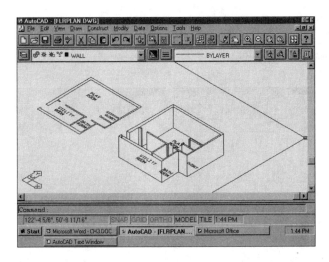

FIGURE 3.2 Creating a crude 3D from a 2D object using thickness.

The problem with this technique is that you can not cut holes in the objects because the objects are only projected (extruded) along the Z axis of the objects Entity Coordinate System (ECS). The ECS is not something you normally need to concern yourself with. Every object created in AutoCAD has its own ECS assigned and stored at the time of creation. AutoCAD uses that information with certain commands, like the Thickness option of the CHPROP command, to determine which way to extrude the object. The positive side to this is that you can get a quick feel for how the plan would look in 3D space.

When you set the thickness with the THICKNESS command, all geometry created has that extruded thickness until you change the thickness to some other setting. Some objects in AutoCAD ignore thickness even when it is assign to them. 3Dfaces (discussed in Chapter 6) and blocks are good examples. Objects inside a block can have thickness but the block itself ignores any thickness assigned to it.

Thickness is more like 2.5D instead of 3D. It is a cheater's way of simulating 3D crudely and quickly. Cheaters never prosper. Use this technique enough and sooner or later you will get burned. You cannot change the thickness other than to another setting or zero. You cannot cut holes in it. It does allow hidden line removal (discussed in Chapter 6) but it is not a solid so the top and bottom of a wall are open. An extruded circle appears solid but does not behave as a solid. Try the THICKNESS command.

Practice Procedure for the THICKNESS Command

1. In a new drawing, position yourself in an isometric view.
2. Type **thickness** and press **Enter** to activate the command.
3. Type **3** and press **Enter** to set a thickness of three.
4. Place a line, an arc, and a circle in the drawing.
5. Type **hide** and press **Enter**.

The result should look similar to Figure 3.3. Notice that each object extrudes 3 units on the Z axis from the bottom of the object and the circle appears solid.

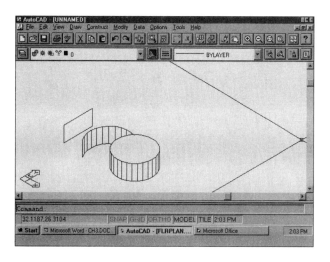

FIGURE 3.3 Practice Results Using the THICKNESS Command.

THE THICKNESS COMMAND MENU LOCATIONS

This command is not present in any menu location as shipped with Release 13. See the "Customizing 3D Toolbars" section in Chapter 12 for information on adding this command to your own toolbar or an existing toolbar.

POINT FILTERS

All points in AutoCAD are expressed in the form X,Y,Z. Point filters allow you to extract any combination, in any form, from any three points to create a new point. It sounds complicated, but in actuality it is simple. Say you have three objects in 3D space that are not located in conjunction. You need to find the theoretical middle point between the midpoints of the objects. Point filters allow you to do this quickly and easily. The steps are to ask AutoCAD to extract the X part of the point on the object on the X axis, the Y part of the point on the object on the Y axis and the Z part of the point on the object on the Z axis. Try drawing a circle at the midpoint intersection of the three sides of a cube.

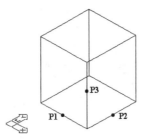

FIGURE 3.4 Point filters practice procedure reference.

Practice Procedure for Using Point Filters

1. In the *Cube3D* drawing, type **circle** and press **Enter** to activate the CIRCLE command.

2. At the <Center point>: prompt, type **.X** and press **Enter**.

3. At the of prompt, select the midpoint object snap.

4. Select a point on the X axis line corresponding to the point P1 shown in Figure 3.4.

5. At the (need YZ): prompt, type **.Y** and press **Enter**.

6. At the of prompt, select the midpoint object snap.

7. Select a point on the Y axis line corresponding to the point P2 shown in Figure 3.4.

8. At the (need Z): prompt, select the midpoint object snap.

9. At the _mid of prompt, select a point on the Z axis line corresponding to the point P3 shown in Figure 3.4.

10. Type **1** at the <Radius>: prompt and press **Enter**.

The result should look similar to Figure 3.5.

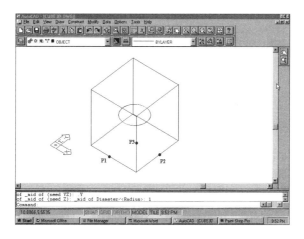

FIGURE 3.5 Point filters results.

Point filters are a lot easier to use when you memorize a simple rule. The rule states:

- The .X filter means you want the X part of a point that is no further to the left or right of a chosen point on the X axis.

- The .Y filter means you want the Y part of a point that is no further above or below a chosen point on the Y axis.

- The .Z filter means you want the Z part of a point that is no further above or below a chosen point on the Z axis.

Given the three points (1,1,1), (2,2,2), and (3,3,3), you can create the new point (1,2,3) by selecting the .X, .Y, and .Z from each respectively. You can use any method of selecting the points. This tool is very powerful for designing because it allows you to position geometry quickly in all three dimensions without the aid of construction lines.

THE POINT FILTERS COMMAND MENU LOCATIONS

The *Point Filters* menu item is located on the *Edit* pull-down menu (shown in Figure 3.6). The toolbar is located on the *Toolbars* menu item under the *Tools* pull-down menu. The toolbar and the menu item pick are shown in Figure 3.7.

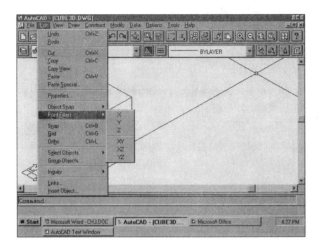

FIGURE 3.6 Point Filters Menu Item.

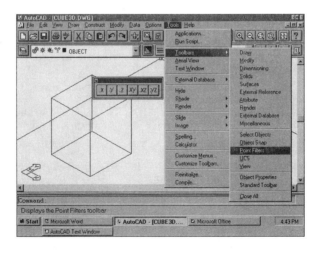

FIGURE 3.7 Point filters toolbar and toolbar menu item.

NOTE

Point Filters are also located on the Standard toolbar as a flyout menu.

COORDINATE SYSTEMS

The Absolute, Relative, and Polar coordinates used in 2D design work the same way in 3D space relative to the current UCS setting. Two additional coordinate systems can be used in 3D design. They are Cylindrical and Spherical. These two systems look like the Relative and Polar system except they have an extra number.

The relative Cylindrical system takes the form @Dist<Ang,Dist. The first distance is the distance *in* the XY plane along the X axis and the angle is measured *in* the XY plane relative to the X axis. The last distance measures along the Z axis. A Cylindrical coordinate of @6<45,4 means a point 6 units from the last point of the current UCS, 45 degrees *in* the XY plane along the X axis, and 4 units *from* the XY plane along the Z axis. Figure 3.8 shows the measurements.

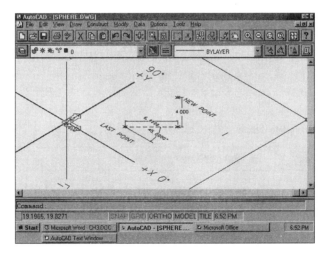

FIGURE 3.8 Cylindrical coordinates.

The relative Spherical system takes the form @Dist<Ang<Ang. The distance is measured along the X axis. The first angle is measured in the XY plane along the X axis and the second angle is measured from the XY plane along the Z axis. A Spherical coordinate of @4<45<60 means a point starting 4 units from the last point at an angle of 45 degrees *in* the XY plane along the X axis and an angle of 60 degree *from* the XY plane along the Z axis.

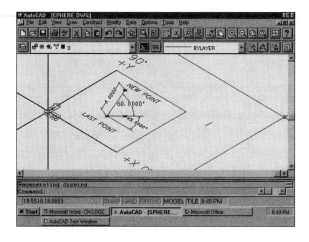

FIGURE 3.9 Spherical coordinates.

GEOMETRIC CALCULATOR

The calculator that started shipping with Release 12 is a powerful tool containing many shortcuts for geometry manipulation. Many geometric manipulation functions are defined in the calculator. They include those shown in Table 3.1.

TABLE 3.1 Geometry Calculator functions.

Function	Description
ang (v)	Angle between the X axis and vector V
ang (p1,p2)	Angle between the X axis and line (p1, p2)
ang (apex, p1, p2)	Angle between the lines (apex, p1) and (apex, p2) projected onto the XY plane
ang (apex, p1, p2, p)	Angle between the lines (apex, p1) and (apex, p2)
cur	Point using the graphics cursor
cvunit (val, from, to)	Converts value from one unit of measurement to another
dee	Distance between two endpoints. Shortcut for dist (end, end)

dist (p1, p2)	Distance between points p1 and p2
dpl (p, p1, p2)	Distance between point p and the line (p1, p2)
dpp (p, p1, p2, p3)	Distance between point p and the plane defined by p1, p2, p3
getvar (var_name)	Reads the value of an AutoCAD system variable
ill (p1, p2, p3, p4)	Intersection of lines (p11, p2) and (p3, p4)
illp (p1, p2, p3, p4, p5)	Intersection of the line (p1, p2) and the plane defined by p3, p4, p5
ille	Intersection of two lines defined by four endpoints. Shortcut for ill(end, end, end, end)
In (real)	Natural log of the number
mee	Midpoint between two endpoints. Shortcut for mid(end, end)/2
nee	Unit vector in the XY plane and normal to two endpoints. Shortcut for nor (vec (end, end))
nor	Unit vector normal to a circle, arc, or arc polyline segment
nor (v)	Unit vector in the XY plane and normal to the vector v
nor (p1, p2)	Unit vector in the XY plane and normal to the line (p1, p2)
nor (p1, p2, p3)	Unit vector normal to plane defined by p1,p2, and p3
pld (p1, p2, units)	Point on the line (p1, p2) that is drawing units away from the point p1
plt (p1, p2, t)	Point on line (p1, p2) that is t segments away from p1. A segment is the distance from point p1 to p2
rad	Radius of the selected entity
rot (p, origin, ang)	Rotates point p through angle ang about point origin
rot (p, p1ax, ang)	Rotates point p through angle ang using line (p1ax, p2ax) as the axis of rotation
rxof (p)	X coordinates of a point (returns a real)
ryof (p)	Y coordinates of a point (returns a real)
rzof (p)	Z coordinates of a point (returns a real)
u2w (p)	Converts point p from the current UCS to WCS

Table 3.1 continued

vec (p1, p2)	Vector from point p1 to point p2
vec1 (p1, p2)	Unit vector from point p1 to p2
vee	Vector from two endpoints. Shortcut for vec(end, end)
vee1	Unit vector from two endpoints. Shortcut for vec1 (end, end)
w2u (p)	Converts point p from WCS to the current UCS
u2w (p)	Converts point p from the current UCS to WCS
xyof (p)	Returns the X and Y coordinates of a point (returns a point). The Z coordinate is set to 0.0
xzof (p)	Returns the X and Z coordinates of a point (returns a point). The Y coordinate is set to 0.0
yzof (p)	Returns the Y and Z coordinates of a point (returns a point). The X coordinate is set to 0.0
xof (p)	Returns the X coordinate of a point (returns a point). The Y and Z coordinates are set to 0.0
yof (p)	Returns the Y coordinate of a point (returns a point). The Y and Z coordinates are set to 0.0
zof (p)	Returns the Z coordinate of a point (returns a point). The Y and Z coordinates are set to 0.0

These functions are the predefined ones in the calculator. You can use the calculator's function language to dynamically create your own functions as you work. One every day function used in 3D design is finding the theoretical center of multiple objects in 3D space. The MEE function is a shortcut for finding the middle between two endpoints (handy for cubes), but you can use any object snap and use as many objects as you wish to find the middle between them. Try placing a circle in the center of three different circles located on three different Z axis.

Practice Procedure for Finding the Center of Objects Using the Calculator

1. In the *Calc* drawing in the *3Dworld* directory, type **circle** and press **Enter** to activate the CIRCLE command.

2. Type **'cal** at the <Center point>: prompt to activate the geometric calculator.

3. Type **(cen+cen+cen)/3** at the Expression: prompt and select each circle.

4. Give the circle a radius of **1**.

The result should look like Figure 3.10. Notice that you added the center points of the three circles together and divided by three. This technique can be used by as many objects as you need as long as you divide by the same number of objects in the formula. You can use any legal object snap in the parenthesis. You are encouraged to experiment with the other standard functions like ANG and ILL.

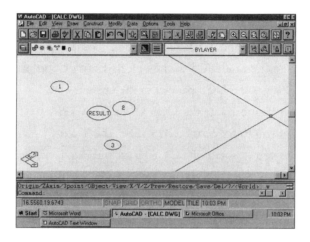

FIGURE 3.10 Calculator results.

OBJECT SNAPS, GRID/SNAP, AND ORTHO MODE IN THE 3D ENVIRONMENT

These tools all work with the current UCS. When you change the UCS, the grid/snap, object snaps, and ortho change with it.

The Endpoint object snap seeks the UCS elevation of a line residing on the Z axis when in plan view. To avoid this situation, use the Endpoint object snap on the line from an ISO view and select near the end that you want.

TIP

The User Coordinate System

The UCS command controls the work surface (XY plane) on which you draw. AutoCAD always draws perpendicular to the UCS work plane. By moving the plane around, you can draw on any surface at any rotation in 3D space. In Chapter 2, you learned how to use the UCS to control your display in 3D space. Here, you are given the opportunity to practice the UCS command for drawing objects in 3D space. The command can also be used to position the working plane for editing. The UCS command has many options that allow you total control over the working plane. The options include:

- Origin—moves the UCS origin to any point selected.
- Zaxis—allows you to tilt the Z axis at an angle relative to the XY plane.
- 3point—positions the UCS around a user selected origin point, X vector (direction) point, and Y vector (direction) point.
- Object—changes the UCS to the objects Entity Coordinate System.
- View—changes the UCS parallel to the current view.
- X—allows you to rotate the UCS about the X axis.
- Y—allows you to rotate the UCS about the Y axis.
- Z—allows you to rotate the UCS about the Z axis.
- Prev—changes the UCS to the previous UCS setting.
- Restore—Allows you to restore a saved named UCS coordinate.
- Save—allows you to save and name a UCS coordinate.
- Del—allows you to delete a saved named UCS coordinate.
- ?—gives you a list of saved named UCS coordinates.
- <World>—sets the UCS to WCS.

The Origin Option

The Origin option moves the UCS origin (0,0,0) to any point selected in 3D space. This is useful for defining the origin of a working plane at the corner of a surface. Another technique is to place the origin and insert a block or external reference at the origin. Many architects developing multi-level buildings use the origin as an anchor and simply move the origin straight up on the Z axis. Try changing the UCS origin in a drawing.

Practice Procedure for Changing the UCS Origin

1. In any drawing, type **ucs** and press **Enter**.
2. Type **or** and press **Enter** to activate the Origin option.

3. Select a point anywhere on the screen using any method you want (Absolute, Relative, Polar, use grid/snap, pick a random point, or use object snaps if objects are present).

Notice how the UCS icon no longer shows a W in the corner. That is because you have now defined your own User Coordinate System that has an origin at the spot you selected.

The Zaxis Option

The Zaxis option allows you to tilt the Z axis at an angle relative to the XY plane. The other axis options of the UCS command allow you to rotate the working plane around an axis. This option allows you to tilt the Z axis relative to the current Z axis. It is handy for creating slopes on an object when you know the slope angle. Figure 3.11 shows how the Zaxis tilts relative to the Z axis.

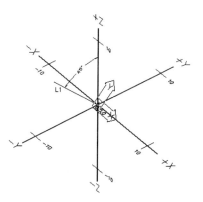

FIGURE 3.11 Zaxis tilt.

The line L1, shown in Figure 3.11, is 10 units long and runs along the positive Z axis of a UCS created using the Zaxis option of the UCS command. Try creating this line in the 3AXIS drawing. The practice procedure gives you two methods of entering the point to tilt the Z axis.

Practice Procedure for Tilting the Z Axis Using the Zaxis Option

1. In the drawing 3AXIS, type **ucs** and press **Enter** to activate the UCS command.

2. Type **za** and press **Enter** to activate the Zaxis option.

3. Accept the default origin by pressing **Enter** at the `Origin point <0,0,0>:` prompt.

4. Use either relative or spherical coordinates to tilt the Z axis, as shown in Figure 3.11.

5. Once the UCS is tilted properly, use the LINE command to place a line from the origin point 10 units along the Z axis. (LINE command, from point at the 0,0,0 origin, and the to point is @0,0,10.)

Step four is the critical step in tilting the Z axis with the Zaxis option. Either suggested method works, and the one you use depends on how comfortable you are with the method. To check your accuracy, turn on the layer ANSWER. The line and dimension shown in Figure 3.11 are on that layer. The UCS was set using the relative method.

The relative method works along the lines of how you calculated your camera position in 3D space using the VPOINT Rotate option. The line's slope is 135 degrees *from* the XY plane (or 45 degrees from the Z axis). To use a relative coordinate, you must calculate the X axis offset from the origin point *in* the XY plane, the Y axis offset from the origin point in the XY plane, and the Z axis offset *from* the XY plane (the line's slope of 135 degrees). The line in Figure 3.11 is parallel with the -Y axis. Therefore, the X axis offset is zero and the Y axis can be any negative number. To get a 45 degree angle from the Z axis (135 degrees from the XY plane), you need to use a positive number for the Z offset. In this case, @0,-10,10 works. The resulting UCS has the Z axis along the imaginary line between the origin point and the one you selected by using the relative coordinate. The XY plane must always remain perpendicular to the Z axis, so it is tilted in relation to the Z axis. When you place the line using a relative coordinate of @0,0,10 in the current UCS, it places the line along the same imaginary line you used to create the working plane.

The method of changing the UCS Z axis using a spherical coordinate demands that you understand how that coordinate method works (see the "Coordinate Systems" section earlier in this chapter). The answer is any positive number, an angle of 270 *in* the XY plane and an angle of 45 from the Z axis (@3<270<45 works).

You might have caught the fact that the line could have been created in 3D space without ever adjusting the UCS first. A line starting at 0,0,0 could be created exactly the same length and direction by using just the spherical coordinate. However, that is not always the case and you need to understand the Zaxis option for those times that you need it. AutoCAD has many tools for working in 3D space and often many of them can be used in a given situation.

The 3point Option

The 3point option positions the UCS around a user selected origin point, X vector (direction) point and Y vector (direction) point, as shown in Figure 3.12.

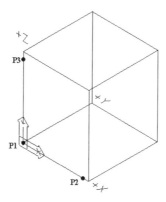

FIGURE 3.12 3point Option.

This option is handy when you already have geometry positioned in 3D space and you need to align your work plane (UCS) with a piece of geometry or several pieces of geometry. Using any combination of object snaps, grid/snap, absolute, relative, or polar coordinates enables you to position your UCS working plane in relation to any combination of objects or points in space. Try using the 3point option.

Practice Procedure for Using the 3point Option

1. Inside the *Wedge* drawing, type **ucs** and press **Enter** to activate the UCS command.
2. Type **3** and press **Enter** to activate the 3point option.
3. Select the endpoint P1 as shown in Figure 3.13.
4. Select the midpoint P2 as shown in Figure 3.13.
5. Select the midpoint P3 as shown in Figure 3.13.
6. Place a circle on the face of the slope of the wedge.

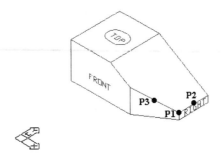

FIGURE 3.13 3point practice procedure reference.

You can check your work by using the VPOINT command's Rotate option and setting it to 255 degrees in the XY plane and 22 degrees from the XY plane. This view shows clearly that circle is on the same work plane as the front slope of the wedge.

NOTE

The X and Y axes always remain at 90 degrees from each other. This trick worked on the wedge slope because the positive X axis is always defined first and the positive Y axis defined only the slope of the face of the wedge, not the exact Y axis along the line selected.

The Object Option

This option aligns the UCS work plane with the object you select. It takes the Entity Coordinate System (ECS) that is stored with each object you create in AutoCAD and positions the UCS to the same position. The ECS is used internally by AutoCAD and you need not concern yourself with it or its operation. The effect of positioning your UCS to it is that the UCS then becomes parallel with the object. This is a must in many situations where you want to edit an existing object. AutoCAD must be on a working plane (UCS) that is parallel to the object for the editing command to work. Using the UCS Object option allows you to quickly position the UCS for editing. Many times the UCS will not look like it did when you created the object when you set it to the ECS. This is not an issue and you can safely ignore the incongruity. Try using the Object option to align the UCS with the slope of the wedge.

Practice Procedure for Using the Object Option

1. In the *Wedge* drawing, type **ucs** and press **Enter** to activate the UCS command.

2. Type **ob** and press **Enter** to activate the Object option.

3. Select the midpoint P2 as shown in Figure 3.13.

4. Place a circle on the face of the slope of the wedge.

The results are the same as the practice procedure using the 3point option. Not all the lines on the face of the wedge's slope would have produced this result. This option is very dependent on how the UCS was set when the object was created.

The View Option

This option forces the UCS parallel to the current view so that you are in plan view to the UCS. This is handy for creating isometric views and then placing text on them that does not look skewed. The text then becomes view-dependent; if you ever change the view, the text looks skewed. This method is used often to fake a simple paperspace technique of annotating the drawing in model space. Many of the examples in this book were created using this technique. Try placing some text in the current view from the last practice using this option.

Practice Procedure Using the View Option

1. In the *Wedge* drawing, type **ucs** and press **Enter** to activate the UCS command.

2. Type **v** and press **Enter** to activate the View option.

3. Use a text command to place some text on the screen.

The text is in plan view (parallel) to the current screen view. Change the view slightly and the text appears skewed.

The X Option, Y Option, and Z Option

Each of these options allow you to rotate the UCS around the desired axis. The hardest thing to remember about these options are which directions are positive degrees. The easiest way to solve the problem is to use the right–hand rule discussed in Chapter 1. AutoCAD measures the angle relative to the axis in a counter-clockwise direction by default (you can change it to clockwise with the UNITS command). When you want to rotate about an axis with the X, Y, or Z option, take your right hand and look down the corresponding finger or thumb. Imagine the XY plane imposed over the digit as if you were looking down from plan view. The UCS will rotate in a counter-clockwise fashion. You can twist your hand in the same fashion to get an idea of how the axis is going to spin.

TIP

The human hand does not twist around 360 degrees, so many users design a tool to help them with this problem. Take the corner of a box and cut it off at a 45 degree angle. Label each axis and place a labeled cube (a disk box works) on the corresponding axis. Figure 3.14 illustrates the concept. Now you can experiment using the tool.

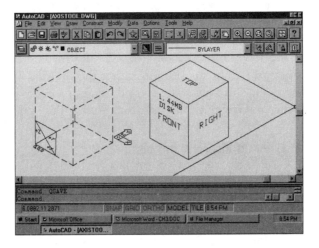

FIGURE 3.14 Axis tool and box.

TIP

Many people just try a positive angle about the axis and if it is wrong, they use the U command and then use a negative angle for the axis option. Crude, but often quicker than playing around with a tool.

NOTE

The *Preset UCS* dialogue box, discussed in Chapter 2, uses the X, Y, or Z axis option to accomplish the selected change.

The Prev Option

This option sets the UCS back to whatever position it was last set in. This is handy when you do not want to use the U command to undo the previous UCS adjustment. The U command would undo any work done after the change of the UCS. The Prev option sets back the UCS but leaves the work done after the last UCS setting intact. Try the Prev option.

Practice Procedure for Using the Prev Option

1. In the *Wedge* drawing, type **ucs** and press **Enter** to activate the UCS command.

2. Type **or** and press **Enter** to activate the Origin option.

3. Select any point on the screen as the new UCS origin.

4. Place a line and a circle in the drawing.

5. Type **ucs** and press **Enter** to activate the UCS command.

6. Type **p** and press **Enter** to activate the Prev option.

The result is that the UCS moves back to the previous UCS setting, but leaves the line and circle. Using the UNDO command would result in losing the line and circle as well as placing the UCS back to its previous setting.

The Restore, Save, and Del Options

You can save, restore, and delete UCS work planes in the same way you can save, restore, and delete views and vports. The process is to position your UCS where you want it and use the Save option to give that work plane a name. You can then restore the named UCS work plane using the Restore option at any time. When you no longer need a work plane, you can delete it using the Del option.

The ? Option

This option allows you to see a list of all named UCS work planes that have been saved in the drawing. The option allows the use of wildcards to see only limited names. Organizing your named UCS work planes is as important as organizing layer names when you create many named UCS work planes. Having a consistent naming structure allows you to use wildcards to see only those named UCS work planes limited by the wildcard. An example would be a setup where you have multiple angles varying by 5 degrees from the front UCS. You could create each UCS at 5 degree intervals, giving each the name FR-5 to FR-45. With a naming standard consistently followed, it becomes easy to limit the scope of your search by using the asterisk (*) in the ? list option. (i.e. FR-* to see all of the FRONT UCS work planes.)

NOTE

Contrary to popular belief, wildcards are for *limiting* the scope of a search, not *expanding* the scope. A wildcard says give me everything that falls within the scope of the name defined. The wildcard * is the exception. Used by itself, it expands the scope of the search to every name.

The <World> Option

This is the default option of the UCS command. When you press **Enter** without typing anything, this option is used. The World option places the UCS back to the World Coordinate System (WCS). You can also type a **w** and the option is activated.

NOTE

The UCS icon has a W appear whenever it is set to the WCS.

The UCS Command Options Menu Locations

The UCS menu locations are shown in Chapter 2. The locations remain the same whether you are using the UCS command options for viewing, drawing, or editing.

3D Wireframe Drawing Commands

There is only one drawing command that is dedicated to only 3D design. That command is the 3DPOLY command, which allows you to create polylines that span different elevations. The LINE drawing commands used in 2D design can be used in 3D design. You must use techniques like changing the UCS working plane, or relative coordinates with the LINE drawing command to effectively use it in 3D design. Try the LINE command in 3D space using relative coordinates, polar coordinates and the ELEVATION command.

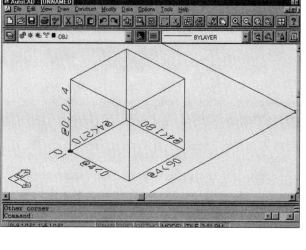

FIGURE 3.15 Practice reference for LINE in 3D space.

Practice Procedure for Using the LINE Command in 3D Space

1. Start a new drawing using the 3D prototype drawing provided in the *3Dworld* directory.

2. Type **line** and press **Enter** to activate the LINE command.

3. Select a point on the screen near the point P1 shown in Figure 3.15.

4. Complete the bottom of the cube using polar coordinates (the lines are 4 units long). Typically you would use @4<0 @4<90 @4<180 @4<270 to place the four lines as shown in Figure 3.15.

5. Type the relative coordinate **@0,0,4** and press **Enter** to create the first leg of the cube as shown in Figure 3.15.

6. Type **'elevation** and press **Enter** to activate the ELEVATION command transparently while still inside the LINE command.

7. Type **4** and press **Enter** to set the current elevation to four units above the WCS.

8. Complete the top of the cube using polar coordinates as you did for the bottom.

9. Press **Enter** to exit the LINE command.

10. Using the endpoint object snap, place the last three Z axis lines from the bottom to the top of the cube.

The technique of combining many different tools to create your object is a commonly-used technique. The same object could be created using the RECTANG command, and the ELEVATION command with the LINE command and object snaps to fill in the Z axis lines. Aligning the top rectangle with the bottom can be accomplished using point filters.

This brings up the issue of planning your design. Even the most experienced 3D design user needs to plan how to approach the design of the object before starting. Simple objects, like the cube, can be done quickly with little planning based upon the user's experience. More complex parts should be thought out before starting. The approach to the design and the tools to be used should be planned ahead. Many 3D designers use a method of design that entails creating simple parts of the object and combining them into one complex object. That method allows checking of the work on a small scale before the assembly of the complete part. The method is discussed in detail in Chapter 4.

Use the elevation command to set the current elevation of your drawing back to zero before proceeding.

N O T E

THE 3D POLYLINE

The 3D polyline accepts points with a Z axis other than the current elevation. The command does not have arc segments like the 2D polyline command. You can place a point anywhere in 3D space by using relative, cylindrical, spherical coordinates, point filters, or the ELEVATION command. Try using the 3DPOLY command to place a continuous line across several elevations.

PRACTICE PROCEDURE FOR THE 3DPOLY COMMAND

1. In the *3Dpoly* drawing, turn on your running nearest object snap.
2. Type **3dpoly** and press **Enter** to activate the 3DPOLY command.
3. Place the polyline on the elevations by snapping on the elevation planes near the points P1, P2, P3, P4, P5, and P6 as shown in Figure 3.16.

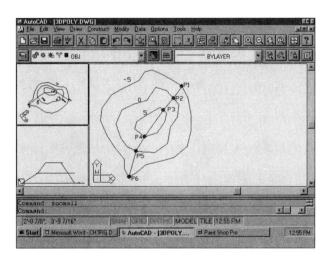

FIGURE 3.16 Practice reference for the 3DPOLY command in 3D space.

In Conclusion

The tools covered in this chapter allow you to design in the 3D world with relative ease. By using many of the same tools that you should be using in 2D design, you are shortening your learning curve. The 3D polyline command is limited by its inability to create arcs. Using 2D drawing commands and controlling the working plane (UCS) gives you more control in the 3D world. In the next chapter, you are given the opportunity to practice several different techniques for creating wireframe objects.

CHAPTER FOUR

Wireframe Construction

This method of creating 3D geometry is much like building your object out of sticks and then having to place an outer surface on the stick frame. You use primitive drawing objects like lines, arcs, and circles to create the frame of the object and then use surface mesh commands to place a "skin" on the frame. Simple pre-built 3D surface primitive objects are introduced as a tool for creating wireframe. These objects have been built by Autodesk to help speed up the production process. Techniques for creating 3D wireframe geometry using the surface primitives are presented and practiced.

Creating Geometry Using 3D Primitives

AutoCAD has predefined 3D objects. These objects define primitive shapes in 3D design construction using surfaces (discussed in detail in Chapter 6 on 3D Surfaces). They can be used to create more complex objects, combining them and using drawing and editing commands to shape the new object. The object created has no wireframe lines—everything is a 3D surface—but you can snap to the edges and create a complex wireframe object from the primitive 3D surfaces. One advantage to this method of wireframe creation is that any 3D surface you do not need to change can be left in place. Wireframe constructions must have 3D surfaces placed on them to hide the sides of the object from the front view. The steps to wireframe construction using these primitive objects is:

1. Place the necessary 3D primitive objects on a faces layer.

2. Use running object snaps and various drawing commands on a different layer to outline the object (frame).

3. Delete any 3D surfaces not needed in the new object outline.

4. Place any new 3D faces needed on the object on the faces layer by snapping them to the outline of the wireframe.

The shapes include:

- Cube
- Pyramid
- Wedge
- Dome
- Sphere
- Cone
- Torus
- Dish

THE 3D BOX AI_BOX COMMAND

This command allows you to form a 3D box by defining the length, height, width, and rotation of the object. Try placing a 3D box.

Practice Procedure for the 3D Box

1. In a new drawing created using the 3DPROTO drawing, type **ai_box** and press **Enter** to activate the 3D box surface primitive command.

2. Select a point near the lower center of the screen at the Corner of box: prompt.

3. Type **2** and press **Enter** at the Length: prompt.

4. Type **2** and press **Enter** at the Cube/<Width>: prompt.

5. Type **2** and press **Enter** at the Height: prompt.

6. Type **0** (zero) and press **Enter** at the Rotation angle about Z axis: prompt.

7. Type **hide** and press **Enter** to activate the hidden line removal command.

The Cube option in step 4 takes the length and applies it to the width and height. This cube is made up of 3D surfaces called *3D faces* (covered in Chapter 6 on 3D Surfaces). To create a wireframe, switch to a frame layer and outline each edge of the cube. Try creating the frame on the cube.

Practice Procedure for the 3D Box Wireframe

1. Create a layer for your wireframe entities called FRAME.

2. Turn on your running object snap **Endpoint**.

3. Type **regen** and press **Enter** to clear the hidden line removal.

4. Type **line** and press **Enter** to activate the LINE command.

5. Outline all edges of the cube by picking each corner of the cube. (You will need to exit and enter the LINE command when you can no longer continue without drawing over a previous wireframe line.)

TIP

It helps to assign a different color to the wireframe layer than is used with the layer on which the 3D surface object was placed.

87

THE PYRAMID AI_PYRAMID COMMAND

This command allows you to build two types of 3D pyramids. You can create a pyramid with a base of three points (the Tetrahedron option at the Fourth Base Point option) or a base of four points (the default when you select the fourth point for the base). The command needs you to define the base points of the base of the pyramid and an apex point. Two other options are provided for the top of the pyramid, Top and Ridge. Try building the great pyramid.

Practice Procedure for the 3D Pyramid

1. In a new drawing created using the 3DPROTO drawing, restore the viewport configuration 3D3R and activate the upper-left viewport as shown in Figure 4.1.

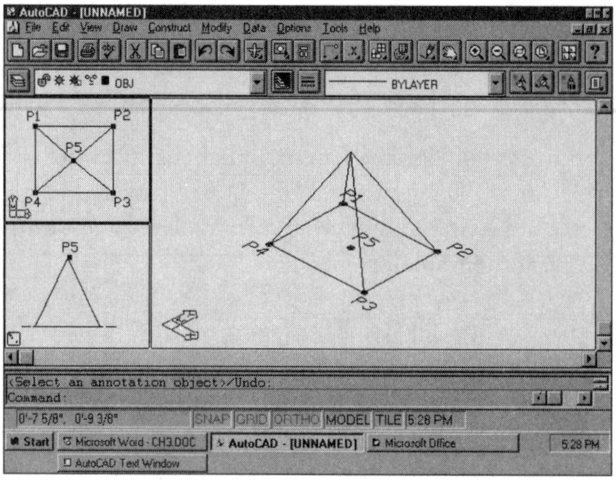

[Figure: AutoCAD application window screenshot]

FIGURE 4.1 Practice reference for the AI_PYRAMID command in 3D space.

2. Type **ai_pyramid** and press **Enter** to activate the 3D pyramid surface primitive command.

3. Select the points P1 through P4 (for the base) shown in the upper-left corner of Figure 4.1.

4. Type **.xy** and press **Enter** to activate the XY filter.

5. Select the point P5 in the upper-left viewport.

6. Activate the lower-left viewport by picking inside the viewport, and select a point near the P5 point shown in the lower-left viewport of Figure 4.1 to define the pyramid's apex point.

The pyramid, like the 3D box and all other primitives in this section, is constructed of 3D face surfaces. You must use commands like LINE and object snaps to place a wireframe on the edges of the object.

TIP

The technique of splitting the point filter between two different viewports (steps 5 and 6 in the last procedure) is effective for all 3D drawing, editing, and viewing commands. Remember, when AutoCAD wants a point, you can use a point filter. Whenever you use a point filter, you can select the parts of the point in different viewports.

CREATING A WEDGE WITH THE AI_WEDGE COMMAND

The AI_WEDGE command allows you to create a 3D wedge. You must specify the length, width, height, and rotation of the object. The length of the wedge is the front of the wedge and the width is the side. Try creating a 3D wedge using the AI_WEDGE command.

Practice Procedure for Using the AI_WEDGE Command

1. In a new drawing created using the 3DPROTO drawing, restore the viewport configuration 3D3R and activate the upper-left viewport as shown in Figure 4.1.

2. Type **ai_wedge** and press **Enter** to activate the 3D wedge surface primitive command.

3. Select a point near the point P1, as shown in the right viewport in Figure 4.2, for the corner of the wedge.

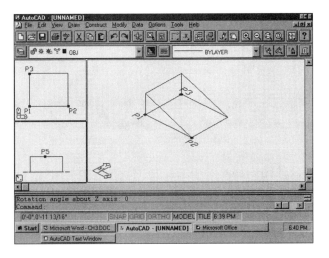

FIGURE 4.2 Practice reference for the AI_WEDGE command in 3D space.

4. Select a point near the point P2, as shown in the right viewport in Figure 4.2, for the length of the wedge.

5. Select a point near the point P3, as shown in the right viewport in Figure 4.2, for the width of the wedge.

6. Use the .XY filter to select the point P1, as shown in the right viewport in Figure 4.2, for the position of the height of the wedge.

7. Select a point near the point P5, as shown in the lower-left viewport in Figure 4.2, for the height of the wedge.

8. Type **0** (zero) and press **Enter** to give the wedge a zero rotation.

THE 3D DOME AI_DOME COMMAND

This command creates the upper half of a sphere. You can define the center point, a radius or diameter, and how many 3D face segments are on the latitude and longitude faces. Try placing a dome.

Practice Procedure for Placing a Dome Using the AI_DOME Command

1. In a new drawing created using the 3DPROTO drawing, type **ai_dome** and press **Enter** to activate the 3D dome surface primitive command.

2. Set your viewport to plan view (use the PLAN command).

3. Select a point near the point P1, as shown in Figure 4.3, for the center of the dome.

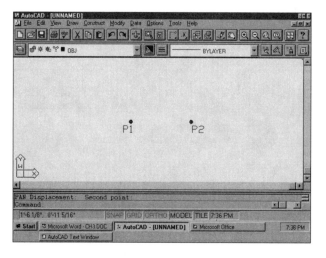

FIGURE 4.3 Practice reference for the AI_DOME command in 3D space.

4. Select a point near the point P2, as shown in Figure 4.3, for the radius of the dome.

5. Press **Enter** twice to accept the default of 16 segments for the longitude and 8 segments for the latitude.

6. Restore the viewport configuration, 3D3R, and zoom extents in each view.

7. Hide all the views to see the results of your work.

TIP

Seeing your work in the various viewports, as shown in steps 5 and 6 of the last procedure, can be time-consuming because you must activate each viewport, set the view, and then hide it. The core AutoCAD commands for this series of events can be slow. Two AutoLISP routines have been provided on the disk with this book for speeding up this process. To position all viewports, load the AutoLISP routine ZOOMALL.LSP (load "zoomall") and run it (zoomall). To hide all of the viewport's hidden lines, load the AutoLISP routine HIDEALL.LSP (load "hideall") and run it (hideall).

CREATING A 3D SPHERE WITH THE AI_SPHERE COMMAND

The AI_SPHERE command creates a 3D sphere. The options are the same as the AI_DOME command, except that the default segments for the latitude 3D faces is 16.

THE 3D CONE USING AI_CONE

This command creates a 3D cone. The command allows you to define a radius for both the base and the top of the cone. A cone top with a radius of 0 (zero) comes to a point. You also control the height and number of 3D face segments of the cone. Try placing a 3D cone.

Practice Procedure for Placing a 3D Cone Using the AI_CONE Command

1. In a new drawing created using the 3DPROTO drawing, type **ai_cone** and press **Enter** to activate the 3D cone surface primitive command.

2. Select a point on the screen near the point P1, as shown in the upper-left viewport in Figure 4.4, to define the base center point.

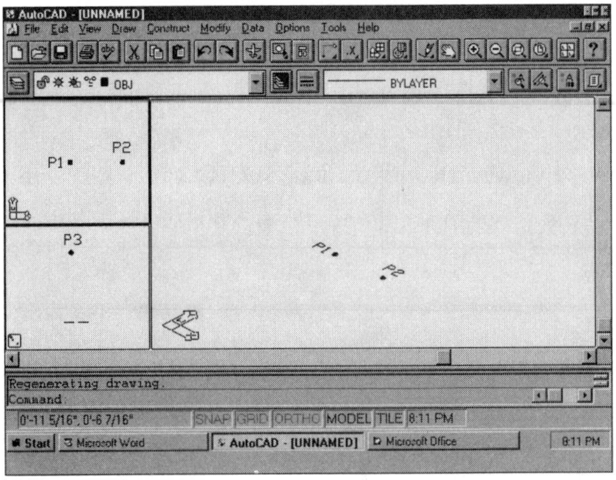

FIGURE 4.4 Practice reference for the AI_CONE command in 3D space.

3. Select a point on the screen near the point P2, as shown in the upper-left viewport in Figure 4.4, to supply the radius of the base.

4. Press **Enter** to accept the default of 0 (zero) for the top radius.

5. Use the .XY point filter and type **@** to start to measure the height.

6. Select a point in the lower-left viewport near the point P3, as shown in Figure 4.4.

7. Accept the default of 16 segments by pressing **Enter**.

8. Restore the viewport configuration, 3D3R, and zoom extents in each view.

9. Hide all the views to see the results of your work.

TIP Step 5 shows a method of using the @ symbol (meaning the last point placed) with a point filter to extract the X and Y part of the last point. This method allows you to position the point in the XY plane and then use the side or front viewport to extract the Z axis from any point selected.

THE 3D TORUS USING THE AI_TORUS COMMAND

The 3D Torus is a three-dimensional version of the 2D DONUT command. You supply the radius of the outside of the Torus ring and the radius of the tube (the 3D ring). You control the number of segments for both the tube and the Torus. Try creating a Torus.

Practice Procedure for Placing a 3D Torus Using the AI_TORUS Command

1. In a new drawing created using the 3DPROTO drawing, type **ai_torus** and press **Enter** to activate the 3D Torus surface primitive command.

2. Select a point on the screen near the point P1, as shown in the upper-left viewport in Figure 4.5, to define the center point of the Torus.

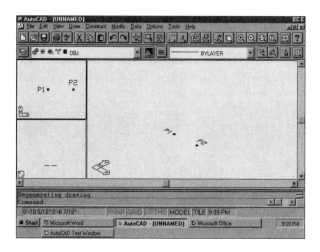

FIGURE 4.5 Practice reference for the AI_TORUS command in 3D space.

3. Select a point on the screen near the point P2, as shown in the upper-left viewport in Figure 4.5, to define the radius of the Torus.

4. Type **1** and press **Enter** to set the radius of the tube to 1 unit.

5. Press **Enter** twice to accept the defaults of 16 segments for both the Torus and the tube.

6. Restore the viewport configuration, 3D3R, and zoom extents in each view.

7. Hide all the views to see the results of your work.

TIP

AutoCAD does not have a dialogue box command for restoring viewport configurations. One has been supplied on the support disk with this book. Load the AutoLISP routine DDVPORTS.LSP (load "ddvports") and run it (ddvports). Select the viewports configuration you wish to restore and select the **OK** button.

THE 3D DISH CREATED BY THE AI_DISH COMMAND

The AI_DISH command creates the lower half of a 3D sphere (the opposite of the AI_DOME command). The options are the same as the AI_DOME command except that the default segments for the latitude 3D faces is 16.

THE 3D SURFACE PRIMITIVES COMMAND MENU LOCATIONS

All the 3D surface primitives are located on the *3D Objects...* menu item on the *Surfaces* menu item under the *Draw* pull-down menu. The sequence of menu picks, *Draw/ Surfaces/3D Objects...*, activates the dialogue box for the 3D surface primitives. Figure 4.6 shows the 3D Surface Primitives dialogue box. You can choose the primitive by selecting either the name from the left list or the image from the images on the right.

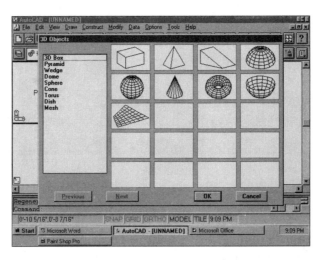

FIGURE 4.6 3D Surface Primitives dialogue box.

Wireframe Construction Techniques

You have now been introduced to the necessary tools to control the display of 3D objects, the tools to control the drawing of wireframe objects, and the primitive 3D surface objects that can be used to create complex 3D objects. Now you need to practice three commonly used techniques using these tools and commands to create wireframe objects.

SIMPLE 2D DRAWING COMMANDS

This technique involves using 2D drawing commands with tools like point filters, object snaps, the calculator, and relative and polar coordinates. The following section walks you through a simple 3D part using these various tools (see Figure 4.7).

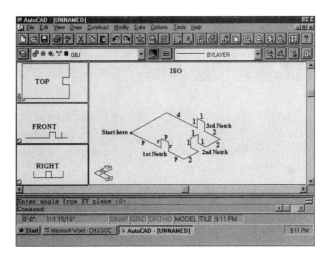

FIGURE 4.7 Simple 2D technique practice drawing.

Practice Procedure for the 2D Drawing Command Method

1. Start a new drawing using the 3DPROTO drawing.

2. Restore the viewport configuration 3D4R. (This technique is easiest from the ISO view.)

3. Use Polar and Relative coordinates (shown in Figure 4.7 as r for relative and p for polar) and the LINE command to create the base of the part. (The line lengths are shown next to each line as typical lengths next to critical lines.)

4. Create the four extruded lines for the sides by placing lines using relative coordinates from each corner, as shown in Figure 4.8.

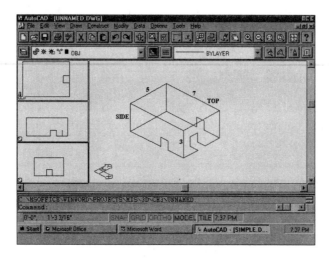

FIGURE 4.8 Simple 2D technique practice drawing continued.

5. Create the top of the object, as shown in Figure 4.8, by endpoint snapping to the extruded side lines at the corners.

6. Create the right side notch, as shown in Figure 4.9, by using the LINE command and a relative coordinate from P1 to P2 and object snap to the top of the notch at P3. (Running object snaps can cause problems in this step.)

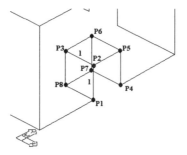

FIGURE 4.9 Simple 2D technique practice drawing right side notch.

7. Do the same for the other side of the notch at P4, P5, and P6.

8. Fill in the bottom line between P6 and P7 and the top front of the notch between P2 and P5 using endpoint object snap.

9.   Finish the part by using your running endpoint object snap to connect the sides and top of the front and rear notch.

10. Save the drawing with the name WIREFRAM.

The finished part is shown in Figure 4.10. It cannot have hidden line removal because it has no 3D surfaces attached. The techniques for placing 3D faces on a wireframe object, such as the one you just created, is covered in Chapter 6 on 3D Surfaces.

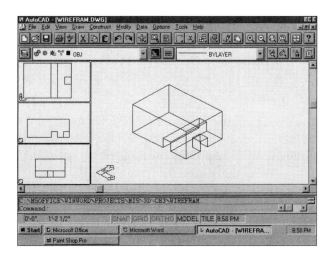

FIGURE 4.10 Simple 2D technique practice drawing finished.

USING THE UCS TO CREATE AN OBJECT IN 3D

This technique involves using the User Coordinate System to rotate the working plane to the side of your part you want to draw. There are two methods of using the UCS for this type of drawing technique. The first and most used method involves placing the object in an ISO view and then doing all of your drawing by manipulating the UCS to the face of the object you wish to create. The second method involves using the UCSFOLLOW system variable to always work in plan view to the UCS. This method can be confusing because even object snaps do not behave as you think they should, and the UCS sometimes appears correct but has actually snapped to another section of the object. This section concentrates on the first method of this UCS technique. A small section walks you through the second method using the UCSFOLLOW variable.

USING THE UCS IN ISO VIEW

The object of this technique is to get set into an ISO view of the object area and change that view as little as possible. You change the UCS working (drawing) plane instead using the UCS command. Then you draw on the working plane. Make the same object as in the 2D drawing command practice procedure shown in Figure 4.10 using the UCS method.

Practice Procedure Using the UCS Method

1. Start a new drawing using the 3DPROTO drawing.

2. Restore the saved named UCS called FRONT (use DDUCS or the menu item that activates it).

3. Start your drawing at 0,0,0 of the FRONT UCS using the LINE command and the lengths shown in Figure 4.11. (You can use Polar coordinates for all the front lines because the UCS (working plane) is parallel to the front of the part.)

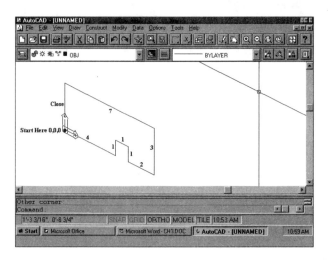

FIGURE 4.11 UCS practice drawing front plane.

4. Restore the RSIDE named UCS using the UCS Restore option or DDUCS and use the UCS command's Origin option to endpoint snap the UCS origin to the far-right bottom line's endpoint shown in Figure 4.12.

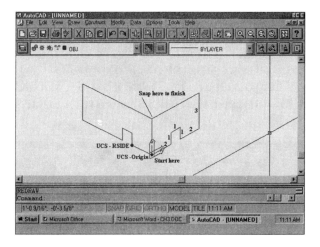

FIGURE 4.12 UCS practice drawing right plane.

5. Construct the right side of the part using the line lengths on the current UCS, as shown in Figure 4.12.

6. You can save time constructing the rear of the object by copying the front to the rear (they are the same). Use the COPY command to select all the front lines except the line at the origin P1 point and endpoint snap to the point P2, as shown in Figure 4.13.

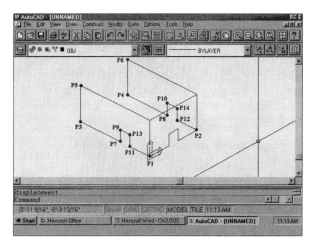

FIGURE 4.13 UCS practice drawing finished sides.

7. Use the endpoint object snap to place the remaining lines finishing the left side and the notches, as shown in Figure 4.13. (Connect the points P3-P4, P5-P6, P7-P8, P9-P10, P11-P12, and P13-P14.)

8. Finish the small notch (a 1x1x1 cube) on the right side by using the same techniques that you just used for the larger box. Set your UCS to World and place the UCS origin at the point P1, as shown in Figure 4.14.

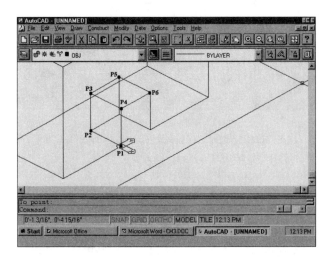

FIGURE 4.14 UCS practice drawing right notch section.

9. Draw the bottom of the notch, using Polar coordinates, starting at the origin point of the UCS, as shown in Figure 4.14 (@1<180, @1<90, @1<0).

10. Copy the right side of the notch cube to the left side of the notch by snapping the base point at the point P1 and the Second point of displacement: at the point P2, as shown in Figure 4.14.

11. Connect the top of the notch using the LINE command and the endpoint object snap from the point P3-P4, P5-P6 as shown in Figure 4.14.

The preceding practice procedure illustrates several ways of designing using the UCS method. Steps 6 and 10 illustrate the use of the COPY command to speed up productivity in 3D production. The Polar coordinate system and object snaps were used extensively when drawing lines, but the snap/grid or any other method could have been substituted in many places.

N O T E

You want to design in 3D quickly and accurately. The method of keeping your view the same as much as possible (usually an ISO view) and only using ZOOM or PAN to maneuver speeds up production. By combining the UCS method and the 2D command method with simple editing tools, you can quickly become proficient in the 3D design environment.

USING THE UCSFOLLOW METHOD

The previous practice procedure for the UCS method can be done using the UCSFOLLOW method. Using the UCSFOLLOW method by itself can cause problems with your object snaps. It is best to use this method in conjunction with the UCS method. To do that you must set up your screen and turn on the UCSFOLLOW system variable before doing the practice procedure.

Setup for the UCSFOLLOW Method

1. Start a new drawing using the 3DPROTO drawing.
2. Create a vertical split viewport screen, as shown in Figure 4.15, using the VPORTS command.

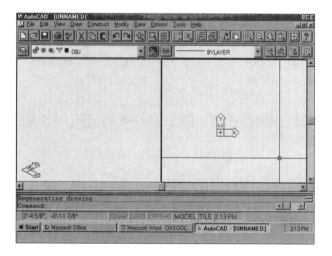

FIGURE 4.15 UCSFOLLOW setup practice procedure screen.

3. Leave the left viewport as an ISO view and make the right viewport into a plan view (select the viewport, if necessary, and use the PLAN command).

4. In the right viewport, type **ucsfollow** and press **Enter** to activate the system variable.

5. Type **1** and press **Enter** to turn on UCSFOLLOW.

6. Use the ZOOM command Scale option (.1x), in the right viewport, to better see your part as you create the first side.

The result should look like Figure 4.15.

Do the UCS method practice procedure steps again (listed in the "Using the UCS in ISO View" section of this chapter), this time working in the right plan view instead of the ISO view. The left view can be used but the object of this practice is to work in the plan view.

TIP

As you change the UCS, you need to adjust one or both of the viewports using the ZOOM and PAN commands. A quick technique is to do a ZOOM Extents, then a ZOOM Scale (.8x) option in each viewport. This is the exact procedure that the supplied routine ZOOMALL does.

Many people do not bother using the UCSFOLLOW method of 3D design. This is unfortunate because the technique can assist in situations where the UCS is distorted into a position that is hard to visualize, even when it is on the screen in front of you. By seeing the object in the left ISO view but working on it in the right plan view, you are assured that the face of the object is in the correct position as you draw by viewing it in the ISO view.

USING 3D SURFACE PRIMITIVES TO CREATE A WIREFRAME OBJECT

Although the surface primitives were created by Autodesk to allow you to quickly create a simple 3D object that you could hide, shade, or render, they can also be used to quickly create the wireframe of more complex objects. As in 2D design, it is usually quicker to edit existing geometry than to create brand new geometry. By placing simple 3D surface objects (that have no wireframe) together into the proper positions, you can "trace" the edges of the surfaces to create the complex wireframe. This technique has the added advantage of already having many of the surfaces in place, eliminating the need to create them by hand later (placing 3D surfaces by hand is covered in Chapter 6 on 3D Surfaces).

T I P

The issue of layer control becomes important with this technique because you do not want your surfaces on the same layer as the wireframe. Use the layer SURFACE to place your surface objects and either the layer OBJ or WIREFRAME to place the wireframe objects.

The box with two notches created in the earlier practice procedures contains three boxes. The first is the large box, the second and third boxes are the notches. Dimensions of the boxes are (XYZ):

- First—7x5x3
- Second—1x5x1
- Third—1x1x1

The notch placement can be accomplished by several different methods. This procedure uses the construction technique introduced in Release 13 called XLINE.

Practice Procedure Using the 3D Surface Primitives to Create a Wireframe

1. Start a new drawing using the 3DPROTO drawing.

2. Turn off any running object snaps and activate the SURFACE layer as the current layer.

3. Create a 3D box with a length of 7, a width of 5, a height of 3, and a rotation of 0 (zero).

4. Place two construction lines using the XLINE command.

5. Type **xline** and press **Enter** to activate the command.

6. Select the point P1, as shown in Figure 4.16, with the From and Endpoint options active.

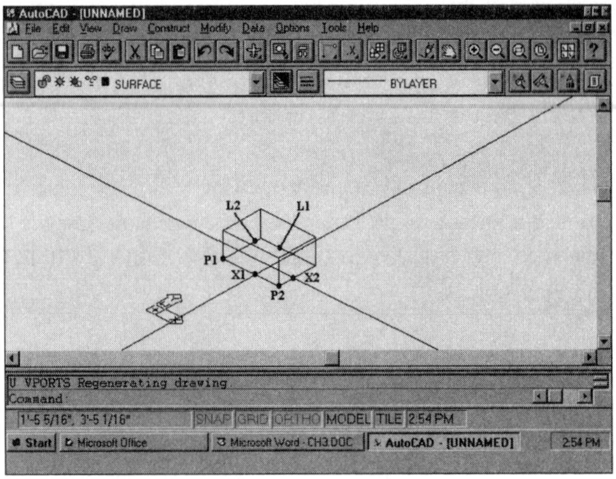

FIGURE 4.16 Surface primitives practice procedure.

7. Type **@4<0** and press **Enter** to place the construction line at an offset from the endpoint P1 that you selected using the Endpoint option.

8. Select the line L1 using the Perpendicular object snap to fix the XLINE in place.

9. Press **Enter** to end the XLINE command and press **Enter** again to reactivate the command.

10. Select the point P2, as shown in Figure 4.16, with the From and Endpoint options active.

11. Type **@2<90** and press **Enter** to place the construction line at an offset from the endpoint P2 that you selected using the Endpoint option.

12. Select the line L2 using the Perpendicular object snap to fix the XLINE in place.

13. Press **Enter** to end the XLINE command.

NOTE

Figure 4.16 illustrates the problem of visualizing 3D wireframe objects with just one viewport. When you look at the object, it can appear as a box in two different views (like the optical illusion of the lady and the chalice). In this case, it is not necessary to have two or more viewports because this procedure is not for a complicated object.

NOTE

Steps 5 through 13 are necessary to place construction lines at precise positions on the box. You can use any technique you want, including no construction lines, to place the two notch boxes. This method was covered as a review of the new Release 13 XLINE feature.

Practice Procedure Continued

1. Create a notch box (AI_BOX) with a length of 1, a width of 5, and a height of 1 at the intersection of X1 (as shown in Figure 4.16) with a rotation of 0 (zero).

2. Create a notch box (AI_BOX) with a length of 1, a width of 1, and a height of 1 at the intersection of X2 (as shown in Figure 4.16) with a rotation of 90 degrees. (A shortcut would be to select the cube option for the second option of the command.)

3. Explode all the objects in the drawing and erase the two construction lines.

4. Using the Crossing option, erase the 3D surfaces at the crossing points P1, P2, and P3, as shown in Figure 4.17.

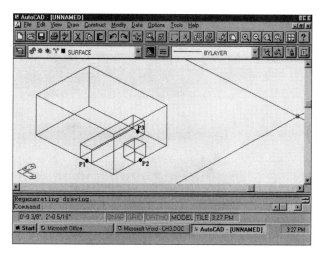

FIGURE 4.17 Erasing crossing points.

The resulting geometry should look like Figure 4.18.

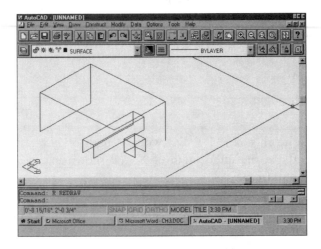

FIGURE 4.18 Results of erasing unneeded 3D surfaces.

Practice Procedure Continued

1. Copy the object L1 from the endpoint P1 to the endpoint P2, as shown in Figure 4.19.

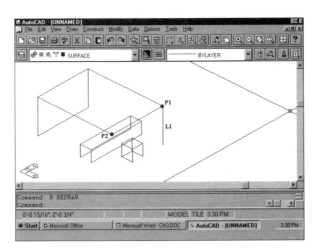

FIGURE 4.19 Add the missing leg.

2. Make the WIREFRAME layer the current layer.

3. Use the LINE command with the Endpoint object snap running to connect the base points P1-P2, P3-P4, P4-P5, P6-P7, P7-P8, P8-P9, and P10-P1, as shown in Figure 4.20.

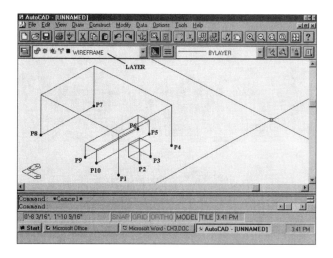

FIGURE 4.20 Construction of the frame base.

4. Using the LINE command and the running Endpoint object snap, finish tracing all the other edges of the box and the notches not already done in step 3.

5. Turn off the SURFACE layer.

The resulting wireframe, shown in Figure 4.21, has all the necessary lines on the WIREFRAME layer and most of the necessary 3D surfaces on the SURFACE layer. Wireframes are built to place 3D surfaces on them. They are really only a means to an end. By themselves, they have little value. The placing of surfaces is covered in Chapter 6 on 3D Surfaces in the "3D Face" section.

TIP

Steps 4 and 5 can be repeated as needed while you are tracing the surface edges. It is easy to miss an edge. Make the color of the SURFACE layer different from the color of the WIREFRAME layer. That way, you can better see which edges have been drawn over.

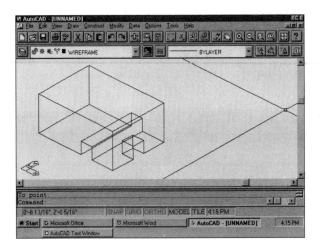

FIGURE 4.21 Practice results.

Chapter Exercise

Create the wireframe shown in Figure 4.22 and save it as CH4EX for later use. Use any technique covered in the last two chapters or any combination of techniques.

Figure 4.22 gives you the dimensions.

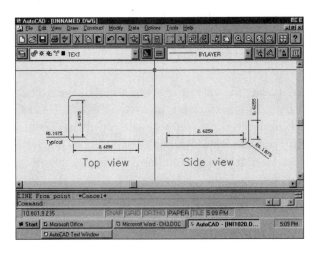

FIGURE 4.22 Chapter exercise dimensions.

TIP

The 3DPOLY command does not have arc segments, you would be better off using the PLINE command in a custom User Coordinate System.

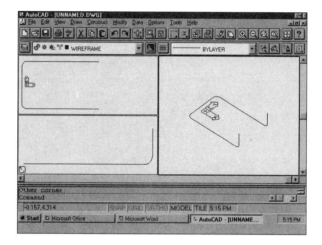

FIGURE 4.23 Chapter exercise result.

In Conclusion

In this chapter, you were introduced to the AutoCAD surface primitives and how they are used in wireframe construction. Many different techniques for creating wireframe construction were covered, and you were given the opportunity to practice them. These techniques are valid for AME solids construction (dropped by Autodesk with Release 13) or the new Release 13 ACIS solids. In the next chapter, you will be given the opportunity to practice editing techniques on wireframe constructions.

CHAPTER FIVE

Wireframe Editing

Editing commands for wireframe objects include any 2D editing commands, as long as the objects being edited are on the same UCS. This means that all the editing commands you already know from designing in two dimensions work as long as the object or objects being edited are on the same work plane. Autodesk has even extended beyond that limitation in Release 13 with some enhancements to the editing commands and the object snap tools. This chapter introduces you to those enhancements and gives you the opportunity to practice the techniques for editing wireframe objects.

N O T E   Several AutoLISP productivity routines are included on your disk. While it is necessary for you to understand and be able to use commands like HIDE, ZOOM, and VPORTS, using routines as productivity tools is preferred. This chapter looks in depth at how some tools work. To better understand, it is necessary to jump around quickly between multiple viewports and views. Load the productivity routines ZOOMALL, HIDEALL, SWAPVP, and DDVPORTS at this time, as they are used extensively in this chapter's practice procedures. Load the menu 3DWORLD, using the MENULOAD command, and activate the toolbar ACAD.3DTOOLS to access the routines.

Tools

To use the 2D editing tools on objects spanning 3 dimensions, you must have the current UCS parallel to the object or objects. If two or more objects to be edited do not share a parallel work plane, they can not be edited.

NOTE

Autodesk actually gets around this problem by building a temporary intermediate work plane for some of its commands by calculating the correct plane internally. This technique is not something you would want to try under normal circumstances.

This section allows you to practice with the FILLET and STRETCH command on a wireframe object. The technique's used to shift the UCS to the correct work plane are valid with all editing commands.

Practice Procedure Using FILLET on a UCS

1. In the drawing *Simple1*, restore the front UCS and place its origin at the point P1, as shown in Figure 5.1.

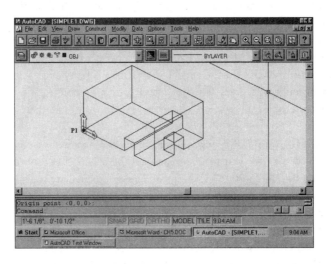

FIGURE 5.1 Fillet on UCS procedure reference.

2. Set your fillet radius to 1 and fillet the lines L1 and L2, L3 and L4, as shown in Figure 5.2.

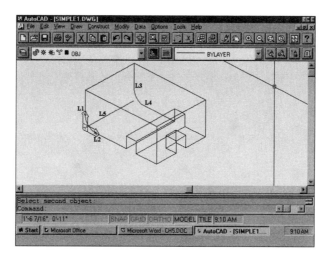

FIGURE 5.2 Fillet on UCS procedure reference.

3. Erase the line L5, as shown in Figure 5.2, and save the drawing for later use as *Simple2*.

Notice that you did not need to set the UCS to the rear of the object to fillet the line L3 and L4. That is because those lines were parallel to the front UCS. The edit commands demand that the geometry is parallel to the current UCS; they do not always need to have the geometry on the current UCS.

The whole last practice took place in an ISO view. Sometimes it is difficult to select the necessary geometry from an ISO view. Try using the STRETCH command and use the UCSFOLLOW method with two viewports to make selection easier in the next practice procedure.

Practice Procedure Using STRETCH, UCS, and UCSFOLLOW

1. In the drawing *Simple2* (that you created in the last procedure), split your screen into two viewports, as shown in Figure 5.3.

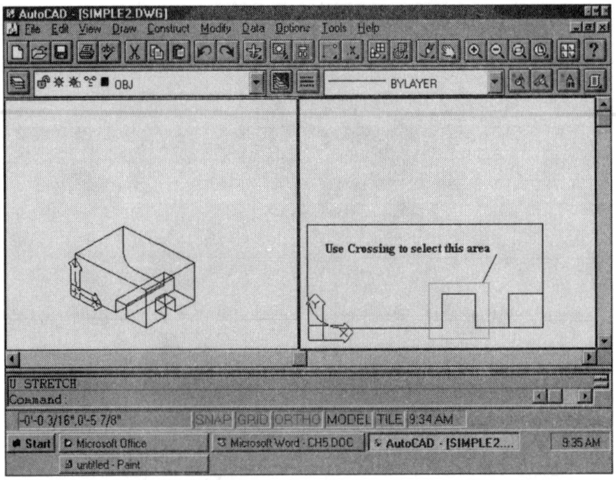

FIGURE 5.3 Stretch on UCS with UCSFOLLOW procedure reference.

2. The viewport on the left should remain in ISO view, the right viewport should have UCSFOLLOW turned on and be in plan view to the current UCS.

3. If your front UCS configuration is not active, restore the front UCS configuration.

4. Use the STRETCH command to select all of the geometry that makes up the notch that runs from the front to the rear of the object, as shown in Figure 5.3.

5. Select any base point on the right viewport screen. (Do not have any running object snaps turned on at this time.)

6. Type **@1<180** and press **Enter** as your second point of displacement.

The result is shown in Figure 5.4. The STRETCH command was used instead of the MOVE command because you needed to stretch the base lines of the object as you moved the notch.

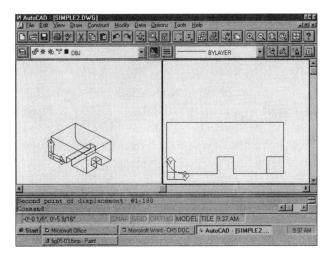

FIGURE 5.4 Stretch on UCS with UCSFOLLOW procedure result.

The message Lines are non coplanar. appears whenever you try to edit two objects that are not on the same work plane.

NOTE

OBJECT PROJECTION USING PROJMODE

The Projmode option is used in the TRIM and EXTEND commands in both 2D and 3D design. Projection mode allows you to control whether or not AutoCAD will extend or trim an object with another object that does not physically intersect. The option has three selections:

- None—default (<None>:) selection allowing no projection mode. This is the same as Release 12 when there was no such thing as projection mode.

- UCS—projects the boundary relative to the current User Coordinate System.
- View—projects the boundary relative to the current view.

The projection mode gives you much more control over TRIM and EXTEND because you can now use the object in conjunction with your UCS work plane, or with your current view, as a boundary. Before PROJMODE, two objects had to physically intersect on the same UCS (working plane) before you could use the TRIM or EXTEND commands on them. Now, you can select the Project option in either command and set the projection mode to View, UCS, or None.

 PROJMODE is a system variable that can be set independent from the TRIM and EXTEND commands' Project option. Set PROJMODE to 1 for the UCS option, 2 for the View option, and 0 (zero) for the None option.

TIP

The UCS selection of the Project option mathematically projects your geometry perpendicular to the current UCS infinitely. The object's projection becomes a temporary work plane that AutoCAD uses as the boundary. Figure 5.5 illustrates a line projecting mathematically perpendicular to the current UCS when this option is active.

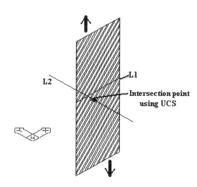

FIGURE 5.5 Projection of a boundary line mathematically illustrated with hatch pattern.

The line L1 in Figure 5.5 is one unit above the line L2. They do not physically intersect. In that situation, the TRIM command could only trim line L2 back to the boundary line L1 if you had the projection mode set to UCS or View. The

UCS option would trim back the line to the point shown in Figure 5.5. The View option would trim back line L2 to the apparent intersection based on the current view. (A "what you see is what you get" operation, conditional on the view.) The EXTEND command works the same way, only line L2 would have to be shorter, enabling it to be extended to line L1. Try the TRIM command using the UCS and View projection option.j5

N O T E Before starting any practice procedures in this chapter, use the MENULOAD command to attach the 3DWORLD menu in your 3DWORLD directory. The toolbar shown in Figure 5.6 should be on the right side of the screen. The buttons are labeled for reference. There might be more buttons on the toolbar than are shown at this time due to possible changes later in the book. Check the "Customizing 3D Toolbars" section in Chapter 12 for greater detail on how to build and modify toolbars.

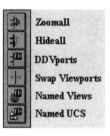

FIGURE 5.6 Custom 3D tools toolbar.

Practice Procedure with TRIM and Projection Mode

N O T E Do all work in the following practice procedure in the upper-left viewport.

1. In the drawing *Appint*, activate the TRIM command.
2. Select line L1 in the upper-left viewport, shown in Figure 5.7, as the cutting edge and press **Enter** to end the selection process.

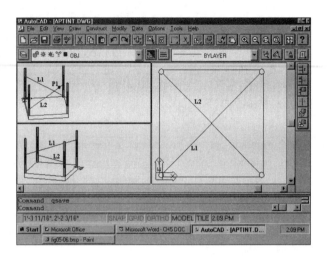

FIGURE 5.7 3D TRIM and projection mode practice reference.

3. Select the line L2 at the point P1, shown in Figure 5.7. A message saying Object does not intersect an edge. appears. This means that the PROJMODE is set to none.

4. Type **p** and press **Enter** to activate the Project option of the TRIM command.

5. Type **u** and press **Enter** to activate the UCS option.

6. Select the line L2 at the point P1 again, shown in Figure 5.7. This time line L2 trims back to the projected line L1 perpendicular to the UCS. Notice how this looks in the other viewports. The right viewport (plan view) clearly shows that the line L2 was trimmed to line L1. That is because the view is perpendicular to the line L1.

7. Type **u** and press **Enter** to undo the trim.

8. Type **p** and press **Enter** to activate the Project option of the TRIM command again.

9. Type **v** and press **Enter** to activate the View option.

10. Select the line L2 at the point P1 again, shown in Figure 5.7. Notice how the line L2 was trimmed back to line L1 relative to the current view in the upper left viewport. The plan viewport shows clearly that the trim took place relative to some other place than the current UCS.

11. Type **u** and press **Enter** to undo the trim.

12. Press **Enter** to exit the TRIM command.

118

In the preceding practice procedure, the lower left viewport shows clearly that the two lines, L1 and L2, do not physically intersect. The trimming that took place was done by AutoCAD temporarily computing an intermediate UCS that would allow the trim based on your projection mode setting. AutoCAD then trimmed the line using the temporary UCS without you ever seeing what took place.

The TRIM and EXTEND commands in 3D design use the same projection mode setting. It is best to get into the habit of checking the Project option of the commands before using them.

TIP

OBJECT SNAPS

Object snaps (osnaps) behave in the 3D environment exactly as they do in the 2D environment. The object snap APPINT is a 3D-specific osnap for finding the apparent intersection between two objects. Selecting both objects with the aperture at the same time results in the snap applying to the lower of the two objects in the WCS.

You can select each object separately to ensure the snap applies to the object you desire. When the two objects are selected individually, the first selected object is always the one that has the snap applied to it. You can select the object individually by ensuring that your aperture is not over both objects at the time you select. Try drawing a line from the apparent intersection in the Figure 5.8.

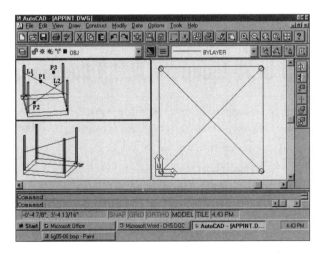

FIGURE 5.8 Apparent Intersection practice reference.

Practice Procedure for Selecting Apparent Intersection Separately

1. In the drawing *Appint*, freeze the layers TRIM and EXTEND and thaw the layer LEVEL-NOT.
2. Start the LINE command.
3. Activate the object snap APPINT from the popup menu (or type it).
4. Select the line L1, at the point P1, as shown in Figure 5.8.
5. Select the line L2, at the point P2, as shown in Figure 5.8.
6. Select a point on the screen near the point P3, as shown in Figure 5.8.
7. Press **Enter** to quit out of the LINE command.
8. Use the production routine ZOOMALL to adjust your viewports.
9. Use the production routine HIDEALL to do hidden line removal in all viewports.

Notice that point P3 creates the line's endpoint at the zero elevation, because the UCS is set to World. The first point, P1 on line L1, dictated to AutoCAD to snap to the top line, using the bottom line as the projected intersection.

Some users confuse themselves between PROJMODE and APPINT. Remember that PROJMODE is for TRIM and EXTEND commands, APPINT is for snapping.

N O T E

Align Objects in 3D Using the ALIGN Command

One of the handiest 3D modifying commands is the ALIGN command. ALIGN can be used to align an object with one set of points (similar to the MOVE command), two sets of points (moving and rotating the object at the same time), and three sets of points (moving and rotating the object *in* the XY plane and *from* the XY plane). The one set of points option works by selecting your two source and target points and pressing **Enter** instead of selecting any more points. The two set of point option works in the same manner. The three sets of points is the 3D alignment. Figure 5.9 shows the three point option. The point prompts are for source and target. Always select the point you want to align first and then the point to which you want to attach.

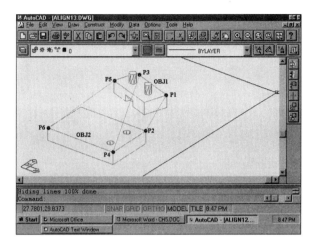

FIGURE 5.9 Alignment practice reference.

Try aligning the top object shown in Figure 5.9 to the bottom plate using the ALIGN command.

Practice Procedure for Selecting Using the ALIGN Command

1. In the drawing *Align 13*, type **align** and press **Enter** to activate the command.

2. Select the object OBJ1 and press **Enter**.

3. Select the point P1, as shown in Figure 5.9, as the *1st source point* (the running object snap is already on).

4. Select the point P2, as shown in Figure 5.9, as the *1st destination point*.

5. Select the point P3, as shown in Figure 5.9, as the *2nd source point*.

6. Select the point P4, as shown in Figure 5.9, as the *2nd source point*.

7. Select the point P5, as shown in Figure 5.9, as the *3rd source point*.

8. Select the point P6, as shown in Figure 5.9, as the *3rd source point*.

The source object aligns with the destination (target) object. The two cube objects demonstrate the use of object snaps to align one object to another. The command does not necessarily need to snap to an object. You can also use known coordinates or snap/grid combinations to guide the source object. There is a trick to using the command with cylindrical objects. The next practice procedure allows you to try the command on a shaft and hole, as shown in Figure 5.10.

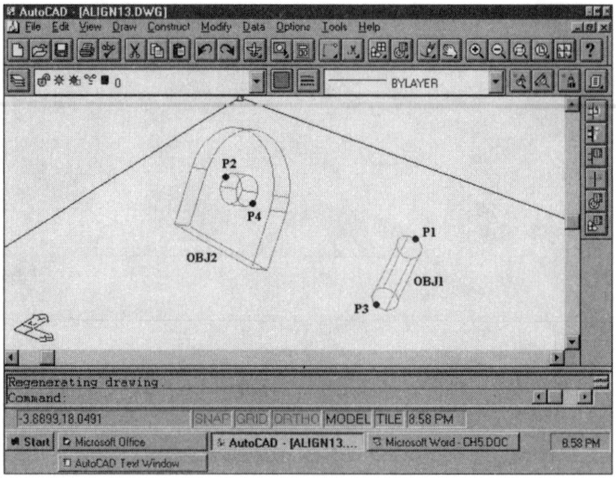

FIGURE 5.10 Alignment practice reference for a round object.

Practice Procedure for Selecting Using the ALIGN Command on a Cylindrical Object

1. In the drawing *Align13*, turn on the running Centerpoint object snap and turn off the running Endpoint.

2. Change the view to the named view ROUND.

3. Type **align** and press **Enter** to activate the command.

4. Select the object OBJ1 and press **Enter**.

5. Select the point P1, as shown in Figure 5.10, as the *1st source point*.

6. Select the point P2, as shown in Figure 5.10, as the *1st destination point*.

7. Select the point P3, as shown in Figure 5.10, as the *2nd source point*.

8. Select the point P4, as shown in Figure 5.10, as the *2nd destination point*.

9. Select the point P4, as shown in Figure 5.10, as the *3rd source point*.

10. Select the point P3, as shown in Figure 5.10, as the *3rd destination point*.

The shaft slides into the hole. The problem with a shaft and hole is that you only have two possible sets of points. The command has the ability to accept an **Enter** key for the last set of points. You are then given the option <2d> or 3d transformation:, selecting **3d** gives you the same results as steps 9 and 10.

The command first moves the object using the first set of points and then rotates the object twice (along the second set of points *in* the XY plane and along the third set of points *from* the XY plane). When you use the **Enter/3D** option, you tell the command to use the second set of points in reverse as the third set of points. This practice procedure had you do the steps manually to illustrate them.

THE ALIGN COMMAND MENU LOCATIONS

The ALIGN command is found on the *Modify* pull-down menu and on the *Modify* toolbar, as shown in Figure 5.11.

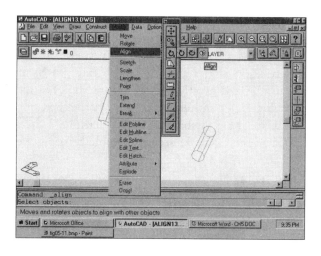

FIGURE 5.11 ALIGN command on the Modify pull-down menu.

Rotate Objects Using the ROTATE3D Command

This command moves objects about all three axes. You control the spin or movement of the object by use of axis instead of source and target points used in the ALIGN command. You have several options for controlling the movement. They include:

- Axis by ObJect—Uses an existing object to align the axis of rotation.
- Last—uses the last rotation axis as the active axis.
- View—aligns the axis of rotation with the viewing direction of the current viewport's plan view.

- Xaxis—rotates the object around the X axis of the current UCS through a selected point.

- Yaxis—rotates the object around the Y axis of the current UCS through a selected point.

- Zaxis—rotates the object around the Z axis of the current UCS through a selected point.

- <2points>:—uses two points to define the axis of rotation. (This is the default option.)

You can enter an option by typing it or specifying a point for the default option of 2points.

It is important that you understand the use of axis in this command. You select two points to define an axis or tell the command to use an axis from the current UCS. All rotation angles are relevant to the chosen axis. The use of angles in rotating an object is exactly like the use of angles in the viewing commands, except that the angles are relative to the axis defined or chosen, not the XY plane. You must use the right-hand rule to determine if the angle should be positive or negative along the axis. An example would be using the X axis option:

- Place your hand into the right-hand rule position and rotate your hand until the thumb is pointing at your face (the camera). See Figure 5.12 for reference.

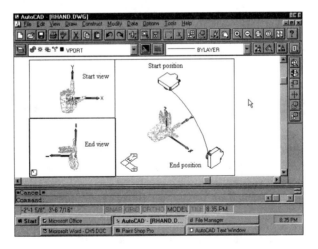

FIGURE 5.12 Right-hand rule positioning.

■ Rotating the object in a positive angle spins the object about your thumb in a counterclockwise direction. Since the front of your object is facing the negative Y axis to begin with (assuming the object is in the WCS and has not been rotated previously), the front of the object begins to rotate toward the bottom while the bottom rotates toward the rear of the object. The rotation takes place along the specified axis in the current UCS (here the WCS and the X axis). Figure 5.13 shows the rotation of the object about the axis.

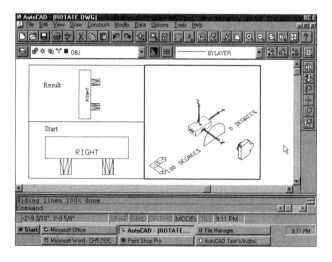

FIGURE 5.13 Rotation motion around the X axis.

The object is shown in the Start viewport in Figure 5.13 as it would appear looking down the X axis. When you use the X axis option of the ROTATE3D command, and specify a positive 90 degree angle, the object rotates around that axis as shown in the Result viewport in Figure 5.13. The large viewport shows the camera looking down the X axis and the arc of the degrees from 0 degrees on the right to 180 degrees on the left (counterclockwise).

TIP

The toughest part of using the 3D modify tools is visualizing the angles about the axis. Many users will rotate guessing the degrees, positive or negative, and retry if it is the wrong way. It is better to get used to visualizing the axis (or use the right-hand rule) and only edit once.

The X, Y, and Z axis options all work in the same manner about their respective axis. They are handy when needing to rotate an object about one of the major axes. The axis options of this command are used most frequently because they are the easiest to use.

Try rotating an object around an axis.

Practice Procedure for Rotating Around an Axis

1. In the *Rotate3D* drawing, type the command **ROTATE3D**.

2. Select the block and press **Enter** to continue.

3. Type **y** and press **Enter** to use the Y axis option.

4. Use the Endpoint object snap to select the corner of the object near the point P1, as shown in Figure 5.14.

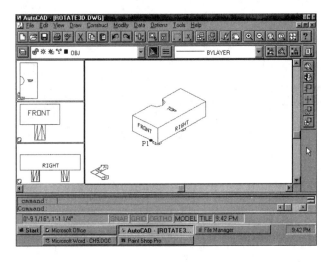

FIGURE 5.14 X axis option practice reference.

5. Type **90** and press **Enter**.

The result is shown in Figure 5.15. This command option does in one step what you would have to do in two steps with the regular ROTATE command (change the UCS and then rotate the object).

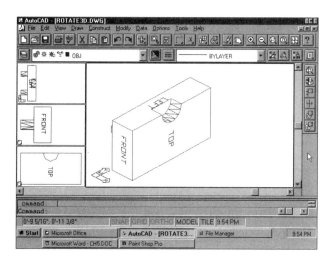

FIGURE 5.15 X axis option practice result.

The ROTATE3D command has many other options as listed above. The Last and 2points options are simple and easy to understand. Follow the prompts to use them. The Axis by Object option works in conjunction with an existing line, arc, circle, or 2D Polyline segment to rotate the selected object around the existing object. The last option that is used frequently is the View option. This option allows you to rotate the object around the current view axis as if it were the current UCS and the command were ROTATE. This is handy, like the axis options, because you can use preset views to set up your rotation. Try the View option of the ROTATE3D command.

127

Practice Procedure for Rotating Around a View

1. Undo back to the beginning of the edit session in the *Rotate3D* drawing.

2. Switch the front viewport (middle left) with the large ISO viewport (right). (The SWAPVP AutoLISP routine is good for this chore.)

3. Type the command **ROTATE3D**.

4. Select the block (in the large viewport) and press **Enter** to continue.

5. Type **v** and press **Enter** to use the View option.

6. Use the Midpoint snap to select the center of the object near the point P1, as shown in Figure 5.16.

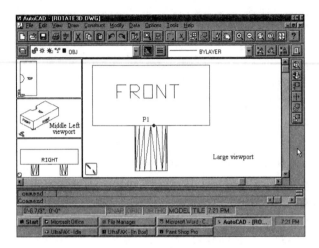

FIGURE 5.16 View option practice reference.

7. Type **90** and press **Enter**.

The result is shown in Figure 5.17. The View option ignores the current UCS and uses the current view as the working plane on which to rotate the object. This works well if the view is parallel with the major axis. The results are less than predictable when the view is not parallel to a major axis.

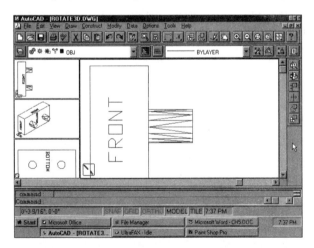

FIGURE 5.17 View option practice results.

The ROTATE3D Command Menu Locations

The ROTATE3D command can be found on the *Modify* toolbar's Rotate flyout and on the *Construct* pull-down menu, as shown in Figure 5.18.

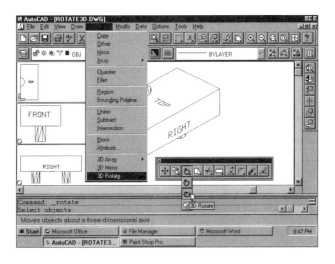

FIGURE 5.18 ROTATE3D command menu positions.

Creating a Duplicate Object with the MIRROR3D Command

The MIRROR3D command allows you to create a copy of an object mirrored about any plane. The 2D MIRROR command is easy to visualize, as it mirrors the object using the 2 points supplied, because the mirroring takes place on the flat surface of the XY plane. The two points defined on the XY plane use an imaginary point on the Z axis to define the three points actually needed by the command. The mirroring plane is defined by the two points on the XY plane and the third imaginary point on the Z axis. Mirroring an object in 3D is harder to visualize because the mirroring plane can extend in any direction (not just in the direction of the Z axis). Figure 5.19 illustrates the working plane and a mirroring plane (as defined by points P1, P2, and P3). Figure 5.20 shows the result of mirroring the object using that plane.

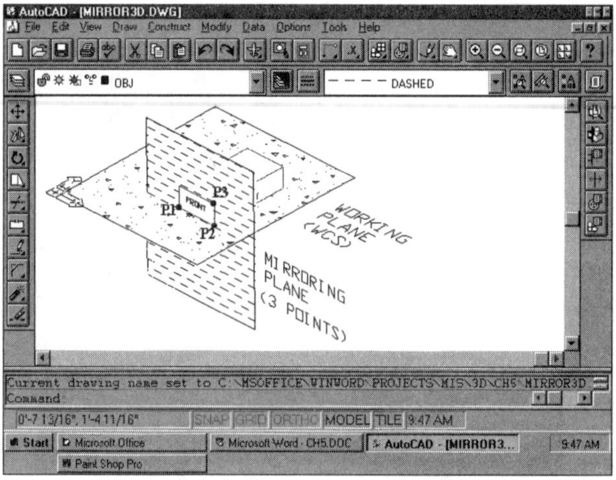

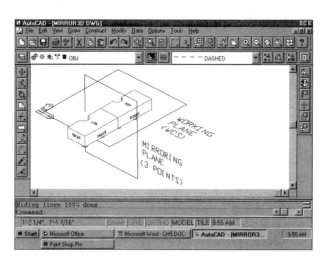

FIGURE 5.19 Working and mirroring planes.

FIGURE 5.20 Object mirrored about the mirroring plane.

Notice that your view is from an ISO position but the mirroring plane extended up along the face of the front of the object. The 3point option was used in this example.

The tricky part of visualizing the mirroring plane comes when you define the mirroring plane on an axis other than a major axis. This would include slopes of a part and angles in the XY plane other than 90 degree vectors.

N O T E

A plane is defined by three points. An axis is nothing more than a theoretical line extending through infinite points. Therefore, an axis can define a plane with the addition of a third point for the tilt of the plane in 3D space.

The MIRROR3D command has many options for defining a plane. They include:

- Plane by Object—uses the plane of an arc, circle or 2D polyline segment as the mirroring plane.
- Last—copies and rotates the selected objects about the last defined plane.
- Zaxis—the mirroring plane is defined by any point on the plane and a point on the Z axis of the plane.
- View—sets the mirroring plane through a point in the current viewing plane.
- XY—sets the mirroring plane to the plane defined between an imaginary point on the X axis, an imaginary point on the Y axis, and through a specified point.
- YZ—sets the mirroring plane to the plane defined between an imaginary point on the Y axis, an imaginary point on the Z axis, and through a specified point.
- ZX—sets the mirroring plane to the plane defined between an imaginary point on the Z axis, an imaginary point on the X axis, and through a specified point.
- <3points>:—sets the mirroring plane by three points. The 1st point on plane prompt does not appear when you specify a point instead of choosing an option.

131

Plane by Object

This option uses the ECS of a Circle, Arc, or 2D Polyline segment as the mirroring plane. Since the ECS is based on how the object was created, you can get unexpected results from the option. Many users try it and undo the result when it is not to their satisfaction. Try using the Plane by Object option of the MIRROR3D command.

Practice Procedure for the Plane by Object Option

1. In the *Mirror3D* drawing, type **mirror3d** and press **Enter** to active the command.
2. Select the object and press **Enter** to end the selection process.
3. Type **o** and press **Enter** to activate the Plane by Object option.
4. Select a point on the circle near the point C1, as shown in Figure 5.21.

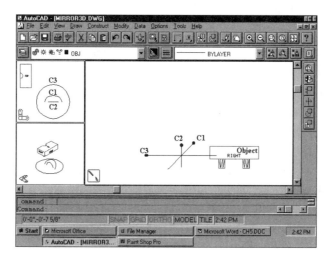

FIGURE 5.21 Plane by Object option practice reference.

5. Press **Enter** to accept the default of no for deleting the original object.
6. Use the HIDEALL supplemental routine to perform hidden line removal in all of the viewports.

Do the same process two more times, from steps 2 through 6, substituting the points C2 and then C3 for C1 in step 5. The results should look like Figure 5.22.

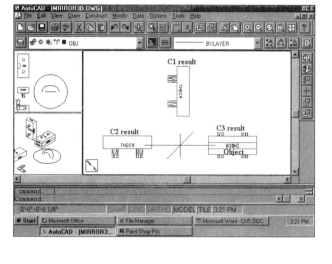

FIGURE 5.22 Plane by Object option practice result.

Zaxis Option

This option requires two points to define the Z axis mirroring plane. Since the XY working plane must be perpendicular to the mirroring plane, the working plane is automatically calculated by AutoCAD. This option works well with objects mirroring about the major axis, but the results are hard to predict when the Z axis is tilted. Try this option on a skewed Z axis angle.

Practice Procedure for the Zaxis Option

1. In the *Mirror3D* drawing (undo back to the beginning or open it again without saving from the last practice procedure), turn off the layer PLANE and turn on the layer ZAXIS.
2. Type **mirror3d** and press **Enter** to activate the command.
3. Select the object and press **Enter** to end the selection process.
4. Type **z** and press **Enter** to activate the Zaxis option.
5. Select the points P1 and P2, as shown in Figure 5.23.

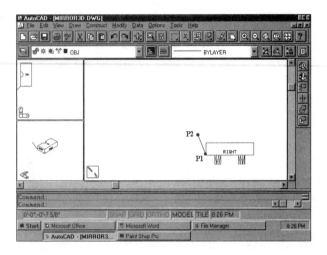

FIGURE 5.24 Zaxis option practice reference.

6. Press **Enter** to accept the default of no for deleting the original object.

7. Use the HIDEALL supplemental routine to perform hidden line removal in all of the viewports.

The results are shown in Figure 5.24.

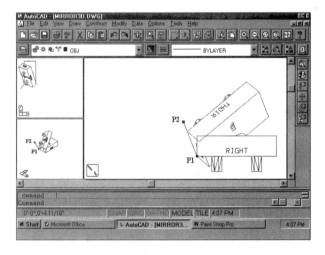

FIGURE 5.24 Zaxis option practice results.

Last Option

The Last option uses the last mirroring plane you defined. You get the message `No plane has been used before.` when you try to use this option without ever having tried the MIRROR3D command.

View Option

This option use the current view as a working plane and requests one point for the mirroring plane. Try a practice procedure using the View option.

Practice Procedure for the View Option

1. In the *Mirror3D* drawing (undo back to the beginning or open it again without saving from the last practice procedure), turn off the layer PLANE.

2. Type **mirror3d** and press **Enter** to activate the command.

3. Select the object and press **Enter** to end the selection process.

4. Type **v** and press **Enter** to activate the View option.

5. Select the points P1(with your endpoint snap on), in view number 1, as shown in Figure 5.25.

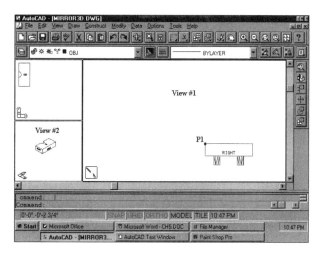

FIGURE 5.25 View option practice reference.

6. Press **Enter** to accept the default of no for deleting the original object.

7. Use the SWAPVP routine to swap the viewports 1 and 2, as shown in Figure 5.25.

8. Use the ZOOMALL routine to adjust all of the viewports.

9. Use the HIDEALL supplemental routine to perform hidden line removal in all of the viewports.

The results are shown in Figure 5.26.

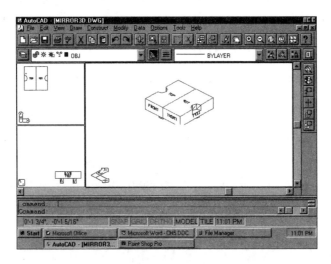

FIGURE 5.26 View option practice results.

The XY, YZ, and ZX Options

These options request one point, to define the origin of the mirroring plane, that runs perpendicular to the work plane requested (XY or YZ or ZX). The XY options is the easiest to predict. Try using the XY option in a practice procedure.

Practice Procedure for the XY Option

1. In the *Mirror3D* drawing (undo back to the beginning or open it again without saving from the last practice procedure), turn off the layer PLANE.

2. Restore the saved UCS configuration named RSIDE.

3. Use the SWAPVP routine to swap the viewports 1 and 2 as shown, already switched, in Figure 5.27.

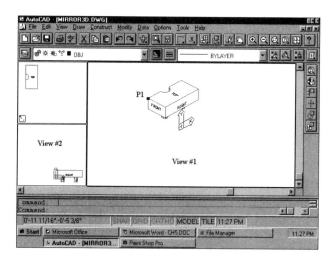

FIGURE 5.27 XY option practice reference.

4. Use the ZOOMALL routine to adjust all of the viewports.

5. Type **mirror3d** and press **Enter** to activate the command.

6. Select the object and press **Enter** to end the selection process.

7. Type **xy** and press **Enter** to activate the XY option.

8. Select the point P1(with your endpoint snap on), in view number 1, as shown in Figure 5.27.

9. Press **Enter** to accept the default of no for deleting the original object.

10. Use the HIDEALL supplemental routine to perform hidden line removal in all of the viewports.

Notice how the object is mirrored along the Z axis (the mirroring plane). The results shown in Figure 5.28 illustrate clearly how the working XY plane and the Z axis mirroring plane work. The object is mirrored along the mirroring plane (turning it inside out). The command option works well in conjunction with the UCS command. Having the preset UCS names to restore speeds the process.

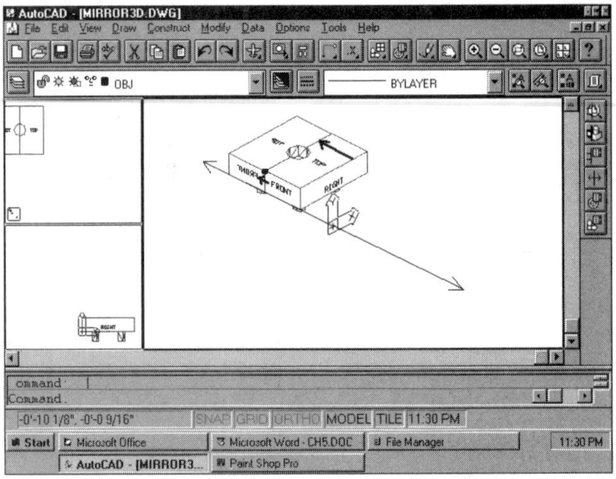

FIGURE 5.28 XY option practice results.

The 3points Option

This option requests three points to define the mirroring plane. It works best with an object and object snaps, although you can select any points you desire.

The advantage of the MIRROR3D command over the ALIGN command is the ability to use the axis without defining target and source points. Many users only use the ALIGN command and ignore the MIRROR3D command because it is easier to edit using other objects to position your object than to become familiar with the various axis options of the MIRROR3D command. The hardest part about learning this command and all of its options is understanding the mirroring plane and how it behaves relative to the working plane. It doesn't help that some options allow you to set up the working plane while other options allow you to set up the mirroring plane. When you understand the relationship between the two planes and practice the options, the command becomes a valuable tool in 3D design.

THE MIRROR3D COMMAND MENU LOCATIONS

The MIRROR3D command is found on the *Construct* pull-down menu and on the *Modify* toolbar, as shown in Figure 5.29.

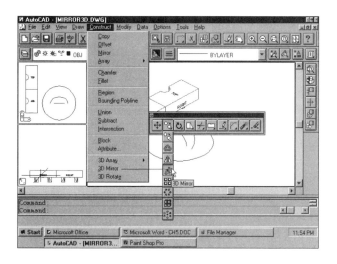

FIGURE 5.29 MIRROR3D command menu locations.

Three-Dimensional Arrays Using the 3DARRAY Command

The 3DARRAY command behaves exactly like its 2D cousin, ARRAY, with the exception that the Z axis is not fixed as it is in the ARRAY command. 3DARRAY requests rows and columns, the same as the ARRAY command, but it also needs information about how many levels (Z axis) you want. 3DARRAY has two options:

- Rectangular—copies the objects in a matrix based on the row, column, and level. One of the matrices must be more than one.
- Angular—copies an object around a center point.

Rectangular Option

The advantage of this option over the two-dimensional ARRAY Rectangular option is that you can create the rows (X axis), columns (Y axis), and levels (Z axis) all at once. See Figure 5.30 for the relationship between rows, columns, and levels and their relative axis. Try using the Rectangular option.

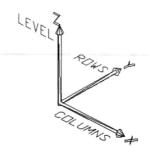

FIGURE 5.30 Matrix relationship.

Practice Procedure for the Rectangular Option

1. In the 3Darray drawing, type **3darray** and press **Enter** to activate the command.

2. Select the object and press **Enter** to end the selection process.

3. Type **r** and press **Enter** to activate the Rectangular option.

4. Type **4** and press **Enter** to request 4 rows.

5. Type **3** and press **Enter** to request 3 columns.

6. Type **3** and press **Enter** to request 3 levels.

7. Type **5** and press **Enter** for the rows distance.

8. Type **3** and press **Enter** for the columns distance.

9. Type **2** and press **Enter** for the levels distance.

10. Use the HIDEALL supplemental routine to perform hidden line removal in all of the viewports.

The results are shown in Figure 5.31. The object has dimensions of 4 on the Y axis, 2 on the X axis and 1 on the Z axis. The numbers entered in steps 7 through 9, allow a unit extra for each side. Like the ARRAY command, you can enter the lengths with any legitimate technique for entering points.

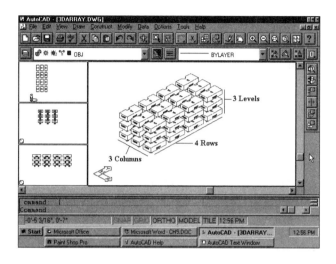

FIGURE 5.31 Rectangular option results.

Polar Option

In the 3D Polar array, you define the Z axis by selecting the origin point for the array and then a second point to define the vector (direction). Figure 5.30 shows the relationship between the three axes and the rows, columns, and levels. The ability to define the Z axis with two points allows you to have a dynamic 3D Polar array. You control the orientation of the array on the fly. Try creating two polar arrays using this option.

Practice Procedure for the Polar Option

1. In the *3Darray* drawing (undo back to the beginning or open it again without saving from the last practice procedure), turn on the layer CENTER.

2. Type **3darray** and press **Enter** to activate the command.

3. Select the object and press **Enter** to end the selection process.

4. Type **p** and press **Enter** to activate the Polar option.

5. Type **12** and press **Enter** for 12 items.

6. Press **Enter** to accept the default of 360 degrees for the angle.

7. Press **Enter** to accept the default of copy the object as it rotates.

8. Select the point P1, as shown in Figure 5.32 (your endpoint snap is running), for the center point of the array.

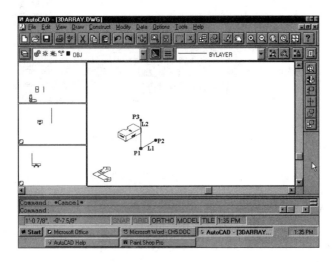

FIGURE 5.32 Polar option reference.

9. Select the point P2, as shown in Figure 5.32, for the second point on the axis of rotation.

Notice how the UCS changed briefly as AutoCAD worked (see Figure 5.33 showing the UCS icon). The command is changing the UCS temporarily to align the Z axis with the origin point and the second point you selected. The rest of the command works exactly the same as the ARRAY command once the UCS is set properly. The 3DARRAY command is saving you the step of changing the UCS before using the regular ARRAY command in the Polar option. Try the last procedure again, but use the point P3 in step eight. The result is shown in Figure 5.34.

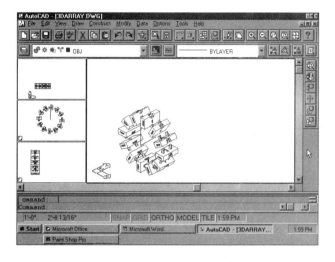

FIGURE 5.33 Polar option results using point P2.

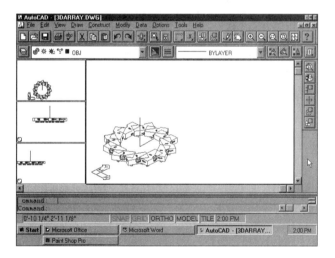

FIGURE 5.34 Polar option results using point P3.

Notice how the P3 result is the same as the regular ARRAY command. That is because the point P3 is above the point P1 forming the Z axis on the WCS.

The 3DARRAY command is not hard to visualize for either the Rectangular or Polar option. It is one of the easier 3D editing commands and it adds a lot to your arsenal of 3D editing tools.

THE 3DARRAY COMMAND MENU LOCATIONS

The MIRROR3D command is found on the _Construct_ pull-down menu and on the _Modify_ toolbar, as shown in Figure 5.35.

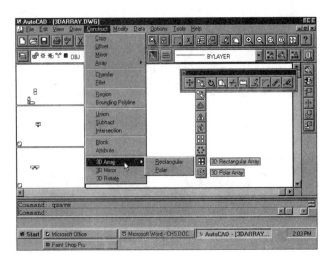

FIGURE 5.35 3DARRAY command menu locations.

In Conclusion

In this chapter you have covered the basic tools (both 2D and 3D) for editing in three dimensions. The 3D editing commands and many techniques for using those commands were introduced. You have many different ways of editing in three dimensions and, through practice, you will develop your own style as you become more proficient with the techniques and commands. In the next chapter, you are introduced to all of the 3D surface commands for creating surfaces and meshes for your wireframe drawings. You are given the opportunity to practice many techniques for controlling and placing surfaces.

CHAPTER SIX

3D Surfaces

In this chapter, you are introduced to all the methods of creating a 3D surface. Surfaces in their basic form are used to hide objects—they are the electronic equivalent to a sheet of paper. When you move a sheet of paper between your eyes and an object you want to see, the object is hidden by the paper. The basic component of a 3D surface is the 3Dface. Many issues arise from the placing of surfaces on an object. The surfaces need to be planar to the side of the object and there are times you need to hide not only the objects behind the surface but the edge of the surface itself.

Hidden Line Removal

You see through a 3D wireframe object because the whole object is nothing but lines and arcs. You make a wireframe appear solid by placing a surface mesh on the wireframe. The HIDE command can then perform hidden line removal, hiding the lines that are behind your faces. One problem that occurs on complex shapes is the desire to have a mesh face with an invisible edge. Faces can only have three or four edges. When an object has a complex surface, it becomes necessary to place several faces to cover the whole surface. The edges of some of the faces show as lines running through the side of the object. The 3DFACE command has the ability to create an edge that is invisible. The DDMODIFY command can make an existing surface edge invisible or visible, and the EDGE command can make an existing surface edge invisible.

There are a few important items to consider when using the HIDE command. Circles and objects that are assigned thickness behave like a 3D surface. They hide objects positioned behind them from your field of view. Text shows through 3D surfaces. Try using the HIDE command on several different views to see the effect it has on different objects.

Practice Procedure for Using the HIDE Command

1. In the *Hide* drawing, type **hide** and press **Enter**.
2. Activate each viewport and use the HIDE command in each.

The results are shown in Figure 6.1. Notice how the text shows through the wedge (which has 3DFACE surfaces on it) and the extruded circle, while the line is hidden by both.

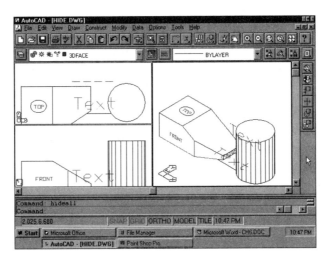

FIGURE 6.1 HIDE command practice results.

TIP The text on the wedge hides because it is not text. It has been converted to line segments using the technique of plotting to a Data eXchange Binary (DXB) file and importing the resulting line segments using the DXBIN command. This technique is handy for situations where you want to hide text behind a face (as in the illustrations for this book). It is not a good idea to use this technique in production, because it leaves your text as tiny line segments that are hard to manage.

The REGEN command restores an object after it has had hidden line removal applied. The command REGENALL applies a regeneration to every viewport on the screen. The REGENALL command has been added to the 3DWORLD.3DTOOLS toolbar in the menu supplied on the companion disk.

The more complex the part, the longer a regeneration takes. Multiply that by the number of viewports and a REGENALL can take a good chunk of production time. Hiding and regening viewports should be done sparingly during production.

TIP

THE HIDE COMMAND MENU LOCATION

The HIDE command is found on the **Render** toolbar, as shown in Figure 6.2.

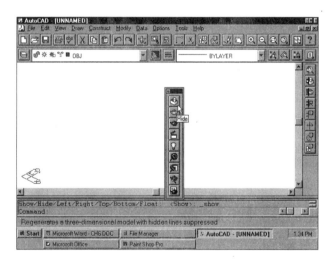

FIGURE 6.2 HIDE command on the Render toolbar menu.

Placing Surfaces with the 3DFACE Command

The 3DFACE command places an electronic sheet of paper with three or four corners. The command is designed to continue placing four corner sheets, using the last two points of the previous sheet as the first two points of the next sheet. This works well for wrapping faces around the outside of a cube, but in normal production that situation is the exception, not the rule. Most users place a three-corner or four-corner face and exit the command. Then they activate the command again to place another face. Try placing 3D faces around a cube.

Practice Procedure for Placing 3D Faces around a Cube

1. In the drawing *3Dface*, type **3dface** and press **Enter** to activate the command.

2. Using the running Endpoint object snap (already turned on), snap to the points P1, P2, P3, P4, P5, P6, P7, P8, P1, P2 (as shown in Figure 6.3) and press **Enter** to exit the command.

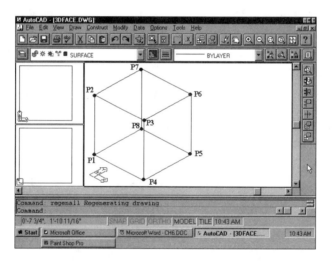

FIGURE 6.3 3DFACE practice reference.

3. Hide the geometry in each viewport (the support routine HIDEALL supplied on the companion disk is good for this).

Notice how the command kept prompting for the third and fourth points once you placed the first face. The HIDE command also shows that you have not completed the top (and the bottom, which you can't see anyhow from this view).

The order of the point selection is critical in the preceding procedure. You must enter the points in a clockwise or counterclockwise fashion to avoid a "bowtie" face.

T I P

The 3DFACE command works well on sides with four corners, but now try it on an object that has sides with more than four corners.

Practice Procedure for Placing 3D Faces around an Object

1. In the drawing *3Dface*, make the layer SURFACE1 the current layer, freeze the layers OBJ and SURFACE, and turn on the layer OBJ1.

2. Type **3dface** and press **Enter** to activate the command.

3. Using the running Endpoint object snap (already turned on), snap to the points P1, P2, P3, P4 (as shown in Figure 6.4) and press **Enter** to exit the command.

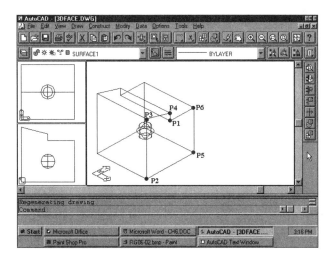

FIGURE 6.4 3DFACE practice reference.

4. Press **Enter** to enter the 3DFACE command again.

5. Snap to the points P1, P2, P5, P6 (as shown in Figure 6.4) and press **Enter** to exit the command.

6. Hide the geometry in each viewport (the support routine HIDEALL supplied on the companion disk is good for this).

Notice that a line runs diagonally across the surface of the side, shown in **Figure 6.5**.

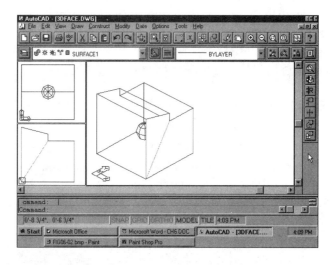

FIGURE 6.5 3DFACE practice results.

The line is the two edges of the two surface faces you placed. You can place the faces and hide the edges by using the I (for invisible) option of the 3DFACE command. Try the last procedure again using the Invisible option.

Practice Procedure for Placing 3D Faces Around an Object Using the Invisible Option

1. Erase the two surfaces you placed in the last procedure and do a REGENALL before starting this procedure.

2. Type **3dface** and press **Enter** to activate the command.

3. Type **I** and press **Enter** to activate the Invisible option.

4. Using the running Endpoint object snap (already turned on), snap to the points P1, P2, P3, P4 (as shown in Figure 6.4) and press **Enter** to exit the command.

5. Press **Enter** to enter the 3DFACE command again.

6. Type **I** and press **Enter** to activate the Invisible option.

7. Snap to the points P1, P2, P5, P6 (as shown in Figure 6.4) and press **Enter** to exit the command.

8. Hide the geometry in each viewport (the support routine HIDEALL supplied on the companion disk is good for this).

Notice that the edge between points P1 and P2 is invisible (see Figure 6.6). The Invisible option is awkward to use because you must activate it before you place the two points defining the edge. There is no way to keep the Invisible option running, you must type **I** before each set of points to make the edge invisible.

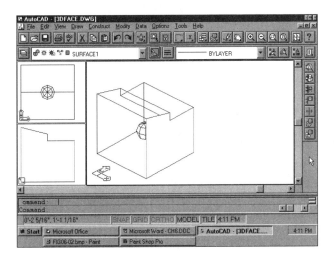

FIGURE 6.6 3DFACE practice results using the Invisible option.

ACIS solids, like surfaces, work with hidden line removal.

N O T E

THE 3DFACE COMMAND MENU LOCATION

The 3DFACE command is found on the *Surfaces* menu item of the *Draw* pull-down menu and on the *Surfaces* toolbar as shown in Figure 6.7.

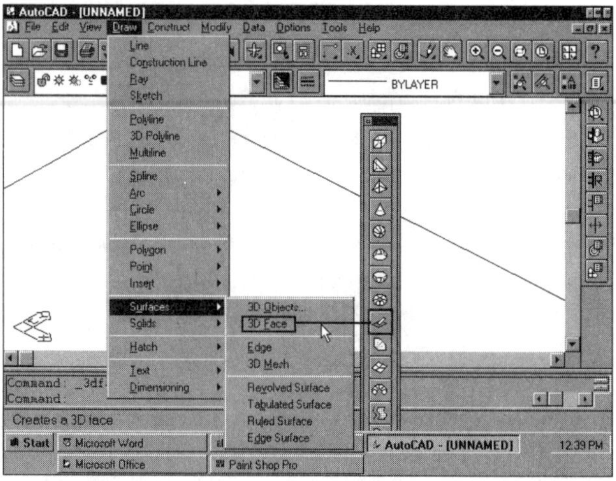

FIGURE 6.7 3DFACE command on the Surfaces toolbar menu.

Using the EDGE Command to Hide 3D Face Edges

There are a couple of methods for controlling the visibility of a 3D face edge after it has been placed. The EDGE command (new to Release 13) changes the face edge selected to invisible. The command displays any edge on a 3D face, or a face created using the PFACE command (discussed later in this chapter) that is already invisible along with the selected edge. When you press **Enter** to exit the command, all selected edges are set to invisible (as if you used the Invisible option during their creation). Try changing some edges to invisible.

Practice Procedure for Using the EDGE Command

1. In the drawing *Hide*, restore the SINGLE Vport configuration.
2. Restore the view EDGE.
3. Type **edge** and press **Enter** to activate the EDGE command.
4. Select the points P1 and P2 as shown in Figure 6.8.

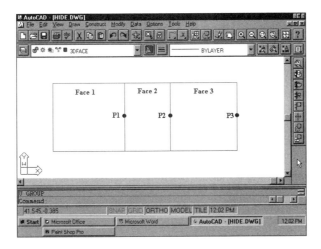

FIGURE 6.8 EDGE command practice reference.

5. Press **Enter** to exit the EDGE command.

The result is shown in Figure 6.9. Try the procedure again and select another edge.

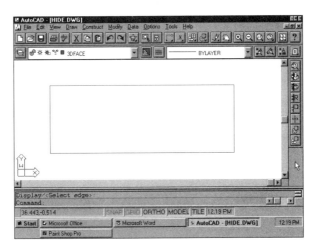

FIGURE 6.9 EDGE command practice results.

Practice Procedure for Using the EDGE Command

1. In the drawing *Hide* using the view called EDGE, type **edge** and press **Enter** to activate the EDGE command.

2. Select the point P3 as shown in Figure 6.8 and press **Escape** to exit the command.

The edge with the point P2 on it should also have appeared as a highlighted edge in Step 2 of the last procedure. This is because the EDGE command shows you all edges of the selected face that are currently hidden, as well as the selected edge that you want to hide.

NOTE This command performs the hide edge even when you use the **Escape** key (or **Cancel** key sequence) in Release 13c3. This is not the behavior you would expect. This is considered a bug by many users and will hopefully be fixed by the time you read this book.

The disadvantage of the EDGE command is that it can only perform the hide edge (invisible edge) function. It can not make an invisible edge visible again. That function is performed by the DDMODIFY command.

TIP The EDGE command only works on primitive faces (3DFACE and PFACE); most meshes are complex objects containing 3D faces. You can explode most meshes and use the EDGE command on any of the 3D face primitives to hide their edges.

THE EDGE COMMAND MENU LOCATION

The EDGE command is found on the *Surfaces* toolbar, as shown in Figure 6.10.

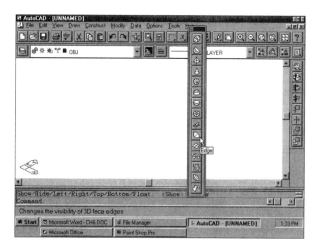

FIGURE 6.10 EDGE command on the Surfaces toolbar menu.

Controlling the Visibility of a Face Edge with DDMODIFY

The DDMODIFY command allows you to change the visibility state of a surface edge. Try setting an invisible edge back to visible with the DDMODIFY command.

155

Practice Procedure for Changing the Visibility State of a Surface Edge

1. In the *3Dface* drawing, after you have completed the last procedure, type **ddmodify** and press **Enter** to activate the command.

2. Select any edge on the 3D surface (near the point P4, as shown in Figure 6.4, is a good choice).

3. The dialogue box appears (as shown in Figure 6.11), allowing you to toggle all four surface edges on or off. Select the *Visibility* toggle for *Edge 1* and click **OK**.

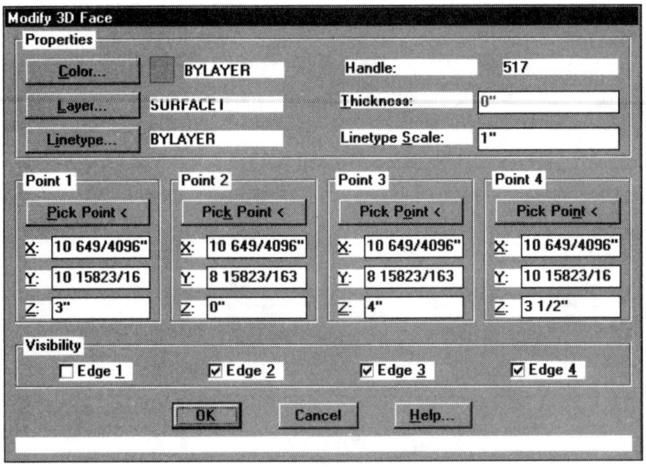

FIGURE 6.11 DDMODIFY dialogue box for a 3Dface.

The surface edge is now showing on the side of the object. The trick to using this command to restore visibility or set invisibility to an edge is the edge number corresponds to the way the face was created. A four-edged face has edge 1 from point 1 to point 2. The problem with this is, when you work on a face that was created by someone else (or by you a long time ago) you do not always know the order in which the face edges were created. In those situations, you must experiment by selecting different edges in the dialogue box until you get the correct one you want changed.

You can make all four edges of a 3D face invisible. This makes it impossible to select the face for editing unless you use the SPLFRAME variable (discussed later in this chapter) to temporarily turn on all the edges to all of the faces in the drawing.

TIP

THE DDMODIFY COMMAND MENU LOCATION

The DDMODIFY command is found on the *Properties* toolbar as shown in Figure 6.12 (it is called the Properties button).

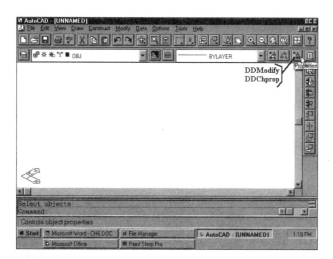

FIGURE 6.12 DDMODIFY command on the Properties toolbar menu.

NOTE

The **Properties** button activates the DDCHPROP command when you select more than one object at a time to modify.

Creating a Polymesh Surface Using the 3DMESH Command

The 3DMESH command defines a three-dimensional Polygon mesh by specifying its M and N size, and the location of each vertex in the mesh. The total number of vertices equals M times N. After all vertices have been specified, AutoCAD draws the mesh. Polygon meshes created by the 3DMESH command are always open in both the M and N directions. You can close the mesh in either or both directions by editing it with the PEDIT command.

NOTE

A 3DMESH reverts to its primitive entities (3D faces) when it is exploded.

Try creating a 3D mesh using the 3DMESH command.

Practice Procedure for Creating a 3D Mesh

1. In the drawing *3Dmesh*, type **3dmesh** and press **Enter** to activate the command.

2. Type **4** and press **Enter** for the M mesh size.

3. Type **5** and press **Enter** for the N mesh size.

4. Starting at P1, as shown in Figure 6.13, select each piece of text (P1, P1A, P1B, etc.) using the running insertion object snap (it is already on).

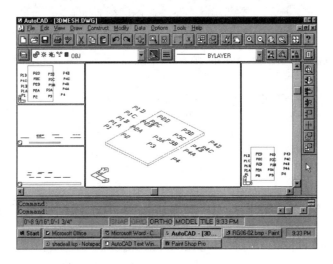

FIGURE 6.13 3DMESH practice reference.

5. Freeze the layer TEXT and select the SHADEALL routine from the 3DTOOLS toolbar.

The result is shown in Figure 6.14.

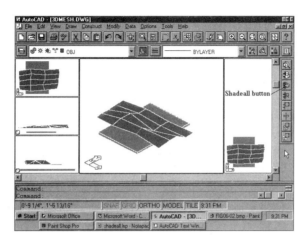

FIGURE 6.14 3DMESH practice results.

THE 3DMESH COMMAND MENU LOCATION

The 3DMESH command is found on the *Surfaces* toolbar, as shown in Figure 6.15.

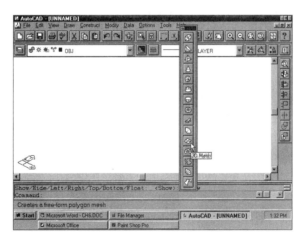

FIGURE 6.15 3DMESH command on the Surfaces toolbar menu.

Produce a Polygon Mesh Using the PFACE Command

The PFACE command allows you to create a 3D polyface mesh, vertex by vertex, similar to the 3DMESH command. A Polyface mesh represents what might appear to be numerous unrelated elements. For example, a Polyface mesh can represent a solid created by Boolean operations consisting of pieces belonging to many different primitives, each with a different layer or color. You specify all vertices used in the mesh. The vertex numbers displayed in the prompts are the numbers used to reference each vertex. Each face is defined by entering vertex numbers for all the vertices of that face. An invisible edge requires a negative number for the beginning vertex of the edge. The SPLFRAME system variable (discussed later in this chapter) controls the visibility of the polyface mesh's edges. Setting SPLFRAME to a non-zero value displays any invisible edges of polyface meshes. You can edit them in the same manner as fully visible polyface meshes.

You can create polyface meshes with any number of edges. PFACE automatically breaks them into multiple face objects with appropriate invisible edges. All Object Snap modes apply to the visible edges of polyface meshes. You can not use PEDIT to edit polyface meshes. The PFACE command is typically used by programmers.

THE PFACE COMMAND MENU LOCATION

This command has no menu location, since it is used mostly in programs by programmers.

3D Primitive Object Surface Commands

These 3D objects were discussed in Chapter 4 as a method for creating wireframe objects. That technique, while legitimate, is actually backwards. The goal of creating a wireframe object is to place a mesh surface on it so that it appears solid.

3D objects are complex objects composed of a polyline mesh. The polyline mesh can be exploded into 3D faces. The techniques presented in the earlier chapter took advantage of this fact. Another technique using 3D objects is to place them together without trimming anything to quickly create a more complex 3D object. This method is good for "sketching" a complex 3D object. Unlike the ACIS solids in AutoCAD, these 3D objects do not have Centerpoints or Midpoints. This makes it a little tricky positioning them, but not impossible. Remember, the objective is to sketch the complex object to see roughly how it is going to look. In this situation, precision is not required but can be applied. Try creating the "sketch" 3D object using the 3D objects as shown in Figure 6.16.

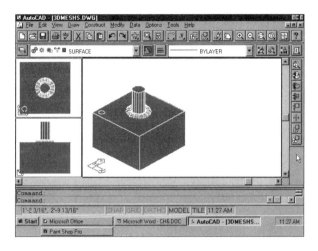

FIGURE 6.16 Complex 3D object sketch reference.

Practice Procedure for Creating Quick Complex 3D Objects

1. In a new drawing using the viewport configuration 3D3R, set your current layer to SURFACE and change the SURFACE layer to the color magenta (turn off any running object snaps).

2. Place a 3D box measuring 5x5x3 (length, width, height) and a rotation of zero in the large viewport on the right, as shown in Figure 6.16.

3. Place a 3D Torus with a center point at the exact center of the top of the 3D box, with a radius of 1 and a tube radius of 0.25. Use the default of 16 segments for the tube and torus circumference. (Use point filters to find the center of the 3D box top, because the calculator does not work inside another ADS routine like the 3D Torus command.)

4. Set the thickness to 3 and place a circle with a radius of 0.25 at the offset (0.5,0.5) from the front left corner of the 3D box.

5. Set the thickness to 5 and place a circle with a radius of 0.5 at the center of the bottom of the 3D box. (Use the calculator or point filters to find the center point.)

6. Set thickness back to zero and use the SHADEALL routine to see the results shown in Figure 6.16.

The last simple practice procedure incorporated many of the techniques covered in this book. The simple widget in the procedure can be created in less than five minutes with these techniques. This object can then be completed using the standard wireframing techniques described in the earlier chapters. Much of what you do in design is dictated by the desired end result. When a pretty picture is all that is needed, slap together the necessary 3D primitive objects and show the picture. When you need detail for production, use the picture as your frame of reference.

NOTE The technique of assembling 3D primitive object together works well unless you need to subtract an area from the surface. Since the objects are only surfaces, you cannot subtract one surface from another without exploding the object and deleting the individual 3D faces that make it up.

THE 3D PRIMITIVE OBJECTS COMMAND MENU LOCATION

The 3D Objects commands are found on the *Draw* pull-down menu under the *Surfaces* cascade menu, as shown in Figure 6.17. The commands are accessed through the dialogue box that appears when you make this menu selection.

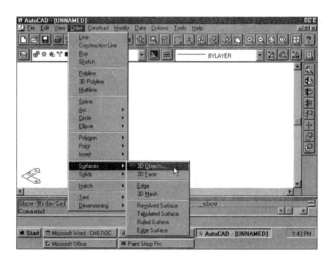

FIGURE 6.17 3D Primitive Objects command menu location.

Variables for Controlling Surfaces and Surface Display

There are several variables you can use to view invisible edges of faces or control the number of faces in a mesh. They include:

- SPLFRAME—global visibility of face edges and mesh frames.
- SURFTYPE—controls the type of surface generated by the Smooth option of the PEDIT command.
- SURFU—controls the accuracy of the surface density in the M direction for the Smooth option of the PEDIT command.
- SURFV—controls the accuracy of the surface density in the N direction for the Smooth option of the PEDIT command.
- SURFTAB1—controls the density of faces in a 3D mesh in the M direction.
- SURFTAB2—controls the density of faces in a 3D mesh in the N direction.

THE SPLFRAME SYSTEM VARIABLE

This variable controls the display of the framework for splined polylines and the edges of 3D meshes (faces). The variable is global in nature: it works on all objects in the drawing when active. When turned off (set to zero) the following objects *do not* display:

- The control polygon for spline-fit polylines.
- The defining mesh for a polygon mesh.
- The invisible edges of 3D faces or polyface meshes.

When SPLFRAME is turned on (set to 1) the following objects *do* display:

- The control polygon for spline-fit polylines.
- The defining mesh of a surface-fit polygon mesh (not the surface).
- Invisible edges of 3D faces or polyface meshes.

SPLFRAME overrides the invisible edge of a 3D face, showing the edge whether or not you have it set to invisible when turned on. This enables you to get at a 3D face edge or the control polygon mesh to edit it. Try setting the SPLFRAME variable in the WEDGE drawing.

Practice Procedure Using SPLFRAME

1. In the *Wedge* drawing, zoom in close to the wedge object.
2. Type **splframe** and press **Enter** to activate the system variable.
3. Type **1** and press **Enter** to turn the variable on.
4. Hide the drawing using the HIDE command.
5. Turn the SPLFRAME variable off by setting it to zero (0).

The 3D face edges on the sloping right side and the front appeared when the variable was set to 1. This makes selecting the face easier and helps in debugging problems with faces that are placed incorrectly. This variable is set to zero (off) by default in any new drawings, unless you change the default in your prototype drawing.

THE SURFTYPE SYSTEM VARIABLE

This variable controls the type of surface-fitting performed by the PEDIT command's Smooth option. It has an initial value of 6. There are three values for the three different types of surface-fitting desired. They are:

- 5—quadratic B-spline surface with a minimum of 3x3 vertices.
- 6—cubic B-spline surface with a minimum of 4x4 vertices.
- 8—Bézier surface with a maximum of 11 vertices in either the M or N direction.

The system variables SURFU and SURFV (discussed later in this chapter) control the density of the mesh in the M and N directions. Try the three different settings for the SURFTYPE system variable.

Practice Procedure for SURFTYPE Control of PEDIT Smooth Option

1. In the drawing *Sysvar*, perform a hide in all of the viewports by using the supplied HIDEALL command. (The hiding is not mandatory but helpful.)

2. Set SURFTYPE to **5** by typing the variable name and assigning it 5.

3. Type **pedit** and press **Enter** to activate the polyline editing command.

4. Select the polyline at the point P1, as shown in Figure 6.18.

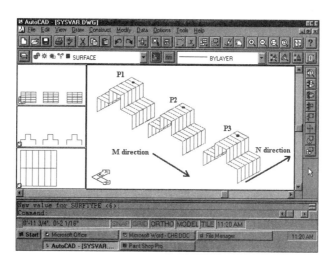

FIGURE 6.18 SURFTYPE practice reference.

5. Type **s** and press **Enter** to activate the Smooth option of the PEDIT command.

6. Press **Enter** to exit the PEDIT command.

7. Repeat steps 2 through 6 two more times, first making SURFTYPE set to **6** and selecting the point P2, and then making SURFTYPE set to **8** and selecting the point P3.

8. Switch the large ISO view with the middle small view (front view) using the SWAPVP routine supplied.

9. Hide all of the viewports using the HIDEALL command supplied.

The results appear as shown in Figure 6.19. Notice that the difference between SURFTYPE 5 and 6 is very small in this example. That is because the example uses faces that are all 1 unit in the N direction. The more difference in the size between each face, the more dramatic the difference in the resulting curve.

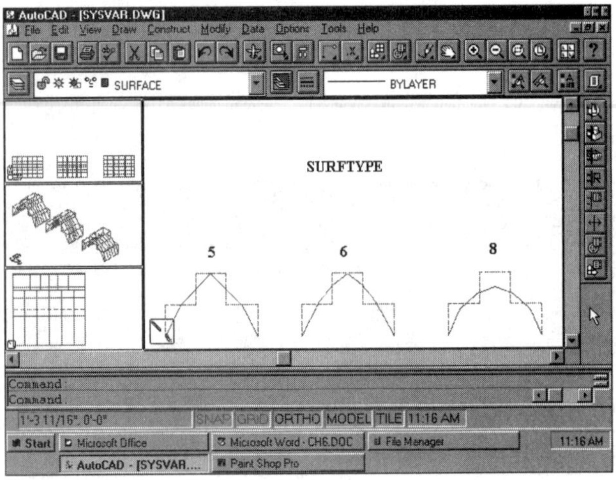

FIGURE 6.19 SURFTYPE practice results.

THE SURFU AND SURFV SYSTEM VARIABLES

The SURFU variable controls the accuracy of the surface density in the M direction for the Smooth option of the PEDIT command, while the SURFV variable controls the accuracy of the surface density in the N direction. The default setting for both variables is **6**. The direction of the mesh in M and N can be confusing. The directions are dependent on how the object was created and how the UCS was set at the time of creation.

> **TIP**
>
> Many users try setting one variable and using the PEDIT Smooth option to experiment. Once they know the correct orientation of the M and N directions, they UNDO the experiment, set everything correctly, and perform the edit.

Try adjusting the density of the mesh on the three objects used in the last procedure.

1. In the *Sysvar* drawing, either UNDO back to the beginning or open the drawing without saving from the last procedure.

2. Set SURFU to **2**.

3. Type **pedit** and press **Enter**.

4. Select the point P1, as shown in Figure 6.18.

5. Type **s** and press **Enter** to activate the Smooth option.

6. Press **Enter** to exit the PEDIT command.

7. Repeat steps 2 through 6 two more times, first setting SURFV to **20** and selecting the point P2, and then setting both SURFU and SURFV to **10** and selecting the point P3.

8. Hide all of the viewports using the HIDEALL command supplied.

The results are shown in Figure 6.20. The M and N directions are very clear when you set the two variables to radically different settings.

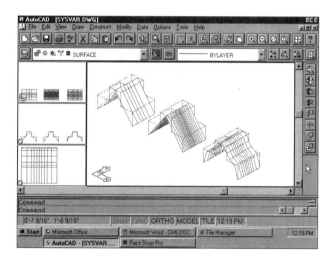

FIGURE 6.20 SURFU and SURFV practice results.

The **SURFTAB1** and **SURFTAB2** System Variables

SURFTAB1 is the system variable that determines the number of tabulations generated for RULESURF and TABSURF commands. SURFTAB1 also determines the mesh density in the M direction for the REVSURF and EDGESURF commands. The value is stored in integer form in the drawing file. You can select from a range of 2 to 256; the default is 6.

SURFTAB2 is the system variable that determines the mesh density in the N direction for the REVSURF and EDGESURF commands. You can select from a range of 2 to 256; the default is 6.

You are given the opportunity to practice using these variable in the surface commands discussed later in this chapter.

THE 3D SURFACE SYSTEM VARIABLES MENU LOCATION

The 3D surface variables discussed in this chapter do not have a menu location in the shipped version of AutoCAD. It is handy to have them on a toolbar, so they have been added to a customized toolbar called *3DWORLD.SURFVARS* in the supplied menu. The technique for creating customized toolbars is discussed in Chapter 12. The toolbar is shown in Figure 6.21.

SPLFRAME
SURFU
SURFV
SURFTYPE
SURFTAB1
SURFTAB2

FIGURE 6.21 3D Surfaces system variables toolbar.

The REVSURF Command

The REVSURF command creates a surface of revolution by rotating a curve path about a selected rotation axis. The path curve can be a Line, Arc, Circle, or 2D or 3D Polyline. The path object is rotated around the selected axis to define the surface. The path curve defines the N direction of the mesh, while the axis of revolution determines the M direction of the mesh. The start angle specification starts drawing the surface of revolution at an offset from the generating path (the default is 0). The included angle specifies the extent of the surface of revolution. The SURFTAB1 system variable controls the number of tabulation lines generated in the M direction, while SURFTAB2 controls the number of tabulations generated in the N direction. Try placing some surfaces using the REVSURF command.

Practice Procedure for Using REVSURF

1. Open the drawing *Surfaces*.

2. Type **revsurf** and press **Enter** to activate the command.

3. Select the Polyline at the point P1, as shown in Figure 6.22, when prompted `Select path curve:`.

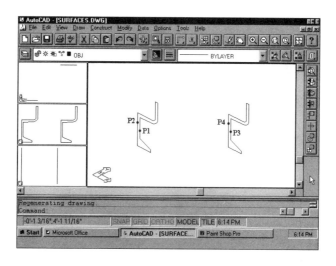

FIGURE 6.22 REVSURF practice reference.

4. Select the Line at the point P2, as shown in Figure 6.22, when prompted `Select axis of revolution:`.

5. Take the defaults for the Start angle and Included angle by pressing **Enter** at each prompt.

6. Set SURFTAB1 and SURFTAB2 to 20 and do steps 2 through 5 using the points P3 and P4, as shown in Figure 6.22.

7. Use the supplied ZOOMALL routine and the supplied HIDEALL routine to view your results.

The results are shown in Figure 6.23. The result of the change to SURFTAB1 is the smoothness of the cup's bowl. The result of the change to SURFTAB2 is not as apparent. The difference is shown in Figure 6.24, where the rounded edge at the bottom of the cup's bowl is enlarged for viewing.

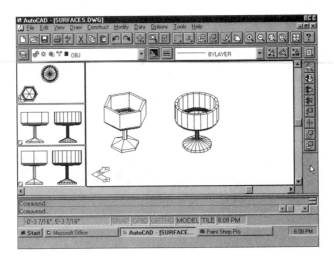

FIGURE 6.23 REVSURF practice results.

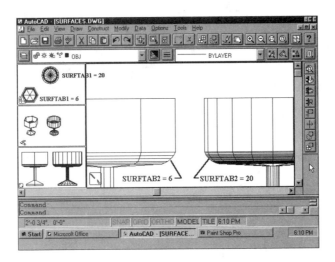

FIGURE 6.24 SURFTAB2 results enlarged for viewing.

TIP

The curve path and axis, for the last practice procedure, were created with the UCS set to the front view so that the end result of the REVSURF command was a glass standing up, not on its side. The current UCS setting when using the REVSURF command is critical to the end result.

THE REVSURF COMMAND MENU LOCATIONS

The REVSURF command is found on the *Surfaces* menu item of the *Draw* pull-down menu and on the *Surfaces* toolbar, as shown in Figure 6.25.

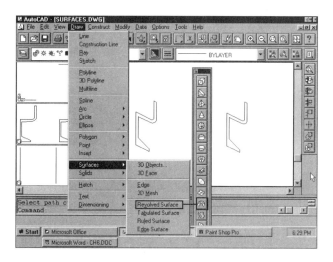

FIGURE 6.25 REVSURF command menu location.

The TABSURF Command

The TABSURF command creates a Polygon mesh representing a general tabulated cylinder defined by a path and a direction vector. The tabulated cylinder is constructed as a 2 x X Polygon mesh, where X is the number of tabulations to be generated in the M direction (specified by the system variable SURFTAB1), while 2 tabulations are generated in the N direction. The path curve can be a Line, Arc, Circle, 2D Polyline, or 3D Polyline. The surface is drawn starting at the point of the path curve closest to your pick point. The direction vector can be a Line, 2D Polyline, or 3D Polyline, determined by subtracting the endpoint of the object closest to your pick point from the object's other endpoint. Figure 6.26 shows a surface created using the TABSURF command with SURFTAB1 set to 80. The path curve is a splined 3D polyline and the direction vector is a line. The line is placed from the base in the +Z direction. The tabulated surface is placed in the same direction as the direction vector. Try create tabulated surfaces using the TABSURF command.

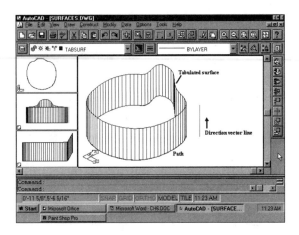

FIGURE 6.26 Surface generated by TABSURF.

Practice Procedure for Creating Tabulated Surfaces

1. In the drawing *Surfaces*, Thaw the layer TABSURF and make it the current layer.

2. Freeze the layer REVSURF.

3. Restore the viewport configuration TABSURF (the supplied routine DDVPORTS is good for this task). The resulting screen layout appears as shown in Figure 6.27.

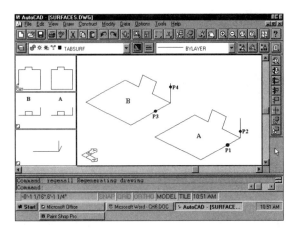

FIGURE 6.27 TABSURF practice reference.

4. Type **tabsurf** and press **Enter** to activate the command.

5. Select the point P1 on object A, as shown in Figure 6.27, for the path curve.

6. Select the point P2 on the line, as shown in Figure 6.27, for the direction vector.

7. Press **Enter** to activate the TABSURF command again.

8. Select the point P3 on object B, as shown in Figure 6.27, for the path curve.

9. Select the point P4 on the line, as shown in Figure 6.27, for the direction vector.

10. Use the supplied routine HIDEALL to view the results.

The results, shown in Figure 6.28, clearly show that the direction vector line selected is important. The resulting surface on object A extruded upward, while the surface on object B extruded downward.

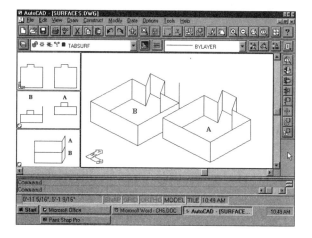

FIGURE 6.28 TABSURF practice results.

TIP   When using TABSURF on objects that have a curved path with many arcs in it, you should use a high setting on the SURFTAB1 variable. The example shown in Figure 6.26 used a setting of 80—while the previous procedure used the default setting of 6. The procedure had no arcs in it, so a low setting was acceptable. Too many tabulated surfaces slow down production, while to few surfaces can look bad. A compromise needs to be found for each object that gives a good representation of the object but does not take to long to REGEN or HIDE.

THE TABSURF COMMAND MENU LOCATIONS

The TABSURF command is found on the *Surfaces* menu item of the *Draw* pull-down menu and on the *Surfaces* toolbar, as shown in Figure 6.29.

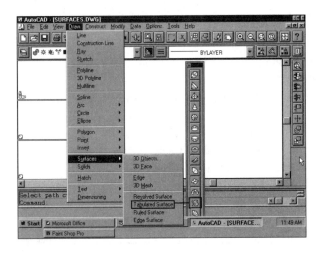

FIGURE 6.29 TABSURF command menu location.

The RULESURF Command

The RULESURF command creates a Polygon mesh representing the ruled surface between two curves. The two curves can be Lines, Points, Arcs, Circles, 2D Polylines, or 3D Polylines. When one curve boundary is closed, the other must also be closed. The exception to this rule is the Point object. A Point can be used as the other boundary for either an open or closed curve, but both boundary curves cannot be Points. The SURFTAB1 system variable controls the density of the surface. The ruled surface is constructed as a 2 x X Polygon mesh, where X is the number of tabulations to be generated in the M direction specified by the system variable SURFTAB1, while 2 tabulations are generated in the N direction. Try placing some ruled surfaces.

Practice Procedure for Placing RULESURF Surfaces

1. In the drawing *Surfaces*, set the variables SURFTAB1 and SURFTAB2 to 6.

2. Make the layer RULESURF the current layer (Thaw it first if necessary) and Freeze the layers REVSURF, TABSURF, RULESURF, RULESURF1A, and EDGESURF (some are already frozen).

3. Restore the viewport configuration called RULESURF (the supplied routine DDVPORTS is good for this task).

4. Type **rulesurf** and press **Enter** to activate the command.

5. Select the point P1 on object A, as shown in Figure 6.30.

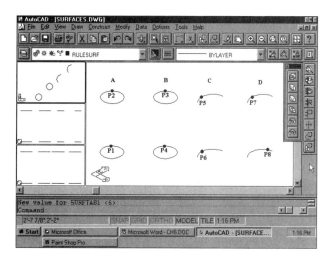

FIGURE 6.30 RULESURF practice reference.

6. Select the point P2 on object A, as shown in Figure 6.30.

7. Set SURFTAB1 and SURFTAB2 each to 20.

8. Repeat steps 3 through 5 three more times using the points P3 & P4 on object B, P5 & P6 on object C, and P7 & P8 on object D.

9. Use the supplied HIDEALL routine to view the results.

The results, shown in Figure 6.31, show an interesting phenomena (object D) when using arcs as your curved boundaries. When using arcs as the curve boundaries, the point selected on the Arc is important. When you select the left side of one Arc and the right side of the other Arc, you get a face that crosses over itself (a bowtie effect). When this happens, you must undo back and try again being careful to select the same side of the arc on both arcs (as done on object C).

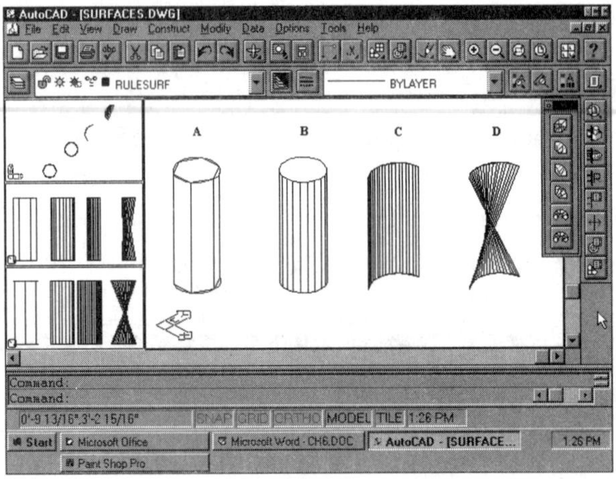

FIGURE 6.31 RULESURF practice results.

The RULESURF command is handy for surfacing rounded corners on a flat surface. There is a point–to–curve technique that allows you to use this command even when you do not have matching curve boundaries on a rounded corner. Try placing a corner surface using the point–to–curve technique.

176

Practice Procedure for Placing RULESURF Surfaces Using Point-to-Curve

1. In the drawing *Surfaces*, set the variables SURFTAB1 and SURFTAB2 to 10.

2. Make the layer RULESURF1 the current layer (Thaw it first if necessary) and Freeze the layers REVSURF, TABSURF, RULESURF, RULESURF1A and EDGESURF (some are already frozen).

3. Restore the viewport configuration called RULESURF1 (the supplied routine DDVPORTS is good for this task).

4. Switch the viewport configuration Large VP with the configuration VP1 (the supplied routine SWAPVP is good for this task).

5. Type **rulesurf** and press **Enter** to activate the command.

6. Select the Point in the viewport labeled Large VP in Figure 6.32.

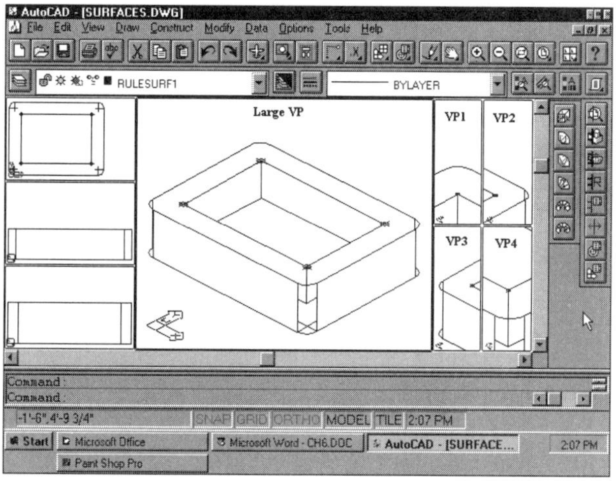

FIGURE 6.32 RULESURF point-to-curve practice reference.

7. Select the Arc in the viewport labeled Large VP in Figure 6.32.

8. Switch back the viewport configuration labeled Large VP with the configuration VP1.

9. Repeat steps 5 through 7 using the viewport configurations VP2, VP3, VP4 respectively with the Large VP viewport configuration.

10. Use the Zoom Extents and Zoom .8x options to enlarge the view of the part in the Large VP viewport configuration, as shown in Figure 6.33.

11. Thaw the layer RULESURF1A.

12. Use the supplied routine called HIDEALL command to view the results.

The results are shown in Figure 6.33. The part was finished using the 3DFACE command for the areas between corners. Unwanted face edges (on the 3Dface) were turned invisible using the DDMODIFY command.

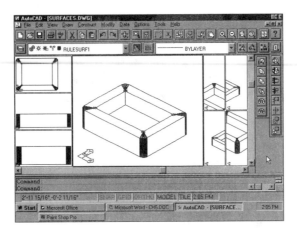

FIGURE 6.33 RULESURF practice results using point-to-curve technique.

The edges of a ruled surface can not be changed to invisible. This means that for the REVSURF, TABSURF, RULESURF, and EDGESURF surfaces, you cannot hide their edges unless you explode the surface to its primitive objects (3D faces).

TIP

The RULESURF Command Menu Locations

The RULESURF command is found on the *Surfaces* menu item of the *Draw* pull-down menu and on the *Surfaces* toolbar, as shown in Figure 6.34.

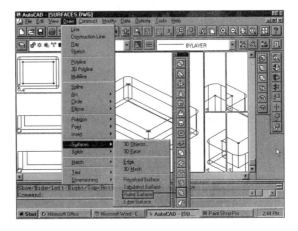

FIGURE 6.34 RULESURF command menu location.

The EDGESURF Command

The EDGESURF command constructs a Coons surface patch from four adjoining space curve edges. The four adjoining edges for selection can be Lines, Arcs, or open 2D or 3D Polylines, and they must touch at their endpoints to form a topological rectangular closed path. The edges can be selected in any order; however, the first edge selected generates the M direction, and the two edges that touch the first edge generate the N direction of the mesh. The system variable SURFTAB1 controls the number of tabulation lines generated in the M direction, while SURFTAB2 controls the number of tabulations generated in the N direction. Try placing a surface using the EDGESURF command.

Practice Procedure for Placing EDGESURF Surfaces Using Point-to-Curve

1. In the drawing *Surfaces*, set the variables SURFTAB1 and SURFTAB2 to 20.

2. Make the layer EDGESURF the current layer (Thaw it first if necessary) and Freeze the layers REVSURF, TABSURF, RULESURF, RULESURF1 and RULESURF1A (some are already frozen).

3. Restore the viewport configuration called EDGESURF (the supplied routine DDVPORTS is good for this task).

4. Type **edgesurf** and press **Enter** to activate the command.

5. Select the points P1, P2, P3, and P4 for each edge prompt (see Figure 6.35).

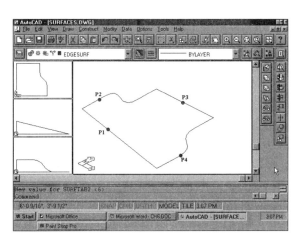

FIGURE 6.35 EDGESURF practice reference.

6. Use the supplied routine HIDEALL to view the results.

The four edges of the last procedure were comprised of two 2D polylines and two lines. One of the polylines was created to span different elevations. The EDGESURF command does not care if the edges are on the same elevation. The command's only concern is that the edges are connected and the type of object is legal. The results are shown in Figure 6.36.

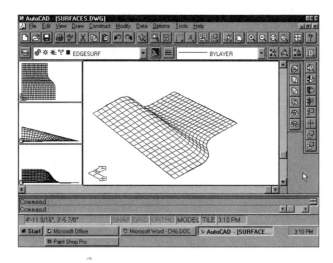

FIGURE 6.36 EDGESURF practice results.

THE EDGESURF COMMAND MENU LOCATIONS

The EDGESURF command is found on the *Surfaces* menu item of the *Draw* pull-down menu and on the *Surfaces* toolbar, as shown in Figure 6.37.

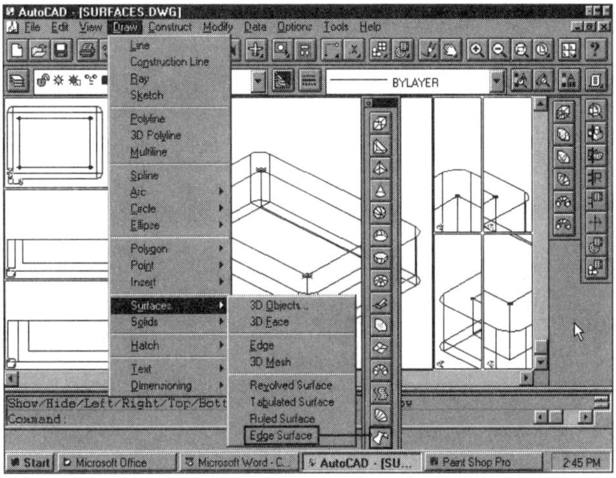

FIGURE 6.37 EDGESURF command menu location.

Using the SOLID Command

The SOLID command creates a filled polygon surface, much like the 3DFACE command. You can select 3 or 4 points to create triangles or rectangles, and the command continues on using the last two points of the last face as the first two point of the next face. The difference in the command's function lies in the order of the points you select. The 3DFACE command wants points selected in clockwise or counter-clockwise fashion or it will create a "bowtie" effect. The SOLID command is exactly opposite. A clockwise or counter-clockwise selection of points creates a "bowtie" effect, while selecting points in a parallel fashion creates the desired face. Both commands create a surface that hides objects from view, and work with the SHADE and RENDER commands. Try using the SOLID command to create a surface.

Practice Procedure for Placing Solids

1. In a new drawing, type **solid** and press **Enter**.

2. Select the points P1, P2, P3, and P4 to create the solid labeled A, shown in Figure 6.38.

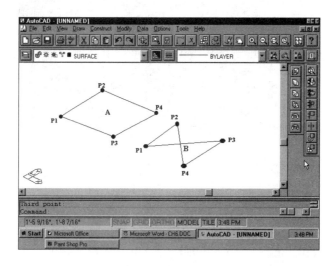

FIGURE 6.38 SOLID practice reference.

3. Press **Enter** to exit the SOLID command.

4. Press **Enter** to activate the SOLID command again.

5. Select the points P1, P2, P3, and P4 to create the solid labeled B, shown in Figure 6.38.

6. Press **Enter** to exit the SOLID command.

The results are shown in Figure 6.38.

THE SOLID COMMAND MENU LOCATION

The SOLID command is found on the *Polygon* flyout of the *Draw* toolbar, as shown in Figure 6.39.

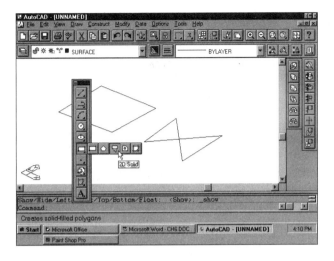

FIGURE 6.39 SOLID command menu location.

Editing Surfaces

Mesh surfaces are edited in two different ways:

- All types of surfaces can be manipulated using basic editing commands such as MOVE, ROTATE, SCALE, MIRROR, STRETCH, and CHPROP.
- Meshes created using 3DMESH, REVSURF, TABSURF, RULESURF, and EDGESURF can be edited with the PEDIT command. Surfaces created using 3DFACE (not a mesh but a mesh primitive) and PFACE (a technique that creates 3D faces from a program) can not be edited using the PEDIT command.

SURFACE EDITING USING BASIC EDITING TOOLS

Commands such as MOVE, ROTATE, SCALE, and MIRROR treat the surface or mesh as a single object and edit them according to the command's options. A command such as STRETCH works on individual vertices in the surface or mesh, and you must select only the vertices you desire to manipulate. This is consistent with the procedures for the editing commands in 2D or 3D.

The PEDIT Command for Editing Meshes

The PEDIT command has several options for editing polyline meshes:

- Edit vertex—allows the movement of individual vertices of a mesh.
- Smooth surface—makes the mesh uniform in the M and N directions.
- Desmooth—places the mesh back to its original configuration before a Smooth operation.
- Mclose—closes the ends of the mesh in the M direction.
- Nclose—closes the ends of the mesh in the N direction.

This command works on surface meshes created with the commands REVSURF, TABSURF, RULESURF, or EDGESURF, but not on individual 3D faces.

Edit Vextex

This option has a series of options that allow you to select the exact vertices you desire to work on and to move that vertices to any position in 3D space. Upon entering this option, a small X appears on the first vertices of the mesh. The X represents the vertices (the first in the mesh when starting) that is to be moved. The vertices selection options are based on the M and N directions of the mesh or a next/previous selection. Once you move the X to the desired vertices, you select the Move option and designate the new position. The mesh is altered accordingly. Try the Edit Vertex option.

Practice Procedure for the Edit Vertex Option of PEDIT

1. In the drawing PEDIT, type **pedit** and press **Enter** to activate the command.
2. Select the 3d mesh.

3. Type **e** and press **Enter** to activate the Edit Vertex option.

4. Type **u** and press **Enter** to move the vertex selection X up in the M direction one vertex, as shown in Figure 6.40.

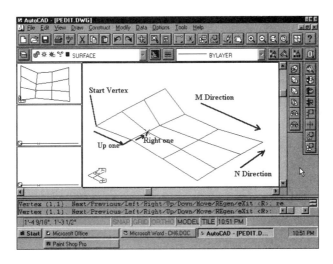

FIGURE 6.40 Edit Vertex practice reference.

5. Type **r** and press **Enter** to move the vertex selection X right in the N direction one vertex.

6. Type **m** and press **Enter** to activate the Move option of the Edit Vertex option.

7. Type **@0,0,1** and press **Enter** to move the vertex on the Z axis.

8. Repeat steps 5 and 6 two more times.

9. Cancel out of the PEDIT command.

The result is shown in Figure 6.41. The three vertices along the second edge are elevated one unit.

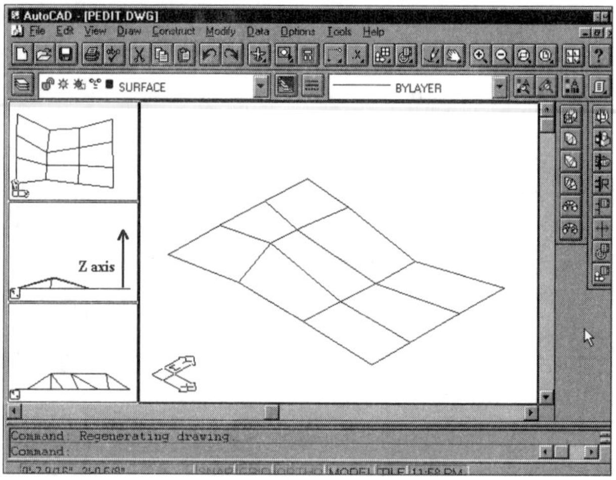

FIGURE 6.41 Edit Vertex practice results.

Smooth Surface

The PEDIT smooth option is a 3D spline performed on mesh surfaces. The type of surface spline used is controlled by the SURFTYPE variable (discussed earlier in this chapter). The mesh density is controlled by the variables SURFU (M direction density) and SURFV (N direction density). Based on the settings of these three variables, the command's option calculates the number of mesh elements (3D faces) in both directions and their position in 3D space. The SURFTYPE practice procedure earlier in this chapter is a good example of smoothing a surface using the Smooth option.

Desmooth

This option undoes the effects of the Smooth option. When no prior Smooth operation has taken place, the Desmooth option has no effect.

Mclose

This option takes an open mesh and closes it in the M direction. When the mesh is already closed, this option changes to Mopen. Try closing the mesh used in the Edit Vertex practice procedure.

Practice Procedure for the Mclose Option of PEDIT

1. In the drawing PEDIT, type **pedit** and press **Enter** to activate the command.

2. Select the mesh, as shown in Figure 6.40.

3. Type **m** and press **Enter** to activate the Mclose option.

4. Press **Enter** to exit the PEDIT command.

5. Use the supplied HIDEALL routine to view the results.

The result is shown in Figure 6.42.

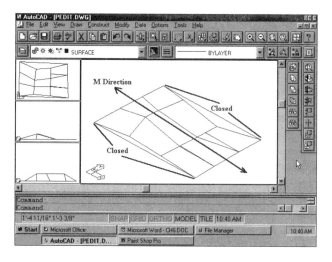

FIGURE 6.42 Mclose practice result.

Nclose

This option takes an open mesh and closes it in the N direction. When the mesh is already closed, this option changes to Nopen.

THE PEDIT COMMAND MENU LOCATION

The PEDIT command is found under the *Modify* pull-down menu and on the toolbar (as the default flyout button and the first button on the flyout) as shown in Figure 6.43.

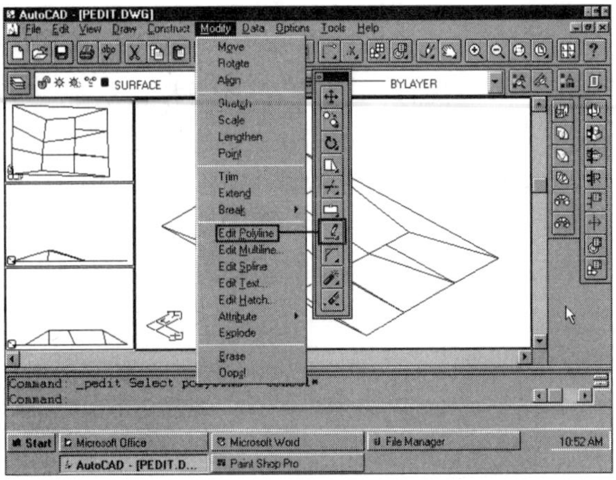

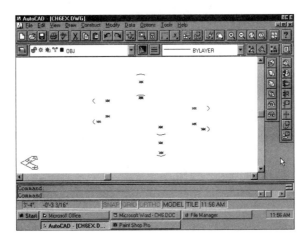

FIGURE 6.43 PEDIT command menu location.

Chapter Exercise

Take the simple wireframe objects (points and arcs) supplied in the drawing CH6EX, as shown in Figure 4.44, and place surfaces on them. The results are shown in Figure 6.45. Place surfaces on the bottom and all sides, since the object should appear solid when viewed from any angle.

FIGURE 6.44 Chapter 6 exercise reference.

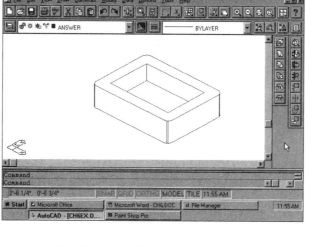

FIGURE 6.45 Chapter 6 exercise result.

Hints:

- You need to using running Node and Endpoint snaps.
- The surfaces can be created using 3DFACE and RULESURF.
- Edges are hidden using the EDGE command.
- You must explode the surfaces created using RULESURF before you can use the EDGE command on them.
- More hints are found on the Text layer in the drawing.
- The surfaces are already in the drawing on the Answer layer for comparison when needed.

In Conclusion

In this chapter, you were introduced to all of the surfacing commands, their support system variables, and the editing tools for surfaces and meshes. The use of these surfacing tools is dictated by your needs and by the style of design you develop. The surface tools, along with wireframes, need not always be used to solve a design problem. With the inclusion of ACIS solids in the core of Release 13, many users are shifting to designing in solids rather than using surfaces or wireframes with surfaces. The more versatile you are with the surface tools and the solids tools introduced later in this book, the better you are able to meet your design needs in a timely fashion. In the next chapter, you are introduced to the new ACIS solids commands and their support system variables.

CHAPTER SEVEN

Solid Geometry

In this chapter, you are introduced to the region modeler, native primitive solids, and supporting system variables. Release 13 introduced the internal region modeler and ACIS solids while dropping AME solids from the package. This controversial switch in solids packages was necessary to bring the AutoCAD software technology into the nineties. ACIS solids have eliminated the useful ability to manipulate the primitive geometry that makes up the solid. This has caused some concern with users, but good design habits can eliminate most problems and it is just a matter of time before Autodesk or some third party developer creates a method to manipulate the primitive geometry that makes up a complex solid. The region modeler is a tool for creating complex 2D regions that you can extrude into solids.

Creating a Region

The REGION command is used to create a bounded planar object. The object can contain holes, islands or be disconnected. You can perform Boolean operations (unions, intersections, and subtractions) on regions and mass property computations. Regions are created from 2-dimensional closed shapes, or loops. Valid object selections are closed polylines, lines, circles, circular arcs, elliptical arcs, 3Dfaces, ellipses, and splines. AutoCAD automatically converts closed 2D and planar 3D polylines to separate regions.

NOTE

Two curves sharing an endpoint can result in an arbitrary region.

The REGION command has several rules about the geometry used to create a region:

- AutoCAD rejects all intersections and self-intersecting curves.
- Each point of the connected geometry must share only two edges.
- Spline or Fit polylines used to create a region contain the line or arc geometry of the smoothed polyline. The actual polyline is not converted into a spline.
- AutoCAD deletes the original objects used to create the regions.

Regions are a benefit because, like solids, you can inquire about mass properties. Try creating some regions.

Practice Procedure for Creating Regions

1. In the drawing REGION, type **region** and press **Enter** to activate the command.
2. Select all three circles and the polyline (the outline) as shown in Figure 7.1.

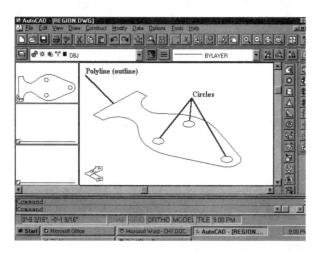

FIGURE 7.1 Region practice reference.

3. Press **Enter** to create the regions and exit the command.

The command line reports back that 4 loops were extracted and 4 regions were created. Use the LIST command to select any of the four objects, and AutoCAD reports back the object as a REGION and the information on the object. Creating a region is only the first step in creating solids using regions. In Chapter 8, you are introduced to editing commands that extrude, subtract, and union regions.

THE DELOBJ SYSTEM VARIABLE

The DELOBJ system variable controls the deposition of the original geometry when a region is created. When set to one (the default), the original geometry is deleted and the region is created. When set to zero, the original geometry is retained and the region is created. Many users create the region with the variable set to zero and then move the region to a separate layer or to another area. They can then create other regions from the same original geometry. This technique is handy when creating libraries of complex parts. Try creating a region using the DELOBJ system variable set to zero.

Practice Procedure for Using DELOBJ with the REGION Command

1. In the drawing REGION, restore the viewport configuration called DELOBJ.
2. Make the layer called BOTTOM current (you need to thaw it first) and freeze the layer OBJ.
3. Set the system variable DELOBJ to zero.
4. Activate the region command.
5. Select all five of the objects, shown in Figure 7.2, and press **Enter** to create the regions and exit the command.
6. Use the CHPROP command and the FILTER command to change all of the new regions to the layer called TOP. (See the Note below for details if you haven't used filters before.)
7. Use the REGENALL command to restore your viewports' views.
8. Set the system variable DELOBJ to one.
9. Activate the region command.
10. Select all of the objects and press **Enter** to create the regions and exit the command.

FIGURE 7.2 DELOBJ practice reference.

The result of the procedure is a set of regions on the TOP layer and a set on the BOTTOM layer. The regions are now available on the appropriate layer (after thawing) for constructing a solid representing the top and bottom of an object.

194

N O T E   Filter is a tool that can be used for selecting objects by properties (color, linetype, and layers), by object type (line, arc, region, and so on), or by any combination (logical OR, AND, and so on). In the above procedure, you use the transparent FILTER command while in the CHPROP command; select the **Region** item from the select filter pop list; use the **Add to list** button; and select the **Apply** button. A crossing or window can be used to select all geometry, and the filter will only select the Region objects and filter out all other objects. This procedure is common and more complex filters, with a little practice, can be designed and saved.

THE DELOBJ SYSTEM VARIABLE MENU LOCATION

The DELOBJ variable does not have a menu location in the shipped version of AutoCAD. It is handy to have them on a toolbar, so they have been added to a customized toolbar called 3DWORLD.SOLIDVARS in supplied menu. The technique for creating customized toolbars is discussed in Chapter 12. The toolbar is shown later in this chapter in Figure 7.6.

Variables for Controlling a Solid Model's Display

Autodesk has introduced several new variables for controlling how the new ACIS solids are displayed. Solids are represented as wireframes in the course of design. You want as few lines in the wireframe representation as possible during production (while still being able to tell what the geometry represents). AutoCAD has two variables for controlling the display of the wireframe representation:

- ISOLINES
- DISPSILH

Solids are automatically meshed when you display them using the HIDE, SHADE, or RENDER commands. The mesh is taken off when the REGEN command is used to change the display back to production design mode. The density of the mesh in this representation is controlled with the variable FACETRES. In the following section, you are given the opportunity to practice the use of all three variables on multiple types of solids.

CONTROL TESSELLATION LINES WITH THE ISOLINES VARIABLE

Tessellation lines are the lines that help you visualize the curves in a solid. These lines are visualization tools and you cannot snap to them. The ISOLINES variable sets the amount of lines to be shown on the curved surface of a solid. The variable has a default value of 4 and it only accepts whole numbers. Another function of the ISOLINES variable is the ability to control the display of spline surfaces. The spline surfaces are controlled by subtracting 4 from the value of the variable. Try different settings for the ISOLINES variable.

Practice Procedure for Using ISOLINES

1. In the drawing *Solids*, set ISOLINES to 4.
2. Activate the viewport marked ISOLINES = 4 in Figure 7.3 and use the REGEN command in that viewport.
3. Activate the viewport marked ISOLINES = 8, as shown in Figure 7.3. Set ISOLINES to 8 and use the REGEN command in that viewport.

4. Activate the viewport marked ISOLINES = 12, as shown in Figure 7.3. Set ISOLINES to 12 and use the REGEN command in that viewport.

5. Activate the viewport marked ISOLINES = 16, as shown in Figure 7.3. Set ISOLINES to 16 and use the REGEN command in that viewport.

6. Set ISOLINES back to 4.

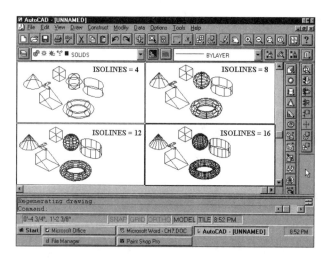

FIGURE 7.3 ISOLINES practice reference.

Notice that the solids with curves (all but the box and the wedge) have the lines that represent them change in each viewport. The viewport with ISOLINES = 4 (the default setting) has few definitions lines, while the viewport with ISOLINES = 16 has many lines.

Tessellation lines, while helping better define a curved solid objects outline, slow down regeneration. Set your ISOLINES low enough to have quick regeneration but high enough to easily identify curved solid objects. A setting of 6 or 8 is a good compromise.

TIP

NOTE

ISOLINES can be set to zero. When this is done, the tessellation lines on objects such as cylinders disappear.

The tessellation lines are for your benefit during the design phase; they have no effect on the results when you hide, shade, or render the object. Keep the ISOLINES to as low a setting as you can to do your work.

CONTROL THE MESH DENSITY OF RENDERINGS WITH THE FACETRES VARIABLE

The FACETRES variable controls how dense a mesh appears on a 3D object that is hidden, shaded, or rendered. The default setting of .5 presents a rather crude visualization of curved objects. Any positive number is acceptable between 0.1 and 10; the higher the number, the more mesh faces are temporarily created for the object. You must balance the need for smooth-looking surfaces on your solid with the need for speed when using a visualization command. Try using the FACETRES variable.

Practice Procedure for Using FACETRES

197

1. In the drawing *Solids*, set FACETRES to .1.
2. Activate the viewport marked FACETRES = .1 in Figure 7.4 and use the HIDE command in that viewport.
3. Activate the viewport marked FACETRES = .5, as shown in Figure 7.4. Set FACETRES to .5 and use the HIDE command in that viewport.
4. Activate the viewport marked FACETRES = 1, as shown in Figure 7.4. Set FACETRES to 1 and use the HIDE command in that viewport.
5. Activate the viewport marked FACETRES = 5, as shown in Figure 7.4. Set FACETRES to 5 and use the HIDE command in that viewport.
6. Set FACETRES back to .5.

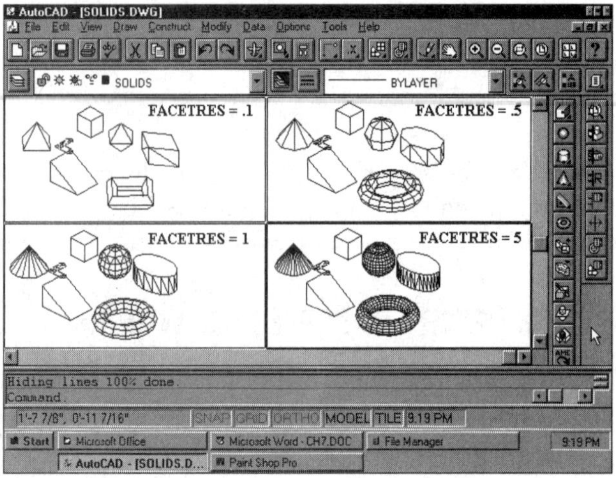

FIGURE 7.4 FACETRES practice reference.

Figure 7.4 shows the results of the practice procedure. The FACETRES variable controls display for the visualization commands as the ISOLINES variable controls the display of tessellation lines for the normal view.

NOTE A mesh is temporarily created on a solid anytime you use the HIDE, SHADE, or RENDER commands on a solid object. The mesh is removed by the REGEN command.

CONTROL SILHOUETTE EDGES WITH THE DISPSILH VARIABLE

Silhouette edges are used to augment isolines, giving solid objects more shape definition when not hidden, shaded, or rendered. The DISPSILH variable controls whether or not the silhouette edges are displayed. Set to zero (the default), the edges do not display. A setting of one displays the edges. Displaying silhouette edges takes longer to calculate and increases regeneration time. Try using the DISPSILH variable.

Practice Procedure for Using DISPSILH

1. In the drawing *Solids*, set FACETRES to .5, set ISOLINES to 4, and DISPSILH to 0 (the defaults setting for all).

2. Activate the viewport marked A, as shown in Figure 7.5, and use the REGEN command in that viewport.

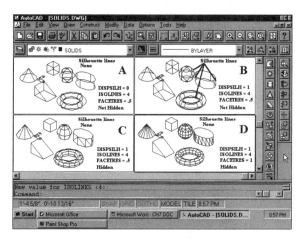

FIGURE 7.5 DISPSILH practice reference.

3. Activate the viewport marked B, as shown in Figure 7.5, and set DISPSILH to 1.

4. Use the REGEN command in viewport B to see the results.

5. Activate the viewport marked C, as shown in Figure 7.5, and use the HIDE command in that viewport.

6. Activate the viewport marked, as shown in Figure 7.5, and set FACETRES to 1.

7. Use the HIDE command in viewport D to see the results.

8. Set FACETRES back to .5 and DISPSILH to 0.

Figure 7.5 shows the results of the practice procedure. Viewport A shows no silhouette lines on the sphere, Torus, and cylinder. The objects have poor definition and are hard to recognize. Viewport B has the silhouette lines showing (DISPSILH = 1) making the objects easier to recognize. Viewports C and D show that the silhouette lines are not used in hidden views (shaded and rendered objects also are included in this group).

SOLIDS DISPLAY VARIABLES SUMMARY

The three variables presented in this chapter give you total control of the way a solid is displayed in "wireframe" representation design mode and in the mesh representation viewing mode. You must balance your need to tell what the object is with the need to keep up your production speed. The ISOLINES variable works well with the DISPSILH variable turned on. You can keep the ISOLINES variable set low (between 4 and 8) and the DISPSILH variable adds the extra lines you need. The FACETRES variable only needs to be set as high as necessary to have smooth-looking curved objects. When your object does not have curved sides, you can leave the variable low. When the object has curved sides, you need to experiment with the setting to find one that allows you a smooth view but does not take too long to hide, shade, or render.

SOLID MODEL'S DISPLAY VARIABLES MENU LOCATION

The 3D solids variables discussed in this chapter do not have a menu location in the shipped version of AutoCAD. It is handy to have them on a toolbar, so they have been added to a customized toolbar called *3DWORLD.SOLIDVARS* in the supplied menu. The technique for creating customized toolbars is discussed in Chapter 12. The toolbar is shown in Figure 7.6.

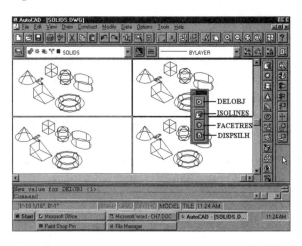

FIGURE 7.6 3D Solids system variables toolbar .

Creating Geometry Using Solids Primitives

Solids have many advantages that are not found using the wireframe/surfaces method of design. Some features of solids are as follows:

- Solids can be queried for information such as mass properties, volume, centroid, moments of inertia, products of inertia, and radii of gyration.

- Solids can be extruded, revolved, sliced, trimmed, and chamfered.

- You can subtract, union, and check for interference with solids.

- Solids can be exported to other CAD systems or converted to Stereo-lithography apparatus format.

The disadvantage in using solids in Release 13 is the inability to edit the primitive solid objects that make up a complex solid model. Solid primitives are the basic building blocks that make up complex solid models. This limitation can be mini-mized by careful planning during the design phase. The following section introduces you to all of the solids primitives available in AutoCAD and allows you to practice creating them. All practice procedures in this section use the following settings for the solids display variables (referred to as the standard settings for the practices) unless otherwise noted.

- ISOLINES = 4 (default)
- DISPSILH = 1
- FACETRES = 1

THE BOX COMMAND

This command allows you to create 3-dimensional boxes of any size. You can create a box by supplying a length, width, and height. The command creates a box from the center or from a defined corner of the box. A shortcut option for creating a cube is also present. Try placing some 3D boxes.

Practice Procedure for Using the BOX Command

1. In a new drawing, using the standard settings for the solids variables, restore the viewport configuration 3D4R, and make the SOLID layer current.

2. Start the box command by typing **box** and pressing **Enter**.

3. Activate the Center option by typing **c** and pressing **Enter**.

4. Place the center of the box at 0,0,0 (on the point P1 as shown in Figure 7.7).

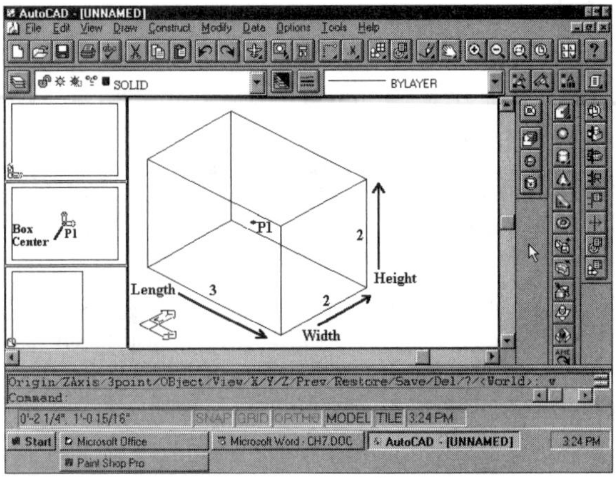

FIGURE 7.7 Box center practice procedure.

5. Type **l** (L) to activate the Length option of the BOX command.

6. Type **3** for the length of the box.

7. Type **2** for the width and height of the box.

202

The result is shown in Figure 7.7. Notice that the Length is the X axis, the Width is the Y axis, and the Height is the Z axis. The center of the box is located at the 0,0,0 point you specified.

A box's length, width, and height can be given in positive, negative numbers, or you can select points on the screen using object snaps, grid/snap, or coordinate systems.

N O T E

The box can also by created using the Corner option (the default option). The resulting box is positioned relative to the corner point selected, not the center point selected as in the Center option. Try using the Corner option of the BOX command. A step in this procedure uses the object created in the last procedure; complete the last procedure before continuing.

Practice Procedure for Using the BOX Command

1. In the same drawing as the last procedure, using the standard settings for the solids variables, restore the viewport configuration 3D4R and make the SOLID layer current.

2. Start the box command by typing **box** and pressing **Enter**.

3. Place the first corner of the box at 0,0,0.

4. Use the point filter .XY and the Endpoint object snap to select the other corner (on the point P1 of the first box as shown in Figure 7.8).

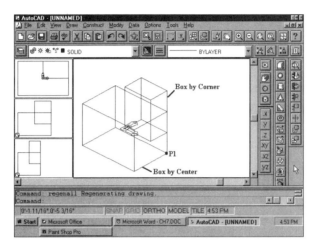

FIGURE 7.8 Box corner practice procedure.

5. Type **@** to complete the point filter point using the current elevation for the Z axis.

6. Type **2** for the Height of the box.

7. Use the supplied ZOOMALL routine to adjust the viewports.

The result is shown in Figure 7.8. Notice that the box by corner resides on the current elevation while the box by center does not. This is because the Center option centers the box on all axes, while the Corner option starts on the current elevation.

TIP

The last procedure combined some of the techniques introduced in Chapters 3, 4, and 5 to place solids (point filters and object snaps). All techniques for placing wireframes and surfaces can be used to place solids.

The Cube option takes the first dimension supplied (the length) and applies it to the width and the height to create a cube. The Cube option is available for both box by center and box by corner.

THE SPHERE COMMAND

This command creates a 3D solid sphere. The central axis of the sphere is parallel to the Z axis of the current UCS, while the latitudinal lines are parallel to the XY plane. This is shown in Figure 7.9. A sphere is defined by a center point and a radius or diameter. You can use any of the available tools for selecting a center point. Try creating a sphere using the SPHERE command.

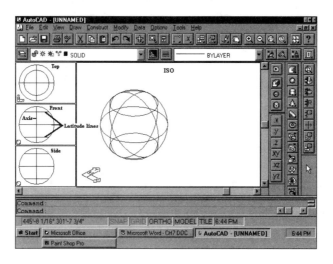

FIGURE 7.9 3D sphere.

Practice Procedure for Using the SPHERE Command

1. In a new drawing, using the standard settings for the solids variables, restore the viewport configuration 3D4R and make the SOLID layer current.

2. Start the sphere command by typing **sphere** and pressing **Enter**.

3. Select a point near the center of the screen.

4. Type **3** to create a sphere with a radius of 3.

To use the Diameter option, you must type **d** and then enter the diameter size. The sphere is one of the curved 3D objects that benefits when the DISPSILH variable is turned on.

THE CYLINDER COMMAND

This command creates a 3D solid cylinder. A 3D solid cylinder is a solid column similar to an extruded circle or ellipse. You can create circular or elliptical cylinders. The CYLINDER command options allow you to use height, center point, and major/minor axis to define a cylinder. Try creating several different types of cylinders using the various options of the CYLINDER command.

Practice Procedure for Using the CYLINDER Command

1. In a new drawing, using the standard settings for the solids variables, restore the viewport configuration 3D4R, make the SOLID layer current, and turn on the Ortho mode.

2. Start the CYLINDER command by typing **cylinder** and pressing **Enter**.

3. Select a point on the screen, near the point P1 as shown in Figure 7.10, for the center of the cylinder.

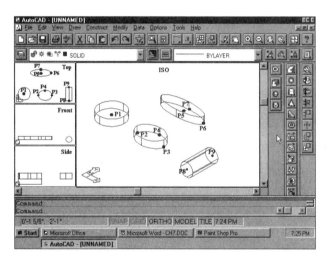

FIGURE 7.10 CYLINDER practice reference.

4. Type **2** for the radius and **1** for the height.

5. Press **Enter** to activate the CYLINDER command again.

6. Type **e** to activate the Elliptical option.

7. Select the points on the screen near the points P2, P3, and P4 as shown in Figure 7.10, for the major and minor axes.

8. Type **1** for the height.

9. Press **Enter** to activate the CYLINDER command again.

10. Type **e** to activate the Elliptical option, and type **c** to activate the Center option.

11. Select the points on the screen near the points P5, P6, and P7 as shown in Figure 7.10, for the center to the major and minor axes.

12. Type **1** for the height.

13. Press **Enter** to activate the CYLINDER command again.

14. Select a point on the screen, near the point P8 as shown in Figure 7.10, for the center of the cylinder.

15. Type **1** for the radius of the cylinder, and type **c** for the center of the other end.

16. Select a point on the screen, near the point P9 as shown in Figure 7.10, for the center of the cylinder.

The results are shown in Figure 7.10 (after using the ZOOMALL routine). The different combinations of options allow you to create a cylinder of any size or shape.

THE CONE COMMAND

This command creates a 3D solid cone. A cone has a circular or elliptical base tapering symmetrically to a point (the apex) perpendicular to its base. The CONE command can also create cones which are non-symmetrical. The CONE command options allow you to use height, center point, and major/minor axis to define a cone. Try creating several different types of cones using the various options of the CONE command.

Practice Procedure for Using the CONE Command

1. In a new drawing, using the standard settings for the solids variables, restore the viewport configuration 3D4R, and make the SOLID layer current.

2. Start the CONE command by typing **cone** and pressing **Enter**.

3. Select a point on the screen, near the point P1 as shown in Figure 7.11, for the center of the cone.

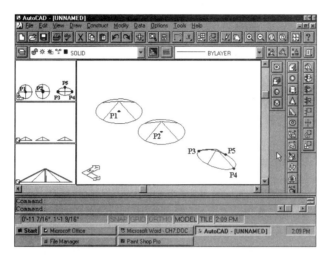

FIGURE 7.11 CONE practice reference.

4. Type **2** for the radius and **1** for the height.

5. Press **Enter** to activate the CONE command again.

6. Select a point on the screen, near the point P2 as shown in Figure 7.11, for the center of the cone.

7. Type **2** for the radius, and **a** to activate the Apex option.

8. Type **@0,0,1** for the apex point.

9. Press **Enter** to activate the CONE command again.

10. Type **e** to activate the Elliptical option.

11. Select the points on the screen, near the points P3, P4, and P5 as shown in Figure 7.11, for the major axis and the minor axis.

12. Type **1** for the height.

As you can see by the options, the CONE command is similar to the CYLINDER command except that it has an Apex option that cylinders do not have. Cones are symmetrical from the base to the apex. The CONE command has the ability to create a non-symmetrical cone (which is not truly a cone since it is not symmetrical).

The trick is to use a cylindrical or spherical coordinate to define the apex point of the cone. With either coordinate system, you can define an apex that is off-center from the center of the base. You can tilt the apex in any direction, at any angle, at any height. Try creating some non–symmetrical cones.

Practice Procedure for Using the CONE Command for Non-Symmetrical Cones

1. In a new drawing, using the standard settings for the solids variables, restore the viewport configuration 3D4R, and make the SOLID layer current.

2. Start the CONE command by typing **cone** and pressing **Enter**.

3. Select a point on the screen, near the point P1 as shown in Figure 7.12, for the center of the cone.

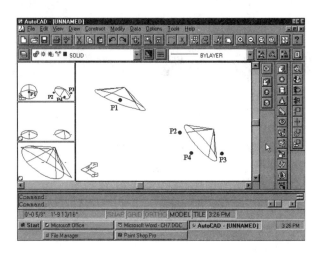

FIGURE 7.12 Non-symmetrical CONE practice reference.

4. Type **2** for the radius, and **a** to activate the Apex option.

5. Type **@1<90<60** for the apex point.

6. Press **Enter** to activate the CONE command again.

7. Type **e** to activate the Elliptical option.

8. Select the points on the screen near the points P2, P3, and P4 (as shown in Figure 7.12) for the major and minor axes.

9. Type **a** to activate the Apex option.

10. Type **@1<60,1** for the apex point.

11. Use the supplied ZOOMALL routine to view the results in all viewports.

By using the spherical and cylindrical coordinate systems, you tilted the apex of the cone on each solid cone.

Using a negative number for the Cone's apex will point the cone upside down.

TIP

THE WEDGE COMMAND

This command creates a 3D solid with a sloped face tapering along the X axis. The command allows you to create the wedge object around a center point or from a specified corner like the BOX command.

Practice Procedure for Using the WEDGE Command

1. In a new drawing, using the standard settings for the solids variables, restore the viewport configuration 3D4R and make the SOLID layer current.

2. Start the wedge command by typing **wedge** and pressing **Enter**.

3. Activate the Center option by typing **c** and pressing **Enter**.

4. Place the center of the box at 0,0,0 (on the point P1 as shown in Figure 7.13).

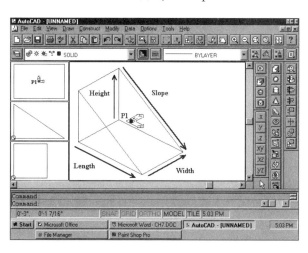

FIGURE 7.13 WEDGE practice reference.

5. Type **l** (L) to activate the Length option of the WEDGE command.

6. Type **3** for the length of the wedge.

7. Type **2** for the width and height of the wedge.

8. Use the supplied ZOOMALL routine to view the results.

The result is shown in Figure 7.13. Notice that the slope of the wedge runs along the X axis. The center of the wedge is located at the 0,0,0 point you specified.

The wedge can also by created using the Corner option (the default option). The resulting box is positioned relative to the corner point selected, not the center point selected as with the Center option. Try using the Corner option of the WEDGE command. A step in this procedure uses the object created in the last procedure; complete the last procedure before continuing.

Practice Procedure for Using the WEDGE Command's Corner Option

1. In the same drawing as the last procedure, using the standard settings for the solids variables, restore the viewport configuration 3D4R and make the SOLID layer current.

2. Start the box command by typing **wedge** and pressing **Enter**.

3. Place the first corner of the wedge at 0,0,0.

4. Use the point filter .XY and the Endpoint object snap to select the other corner (on the point P1 of the first box as shown in Figure 7.14).

5. Type **@** to complete the point filter point using the current elevation for the Z axis.

6. Type **2** for the Height of the wedge.

7. Use the supplied ZOOMALL routine to adjust the viewports.

The results are shown in Figure 7.14. Notice that the wedge by corner resides on the current elevation while the wedge by center does not. That is because the Center option centers the wedge on all axes while the Corner option starts on the current elevation.

The Cube option takes the first dimension supplied (the length) and applies it to the width and the height to create a cube wedge. The Cube option is available for both wedge by center and wedge by corner.

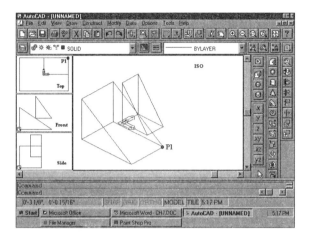

FIGURE 7.14 WEDGE corner practice reference.

THE TORUS COMMAND

This command creates a 3D donut solid. You define a torus by supplying a radius for the tube and a radius measured from the center of the object to the center of the tube. A torus with no inside hole results when you make the tube radius larger than the radius of the torus. Try creating some torus solids.

Practice Procedure for Using the TORUS Command

1. In a new drawing, using the standard settings for the solids variables, restore the viewport configuration 3D4R and make the SOLID layer current.
2. Start the torus command by typing **torus** and pressing **Enter**.
3. Press **Enter** to accept the default of 0,0,0 for the center of the torus.
4. Type **4** for the torus radius and type **1** (one) for the tube radius.
5. Use the supplied ZOOMALL routine to view your results in all viewports.

The result appear as shown in Figure 7.15. Try a torus with no center hole.

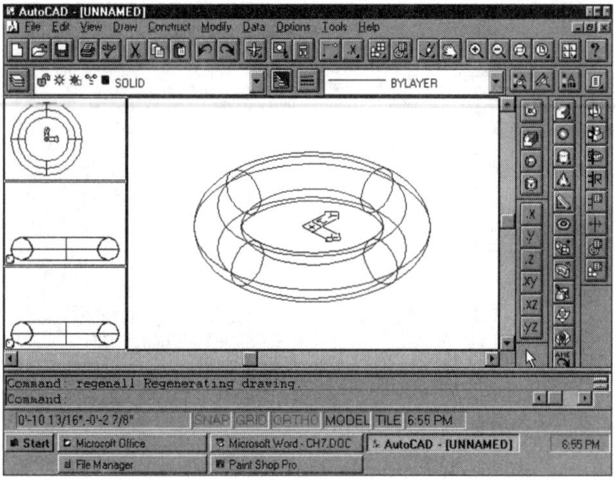

FIGURE 7.15 Torus practice results.

Practice Procedure for Creating a Torus with No Center Hole

1. In a new drawing, using the standard settings for the solids variables, restore the viewport configuration 3D4R and make the SOLID layer current.

2. Start the torus command by typing **torus** and pressing **Enter**.

3. Press **Enter** to accept the default of 0,0,0 for the center of the torus.

4. Type **4** for the torus radius and type **5** for the tube radius.

5. Use the supplied ZOOMALL routine to view your results in all viewports.

The result appears as shown in Figure 7.16. The only difference in the creation of a torus with no center hole and a normal torus is the specification of a tube radius larger than the torus radius.

The TORUS command can be used to create a solid football shape. Use a negative number for the radius of the torus and a positive tube radius greater than the torus radius negative number. Try creating a football solid with the TORUS command.

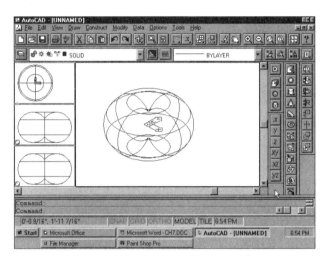

FIGURE 7.16 Torus with no hole practice results.

Practice Procedure for Creating a Torus Football

1. In a new drawing, using the standard settings for the solids variables, restore the viewport configuration 3D4R and make the SOLID layer current.

2. Start the torus command by typing **torus** and pressing **Enter**.

3. Press **Enter** to accept the default of 0,0,0 for the center of the torus.

4. Type **–4** for the torus radius, and type **5** for the tube radius.

5. Use the supplied ZOOMALL routine to view your results in all viewports.

The result appears as shown in Figure 7.17. This feature is interesting, but the dimensions of the object are hard to predict.

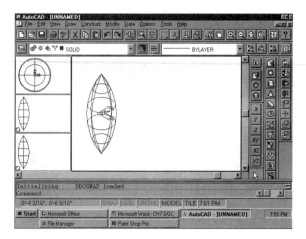

FIGURE 7.17 Torus football practice results.

SOLID PRIMITIVES MENU LOCATION

The 3D primitives discussed in this section are located on the _Draw_ pull-down menu under the _Solids_ menu cascade item and on the _Solids_ toolbar menu, as shown in Figure 7.18. The Solids toolbar can be activated by typing **toolbar** and **ACAD.SOLIDS** for showing or by selecting the _Solids_ menu item from the _Tools_ pull-down menu, and under the _Toolbars_ cascade item.

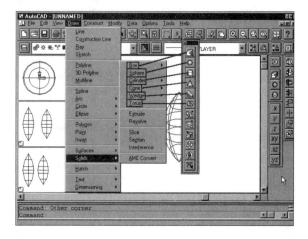

FIGURE 7.18 3D primitives menu locations .

Chapter Exercise

Practice the various solid primitives by creating a brake disk. The drawing *CH7EX.DWG* is supplied containing hints and a created brake disk. The dimensions in Figure 7.19 are all in the supplied drawing on the layer ANSWERS. To view the hints and answers, restore the viewport configuration ANSWERS and thaw the layer ANSWERS. The finished drawing should be saved to another drawing.

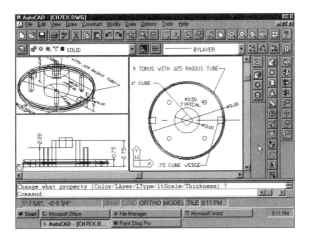

FIGURE 7.19 Chapter 7 exercise reference .

In Conclusion

In this chapter, you were able to practice the REGION command, the various display variables for solids, and the 3D solids primitives. These are the basic building blocks for creating all complex 3D solid parts. All editing commands can be used to maneuver the solids into position. The more comfortable you become using commands such as the calculator, point filters, and filters the faster you are able to design in 3D space. In the next chapter, you are introduced to the 3D solids editing commands.

CHAPTER EIGHT

Solids Editing Commands

Most editing commands work on solids. You can use the MOVE, COPY, SCALE, ERASE, FILLET, CHAMFER, ROTATE, CHPROP, DDMODIFY, and ARRAY commands on a solid in the same way you would use them on 2D objects. Some editing commands do not work on solids. These commands include the TRIM, EXTEND, BREAK, EXPLODE, LENGTHEN, STRETCH, OFFSET, and PEDIT commands. There are many commands dedicated to editing solids. In this chapter, you are introduced to the various editing commands dedicated to solids, along with the FILLET and CHAMFER editing commands. The dedicated solids editing commands covered include:

- SUBTRACT—removes one solid or region from another.

- UNION—adds one solid or region to another.

- INTERSECTION—creates a new region from the intersection of two regions, or a new solid from the intersection of two solids.

- EXTRUDE—creates a solid from a region by assigning it a height.

- SLICE—divides a solid into two solids.

- SECTION—creates a flat 2D outline of a solid section.

- REVOLVE—creates a solid from a region by revolving the geometry around an axis.

- INTERSECT—creates a new solid from the intersection of two solids or regions.

- MASSPROP—lists the properties of a region or solid.

A region is not a solid, although it behaves like a 2-dimensional solid, and many of the same editing commands used for solids are available for a region.

Region Editing

The main purpose of regions is to create 3D solids. You can create a region using the REGION command and then edit it to create the base for a solid. Solids editing commands can be used on the region to add, subtract, extrude, and find the intersection of regions before the region is converted into a solid. In this chapter, you are introduced to the techniques of adding (UNION), subtracting (SUBTRACT), finding the intersection (INTERSECT), finding information about a region (MASSPROP), and extruding (EXTRUDE) regions.

N O T E   A very common error message that occurs when trying to edit regions is "At least 2 solids or coplanar regions must be selected." This message occurs when at least one of the objects selected is not a solid or region, or because the legal objects are on different working planes. Use the region command to convert the illegal objects into regions to solve the problem when the objects are not legal. The objects must be on the same working plane to solve the other problem.

THE SUBTRACT COMMAND

This command allows you to create islands (holes) in a region or remove one solid object from another solid. An ideal situation for the use of this command on a region is when you are going to create a solid with a hole that runs through it. You subtract the hole from the overall region and then use the EXTRUDE command to create the solid. Try using the SUBTRACT command on a region.

Practice Procedure for Using SUBTRACT on Regions

1. In the drawing *Editsols*, type **subtract** and press **Enter** to activate the SUBTRACT command.

2. Select the large base plate labeled B1 in the Figure 8.1.

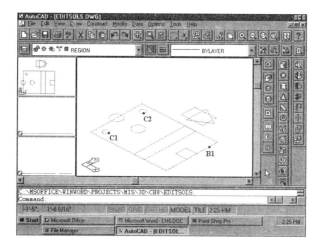

FIGURE 8.1 SUBTRACT practice reference.

3. Press **Enter** to end the selection process.

4. Select the circles C1 and C2 as shown in Figure 8.1.

5. Press **Enter** to end the selection process and exit the command.

You can use the LIST command to check the result. When you select either circle (region) or the base plate, all three objects are attached to each other as one region. The circles have become holes (islands) in the plate. The command is simple to use because you only have to select the objects you want to subtract from and then select the objects that are to be subtracted.

THE UNION COMMAND

This command allows you to create one region or solid from two or more regions or solids. This command is ideal for attaching protrusions onto a region or solid. Try using the UNION command.

Practice Procedure for Using UNION on Regions

1. In the drawing *Editsols*, type **union** and press **Enter** to activate the UNION command.

2. Select the large base plate labeled B1 and the circle labeled C1 as shown in the Figure 8.2.

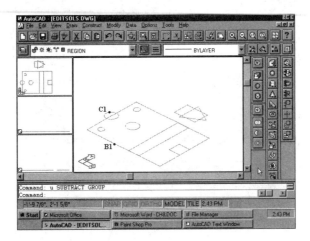

FIGURE 8.2 UNION practice reference.

3. Press **Enter** to exit the command and perform the union.

The results are shown in Figure 8.3. Notice how the part of the circle inside the base disappears and the protrusion becomes part of the base. The LIST command shows the base and circle (now an arc) to be one region object.

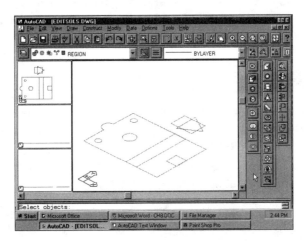

FIGURE 8.3 UNION practice results.

NOTE

You can add region objects that are not intersecting each other with the UNION command. This ability comes in handy for small objects that might be combined later with larger objects, thus becoming protrusions of the larger object.

THE INTERSECT COMMAND

This command allows you to create a region out of the intersection of two intersecting regions. Try creating an intersection region using the INTERSECT command.

Practice Procedure for Using INTERSECT on Regions

1. In the drawing *Editsols*, type **intersect** and press **Enter** to activate the INTERSECT command.

2. Select the rectangle labeled R1 and the triangle labeled T1 as shown in the Figure 8.4.

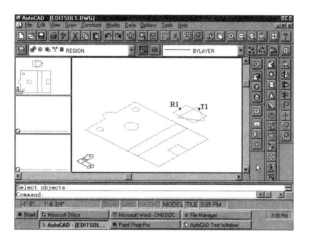

FIGURE 8.4 INTERSECT practice reference.

3. Press **Enter** to exit the command and perform the intersection.

The results are shown in Figure 8.5. Notice how only the area that intersected between the two objects is left. This command allows you to quickly create unusual shaped primitive regions, but removing the original objects is sometimes a problem. The routine INTERSEC.LSP has been included on the support disk to solve this problem. The routine takes the selected region objects and creates copies on a result layer, turning off the originals. Then the routine performs the intersection on the copies and turns back on the originals. You are left with the original objects and the intersection area on a separate layer. Try the routine on the same objects used in the last procedure.

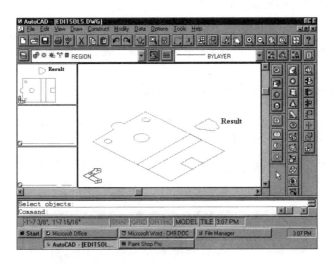

FIGURE 8.5 INTERSECT practice results.

Practice Procedure for Using Supplied Routine INTERSEC on Regions

1. Undo back or open the drawing Editsols without saving after the last procedure.

2. Type **(load "intersec")** and press **Enter** to load the supplied routine.

3. Type **intersec** and press **Enter** to activate the supplied INTERSEC routine.

4. Select the rectangle labeled R1 and the triangle labeled T1 as shown in the Figure 8.4.

5. Press **Enter** to exit the command and perform the intersection.

The results are shown in Figure 8.6. Notice how the results now include both the original objects and the area that intersected between the two original objects.

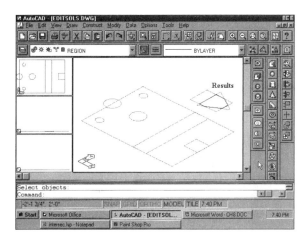

FIGURE 8.6 Supplied INTERSEC routine practice results.

NOTE

This routine does not check to see if the selected objects are regions before it processes the objects. When nonregions are selected the command will not work, since the INTERSECT command is being used inside the command and must have regions with which to work.

223

THE SUBTRACT, UNION, AND INTERSECTION COMMANDS MENU LOCATIONS

These three solids editing commands are found on the _Construct_ pull-down menu and on the _Explode_ flyout menu of the _Modify_ toolbar, as shown in Figure 8.7.

For expediency's sake, these three editing commands have been added to a custom toolbar called 3DWORLD.SOLID_EDIT along with the REGION command. The toolbar is activated by typing **toolbar** and then typing the full name of the toolbar to show the toolbar. The custom toolbar is shown in Figure 8.7, along with the other command menu locations.

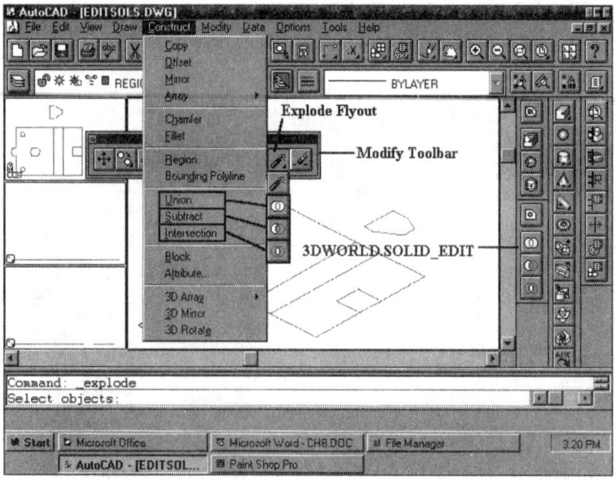

FIGURE 8.7 Solids editing commands menu locations.

THE MASSPROP COMMAND

This command calculates the mass properties of regions or solids. These properties of solid and region objects are essential to analyzing the characteristics of the object. The command only accepts those objects that are coplanar with the first selected object. The results are displayed in the text screen. The command allows you to write the results to a text file. There are some rules that the command follows. Coplanar and noncoplanar regions display the following properties:

- Area
- Perimeter
- Bounding box
- Centroid

When the regions are coplanar with the XY plane of the current UCS, AutoCAD also displays these additional properties:

- Moments of inertia
- Products of inertia
- Radii of gyration
- Principal moments and directions about a centroid

Solids display the following properties:

- Mass
- Volume
- Bounding box
- Centroid
- Moments of inertia
- Products of inertia
- Radii of gyration
- Principal moments and X,Y,Z directions about a centroid

This information is not available with the LIST command. The LIST command only gives you basic information about the object. Try using the MASSPROP command to obtain information from the regions created earlier in this chapter.

Practice Procedure for Using MASSPROP on Regions

1. In the drawing *Editsols*, do the previous practice procedures in this chapter if you have not done them already.
2. Type **massprop** and press **Enter** to activate the MASSPROP command.
3. Select the object labeled P1, as shown in Figure 8.8, and press **Enter** to end the selection process.
4. Press **Enter** to accept the default (no) for writing the results to a file.
5. Press **Enter** to activate the MASSPROP command again.
6. Select the objects labeled P1 and B1, as shown in Figure 8.8, and press **Enter** to end the selection process.
7. Press **Enter** to accept the default (no) for writing the results to a file.

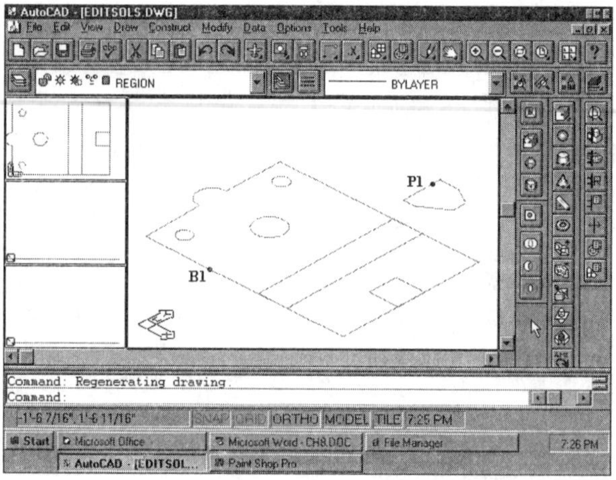

FIGURE 8.8 MASSPROP practice reference.

The results of step 3 are shown in Figure 8.9. Step 6 illustrates that you can add the properties of two or more objects together.

```
-------------------        REGIONS        -------------------
Area:                      1.3606 sq in
Perimeter:                 4.5804 in
Bounding box:              X: -24.6965  --  -23.4268 in
                           Y: 22.4972  --   23.8429 in
Centroid:                  X: -24.1561 in
                           Y: 23.2006 in
Moments of inertia:        X: 732.5149 sq in sq in
                           Y: 794.0813 sq in sq in
Product of inertia:       XY: -762.5077 sq in sq in
Radii of gyration:         X: 23.2031 in
                           Y: 24.1585 in
Principal moments (sq in sq in) and X-Y directions about centroid:
                           I: 0.1462 along [0.6872 0.7264]
                           J: 0.1693 along [-0.7264 0.6872]

Write to a file ? <N>:
```

FIGURE 8.9 MASSPROP practice results from step 3.

THE MASSPROP MENU COMMAND LOCATIONS

The MASSPROP command is found on the *Object Property* toolbar menu under the *Inquiry* flyout. This command is added to a customized toolbar only when needed. The menu location is shown in Figure 8.10.

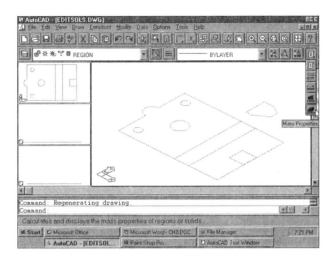

FIGURE 8.10 MASSPROP Command Menu Location.

THE EXTRUDE COMMAND

This command allows you to create a 3D solid out of a region by assigning a height to the region or by pulling the region along a path.

This practice procedure builds upon the previous procedures in this chapter. The selections are based upon the previous procedures having been completed successfully.

N O T E

Practice Procedure for Using EXTRUDE on Regions

1. In the drawing *Editsols*, do the previous practice procedures in this chapter if you have not done them already.

2. Type **extrude** and press **Enter** to activate the EXTRUDE command.

3. Select the base plate at the point B1, as shown in Figure 8.11, and press **Enter** to end the selection process.

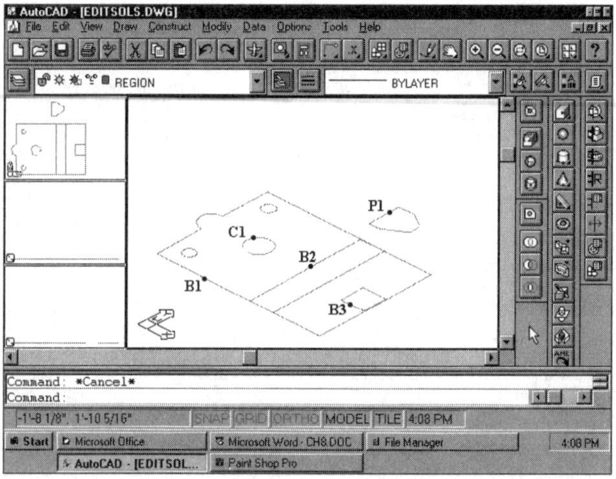

FIGURE 8.11 EXTRUDE practice reference.

4. Type **3** and press **Enter** to assign a height to the solid.

5. Press **Enter** to accept the default of zero for the taper of the extrude.

6. Extrude the objects labeled B2 and B3 in Figure 8.11 following steps 2 through 5, selecting B2 and B3 instead of B1 in step 3 and assigning 1 (one) for the height in step 4.

This process results in a large rectangular solid with two small rectangular solids inside. You are also given the ability to taper the extrusion. The Taper option allows you to assign an angle to the Z axis height when the object is extruded. Try adding a taper to the next objects.

Practice Procedure for Using EXTRUDE on Regions with the Taper Option

1. In the drawing *Editsols*, do the previous practice procedures in this chapter if you have not done them already.

2. Type **extrude** and press **Enter** to activate the EXTRUDE command.

3. Select the large circle labeled C1, as shown in Figure 8.11, and press **Enter** to end the selection process.

4. Type **3** and press **Enter** to assign the height.

5. Type **-5** and press **Enter** to assign a taper of negative five to the Z axis height.

6. Press **Enter** to activate the EXTRUDE command again.

7. Select the large object labeled P1, as shown in Figure 8.11, and press **Enter** to end the selection process.

8. Type **-.5** and press **Enter** to assign the height.

9. Type **20** and press **Enter** to assign a taper of twenty to the Z axis height.

10. Use the supplied ZOOMALL routine to view your results from different angles.

The results of the last two procedures are shown in Figure 8.12. Notice that you can use a negative height or negative taper angle, as shown in steps 5 and 8 in the last procedure. Once a region is extruded, it is a solid.

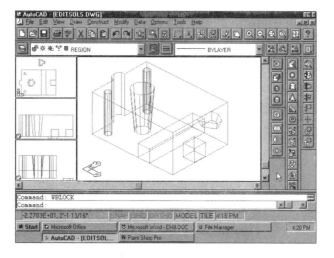

FIGURE 8.12 EXTRUDE practice results.

NOTE

The original region is deleted by AutoCAD automatically unless the DELOBJ system variable is turned off (the default is on).

The EXTRUDE command has a Path option that allows you to extrude a region along an object used as a path. Legal objects that can be used as paths are lines,

229

circles, arcs, ellipses, elliptical arcs, polylines, or splines. Two other rules that need to be followed are:

- Paths should not be on the same plane as the profile.
- Paths should not have sharp curves in them.

Try using the Path option of the EXTRUDE command.

Practice Procedure for Using EXTRUDE on Regions with the Taper Option

1. In the drawing *Editsols*, make the layer EXTRUDE-PATH current (you need to thaw it first) and freeze the layers CHAMFER, FILLET, HVAC, INTER-SECT, INTERSECTION, REGION, REVOLVE, SOLIDS, and SURFACE. Restore the viewport configuration called 3D4R-EXTRUDE-PATH.

2. Type **extrude** and press **Enter** to activate the EXTRUDE command.

3. Select the region labeled C1, as shown in Figure 8.13, and press **Enter** to end the selection process.

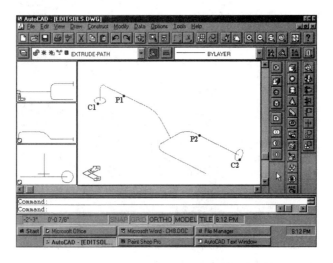

FIGURE 8.13 EXTRUDE Path options practice reference.

4. Type **p** and press **Enter** to activate the Path option.

5. Select the polyline labeled P1 as shown in Figure 8.13.

6. Press **Enter** to activate the EXTRUDE command again.

7. Select the region labeled C2, as shown in Figure 8.13, and press **Enter** to end the selection process.

8. Type **p** and press **Enter** to activate the Path option.

9. Select the polyline labeled P2 as shown in Figure 8.13.

The results are shown in Figure 8.14. The paths used in this procedure do not have angles or bends that exceed 90 degrees. Paths that contain angles or bends that exceed 90 degrees can often cause the solid to pinch in on itself.

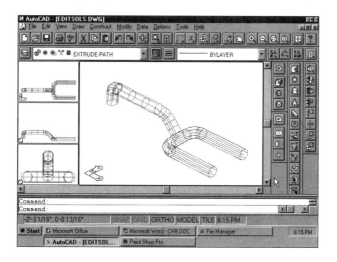

FIGURE 8.14 EXTRUDE Path option practice results.

THE EXTRUDE MENU COMMAND LOCATIONS

The EXTRUDE command is found on the *Solids* toolbar as shown in Figure 8.15.

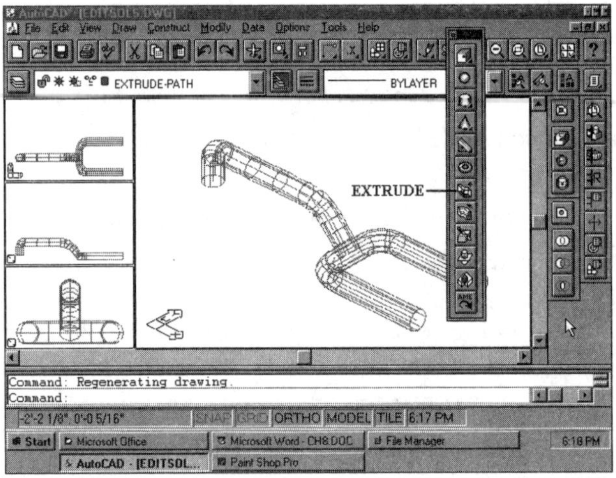

FIGURE 8.15 EXTRUDE command menu locations.

REGIONS IN REVIEW

232

The ability to create and edit regions gives you a powerful tool for creating 3D solids. The technique of constructing complex objects from more primitive basic regions is widely used and both efficient and productive. The two basic rules to creating complex solids from the regions are that the regions must be coplanar and they must all be regions. The various commands discussed in this section allow you full control over regions. Many of the commands also apply to solids.

In the next section, you are given the opportunity to practice some of the same editing commands that work on both regions and solids, and some new commands that only work on solids.

Solids Editing

As stated at the beginning of the chapter, most property editing commands work on solids. You can move them around onto different layers, or change their color or linetype. Changing their position, copying them, or scaling them are all legal operations. In this section, you are presented with the various specific commands for editing a solid. You are also given the opportunity to practice the FILLET and CHAMFER commands as they apply to solids.

THE FILLET COMMAND

This command has been adjusted in Release 13 to include the ability to fillet a solid. The two planes to be filleted must be coincidental (share a common edge). When the radius specified for the fillet is too large for the object, the command displays an error message and aborts. Try placing a fillet on a solid.

Practice Procedure for Using FILLET on a Solid

1. In the drawing *Editsols*, make the layer FILLET current (you need to thaw it first) and freeze the layers CHAMFER, EXTRUDE-PATH, HVAC, INTERSECT, INTERSECTION, REGION, REVOLVE, SOLIDS, and SURFACE. Restore the viewport configuration called 3D4R-FILLET.

2. Type **fillet** and press **Enter** to activate the FILLET command.

3. Select the solid edge labeled E1, as shown in Figure 8.16.

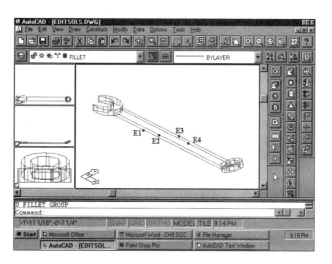

FIGURE 8.16 FILLET a solid practice reference.

4. Type **1/16** and press **Enter** to set the radius to 1/16 of an inch.

5. Select the solid edge labeled E2, E3, and E4, as shown in Figure 8.16.

6. Press **Enter** to end the selection process and exit the command.

The results are shown in Figure 8.17. Notice that the edges between E1 and E2 and the edges between E3 and E4 were filleted.

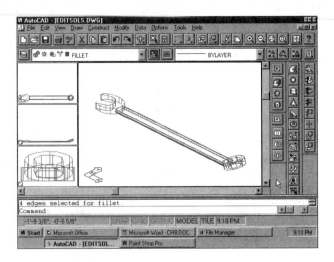

FIGURE 8.17 FILLET a solid practice results.

THE CHAMFER COMMAND

This command has been adjusted in Release 13 to include the ability to chamfer a solid. The two planes to be chamfered must be coincidental (share a common edge). When the chamfer specified is too large for the object, the command displays an error message and aborts. Try placing chamfers on a solid.

Practice Procedure for Using CHAMFER on a Solid

1. In the drawing *Editsols*, make the layer CHAMFER current (you need to thaw it first) and freeze the layers EXTRUDE-PATH, FILLET, HVAC, INTERSECT, INTERSECTION, REGION, REVOLVE, SOLIDS, and SURFACE. Restore the viewport configuration called 3D4R-CHAMFER.

2. Type **chamfer** and press **Enter** to activate the CHAMFER command.

3. Select the solid edge labeled E1, as shown in Figure 8.18.

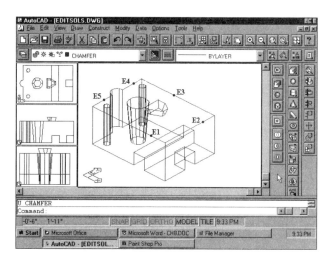

FIGURE 8.18 CHAMFER a solid practice reference.

4. Type **n** and press **Enter** until the top face of the solid is highlighted (probably one time).

5. Press **Enter** to end the selection process.

6. Type **.25** and press **Enter** to set the radius to 1/4 of an inch on the selected face.

7. Type **.5** and press **Enter** to set the radius to 1/2 of an inch on each of the other faces to be selected.

8. Select the solid edges labeled E1, E2, E3, E4, and E5, as shown in Figure 8.18.

9. Press **Enter** to end the selection process and exit the command.

The results are shown in Figure 8.19. Notice that the top face has the chamfer of .25 and the side edges have the chamfer of .5. The order is important because the command works on the first face using the first chamfer measurement and all other faces selected using the second chamfer measurement.

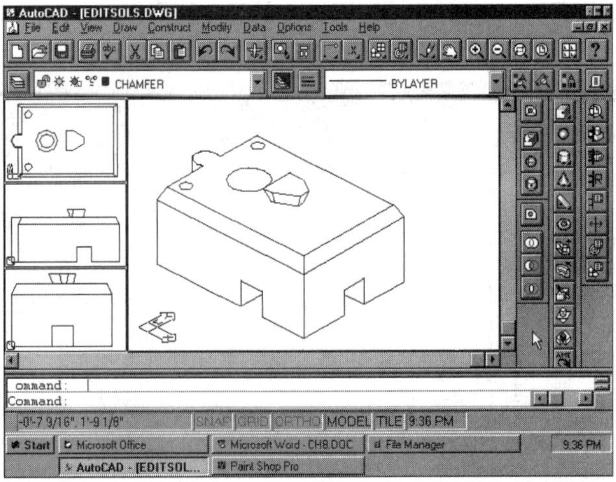

FIGURE 8.19 CHAMFER a solid practice results.

THE MASSPROP COMMAND

This command calculates the mass properties of regions or solids, as discussed earlier in this chapter. Try using the MASSPROP command on a solid.

Practice Procedure for Using MASSPROP on a Solid

1. In the drawing *Editsols*, make the layer CHAMFER current (you need to thaw it first) and freeze the layers EXTRUDE-PATH, FILLET, HVAC, INTERSECT, INTERSECTION, REGION, REVOLVE, SOLIDS, and SURFACE. Restore the viewport configuration called 3D4R-CHAMFER.

2. Type **massprop** and press **Enter** to activate the MASSPROP command.

3. Select the object and press **Enter** to end the selection process.

The results are shown in Figure 8.20. As you can see, the results listed are the same as the region results, with a few extra listings unique to a solid.

```
-------------- SOLIDS --------------
Mass:            94.2857 lb
Volume:          94.2857 cu in
Bounding box:      X: -15.0976 -- -7.5976 in
                   Y: 14.9825 -- 19.9825 in
                   Z: 0.0000 -- 3.5000 in
Centroid:          X: -11.1337 in
                   Y: 17.4827 in
                   Z: 1.5449 in
Moments of inertia:   X: 29309.0598 lb sq in
                      Y: 12383.4346 lb sq in
                      Z: 41105.9406 lb sq in
Products of inertia: XY: -18352.3390 lb sq in
                     YZ: 2546.6012 lb sq in
                     ZX: -1612.3988 lb sq in
Radii of gyration:   X: 17.6310 in
                     Y: 11.4603 in
                     Z: 20.8800 in
Principal moments (lb sq in) and X-Y-Z directions about centroid:
        I: 265.9659 along [0.9996 0.0001 0.0280]
        J: 470.8738 along [-0.0001 1.0000 0.0002]
        K: 600.8815 along [-0.0280 -0.0002 0.9996]
Write to a file ? <N>:
```

FIGURE 8.20 MASSPROP on a solid practice results.

THE SUBTRACT COMMAND

This command allows you to create islands (holes) in a region or remove one solid object from another solid as discussed earlier in this chapter. Try using the SUBTRACT command to remove some solids.

Practice Procedure for Using SUBTRACT a Solid

1. In the drawing *Editsols*, make the layer SOLIDS current (you need to thaw it first) and freeze the layers CHAMFER, EXTRUDE-PATH, FILLET, HVAC, INTERSECT, INTERSECTION, REGION, REVOLVE, and SURFACE. Restore the viewport configuration called 3D4R-SOLIDS.

2. Use the supplied routine ZOOMALL to adjust the views.

3. Type **subtract** and press **Enter** to activate the SUBTRACT command.

4. Select the first object labeled W1 as shown in Figure 8.21.

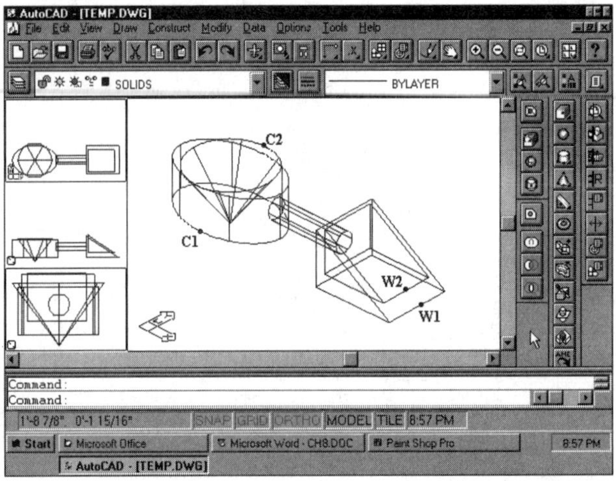

FIGURE 8.21 SUBTRACT a solid practice reference.

5. Press **Enter** to end the selection process.

6. Select the object labeled W2 as shown in Figure 8.21.

7. Press **Enter** to end the selection process and exit the command.

8. Select the object labeled C1 as shown in Figure 8.21.

9. Press **Enter** to end the selection process.

10. Select the object labeled C2 as shown in Figure 8.21.

11. Press **Enter** to end the selection process and exit the command.

12. Use the supplied routine SHADEALL to view the results of your work.

The results are shown in Figure 8.22. Notice that complex shapes were formed by taking simple solids and subtracting other simple solids from them. The only trick to this method of creating complex solids is the positioning of the solids in relation to each other. Object snaps, grid/snap, and all of the other regular tools are used to position objects in 3D space.

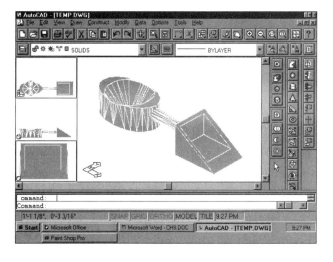

FIGURE 8.22 SUBTRACT a solid practice results.

THE UNION COMMAND

This command allows you to create one region or solid from two or more regions or solids as discussed earlier in this chapter. The solids to not have to be connected to be made into a union. Try creating a union of solids using the UNION command.

Practice Procedure for Using UNION with Solids

1. In the drawing *Editsols*, start this procedure after doing the SUBTRACT procedure above.

2. Use the supplied routine ZOOMALL to adjust the views.

3. Type **union** and press **Enter** to activate the UNION command.

4. Select the first object labeled W1 as shown in Figure 8.23.

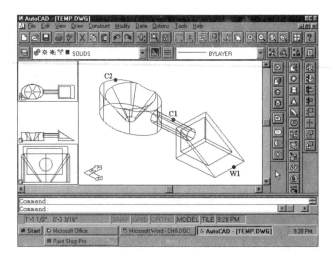

FIGURE 8.23 UNION solids practice reference.

5. Select the object labeled C1 as shown in Figure 8.23.

6. Select the object labeled C2 as shown in Figure 8.23.

240

7. Press **Enter** to end the selection process and exit the command.

The result appears just like the result from the SUBTRACT command procedure shown in Figure 8.22. You can use the LIST or MASSPROP command to see that all three solids have been combined into one solid.

THE INTERSECT COMMAND

This command allows you to create a solid out of the intersection of two intersecting solids, the same as the command does for regions, discussed earlier in this chapter. This is a handy way to check if piping or other solids are touching each other. The disadvantage to this command is that it removes all of the solids that are not intersecting. Many users place a copy of the solids to be checked on a separate layer and do the check there. They then turn on the original objects (usually a different color) to see the interference areas. Try using the INTERSECTION command to check some solid piping for interference.

Practice Procedure for Using INTERSECT on Solids

1. In the drawing *Editsols*, make the layer INTERSECTION current (you need to thaw it first) and freeze the layers CHAMFER, EXTRUDE-PATH, FILLET, HVAC, INTERSECT, REGION, REVOLVE, SOLIDS and SURFACE. Restore the viewport configuration called 3D4R-INTERSECT.

2. Type **intersect** and press **Enter** to activate the INTERSECT command.

3. Select the first object labeled T1 as shown in Figure 8.24.

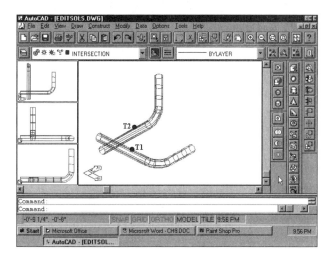

FIGURE 8.24 INTERSECT solids practice reference.

4. Select the object labeled T2 as shown in Figure 8.24.

5. Press **Enter** to end the selection process and exit the command.

6. Thaw the layer INTERSECT to see the original objects.

The results are shown in Figure 8.25. It is unfortunate that Autodesk has not given you the tools to make this process easier. The steps to create a copy and place it on another layer are time-consuming and necessary, since the command deletes the original solids.

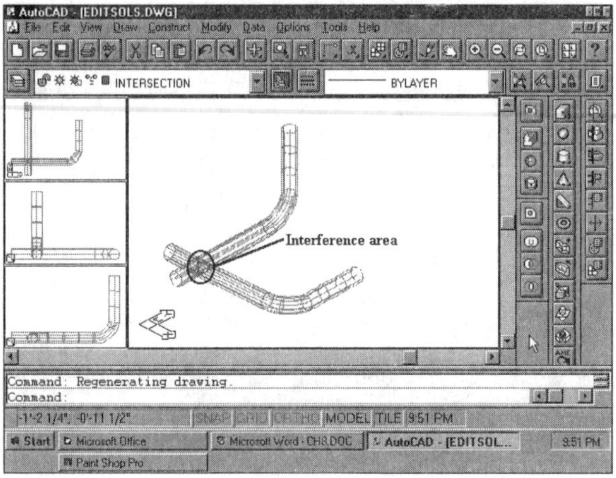

FIGURE 8.25 INTERSECT solids practice results.

THE SLICE COMMAND

This command cuts a set of solids with a plane, creating two sets of solids. Regions are ignored by this command. The command has several options used to define a cutting plane:

- By Object—uses a circle, ellipse, circular or elliptical arc, 2D spline, or 2D polyline segment to define a cutting plane.

- Zaxis—uses a specified origin point to define an XY plane (normal) and a point on the Z axis to define the cutting plane.

- View—uses a specified point and the current view to define the cutting plane.

- XY—uses the current XY plane and a specified point to define the cutting plane.

- YZ—uses the current YZ plane and a specified point to define the cutting plane.

- ZX—uses the current ZX plane and a specified point to define the cutting plane.

- <3points>—uses the supplied three points to define a cutting plane.

Each option has advantages and disadvantages; the trick is to understand how each works and select the option you need for the job at hand. The cutting plane behaves like the UCS. Just as the UCS has an XY plane and a Z axis that must remain perpendicular, the cutting plane is defined by a minimum of two points: one representing the cutting plane, and the other representing the perpendicular axis. All of the following options allow you to define the cutting plane (and the perpendicular) in various ways.

The By Object Option

These options allows you to use a variety of objects as a cutting plane. One method of using this option is to create a cutting plane object from one of the legal objects and insert it onto the object or objects you wish to slice. This technique requires you to set the current UCS to the desired cutting plane before you insert the cutting plane object. The cutting plane object must also be exploded before you use it. Try using a supplied cutting plane to slice some objects.

Practice Procedure for Using the SLICE by Object Option on Solids

1. Open the drawing EDITSOLS, make the layer CHAMFER current (you need to thaw it first) and freeze the layers EXTRUDE-PATH, FILLET, HVAC, INTERSECT, INTERSECTION, REGION, REVOLVE, SOLIDS and SURFACE. Restore the viewport configuration called 3D4R-CHAMFER. The results are shown in Figure 8.26.

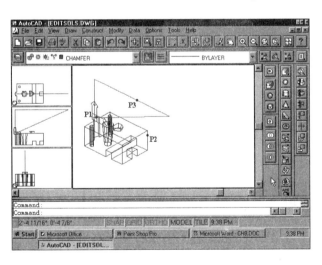

FIGURE 8.26 SLICE by Object option practice reference.

2. Set the current UCS to **Front** using the Named UCS dialogue box.

3. Use the UNDO command's Mark option to place an Undo mark.

4. Use the UCS command to move the origin of the current UCS to the point P1 on the top Arc as shown in Figure 8.26 (the object snap Midpoint works well).

5. Make sure that no running object snaps are turned on, and use DDINSERT to insert the CUTPLANE drawing from your 3DWORLD directory (turn off the Specify parameter on screen button and turn on the Explode button).

6. Use the supplied ZOOMALL routine to adjust the viewports view.

7. Type **slice** and press **Enter** to activate the SLICE command.

8. Select the object at the point P2 as shown in Figure 8.26.

9. Press **Enter** to end the selection process.

10. Type **o** and press **Enter** to activate the Object option.

11. Select the cutting plane object at the point P3 as shown in Figure 8.26.

12. Type **b** and press **Enter** to exit the command and leave both sides of the object.

13. Select one side of the original object using the MOVE command, and reposition the side you select.

The results are shown in Figure 8.27. The command cut the object as if a cutting edge was extended down from the defined cutting plane.

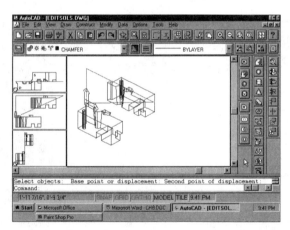

FIGURE 8.27 SLICE by Object option practice results.

You can also select any legal object already in your drawing to be the cutting plane.

The Zaxis Option

This command uses the Z axis as the cutting plane. Since AutoCAD knows that the Z axis must be perpendicular to the normal plane (and the normal plane must be perpendicular to the cutting plane), the cutting plane is defined by the two points selected on the normal plane. Try using the Zaxis option to define a cutting plane.

NOTE

This procedure picks up where the last procedure leaves off. You can start fresh by substituting steps one and two from the Slice by Object procedure for the first two steps of this procedure.

Practice Procedure for Using SLICE Using the Zaxis Option on Solids

1. Use the UNDO command's Back option to remove the work from the last procedure.

2. Set the current UCS to World.

3. Use the UNDO command's Mark option to place an Undo mark.

4. Type **slice** and press **Enter** to activate the SLICE command.

5. Select the object at the point P1 as shown in Figure 8.28.

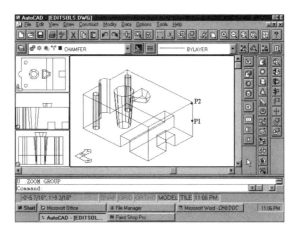

FIGURE 8.28 SLICE using the Zaxis option practice reference.

6. Press **Enter** to end the selection process.

7. Type **z** and press **Enter** to activate the Zaxis option.

8. Use the Midpoint object snap to select the object at the point P1 as shown in Figure 8.28.

9. Use the Endpoint object snap to select the object at the point P2 as shown in Figure 8.28.

10. Type **b** and press **Enter** to leave both sides.

11. Select one side of the original object using the MOVE command, and reposition the side you select.

The results are shown in Figure 8.29. The cutting plane bisected the object because the normal plane was defined as running along the UCS Z axis of the object. The perpendicular (cutting plane) was calculated along the perpendicular to the UCS Z axis (which is the XY plane).

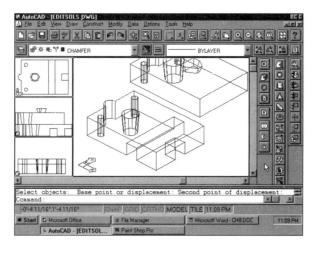

FIGURE 8.29 SLICE using the Zaxis option practice results.

This example is rather simple (if confusing) because the two points selected were on a major axis (the Z axis) of the object. Try doing the same procedure using a different point not on a major axis.

This procedure picks up where the last procedure leaves off. You can start fresh by substituting steps one and two from the Slice by Object procedure for the first two steps of this procedure.

N O T E

Practice Procedure for Using SLICE Using the Zaxis Option on Solids

1. Use the UNDO command's Back option remove the work from the last procedure.

2. Use the UNDO command's Mark option to place an Undo mark.

3. Type **slice** and press **Enter** to activate the SLICE command.

4. Select the object at the point P1 as shown in Figure 8.30.

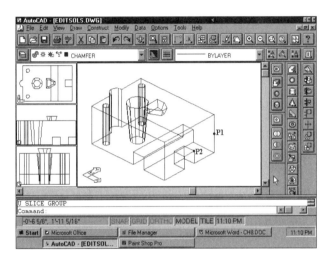

FIGURE 8.30 SLICE using the Zaxis option practice reference.

5. Press **Enter** to end the selection process.

6. Type **z** and press **Enter** to activate the Zaxis option.

7. Use the Midpoint object snap to select the object at the point P1 as shown in Figure 8.30.

8. Use the Endpoint object snap to select the object at the point P2 as shown in Figure 8.30.

9. Type **b** and press **Enter** to leave both sides.

10. Select one side of the original object using the MOVE command, and reposition the side you select.

The results are shown in Figure 8.31. The cutting plane and normal plane are also shown to give a better view of how the option works. Notice that the normal plane goes through the points P1 and P2 (you selected) and that the cutting plane is perpendicular to that plane. It takes some practice to use this option effectively when not on a major axis.

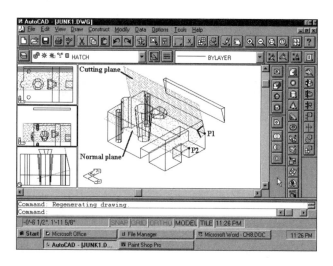

FIGURE 8.31 SLICE using the Zaxis option practice results.

The View Option

This option positions the cutting plane parallel to the current view along a point you select on the object. This means that you can position your view of the object, using any precision means you like, and then project the view parallel (as a cutting plane) through a point you select on the object. Try using the View option of the SLICE command.

This procedure picks up where the last procedure leaves off. You can start fresh by substituting steps one and two from the Slice by Object procedure for the first two steps of this procedure.

N O T E

Practice Procedure for Using SLICE Using the View Option on Solids

1. Use the UNDO command's Back option remove the work from the last procedure.

2. Use the UNDO command's Mark option to place an Undo mark.

3. Type **slice** and press **Enter** to activate the SLICE command.

4. Select the object at the point P1 as shown in Figure 8.32.

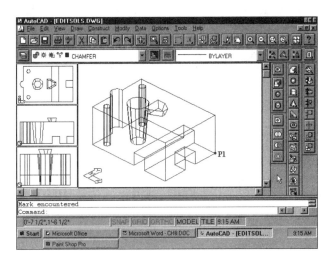

FIGURE 8.32 SLICE using the View option practice reference.

5. Press **Enter** to end the selection process.

6. Type **v** and press **Enter** to activate the View option.

7. Use the Endpoint object snap to select the object at the point P1 as shown in Figure 8.32.

8. Type **b** and press **Enter** to leave both sides.

9. Select one side of the original object using the MOVE command, and reposition the side you select (see Figure 8.33 for reference).

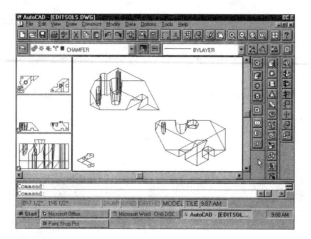

FIGURE 8.33 SLICE using the View option practice results.

10. Use the supplied routine ZOOMALL to view your results in all viewports.

The results are shown in Figure 8.33. Notice how the slice took place parallel to the view intersecting the point you selected. Since the view is set to 313 degrees *in* the XY plane and 31 degrees *from* the XY plane, the slice is 31 degrees *from* the XY plane.

The XY, YZ, and ZX Options

These three options allow you to define a cutting plane parallel to the respective UCS axis running through a point selected by you. These options are handy for defining a cutting plane on a major axis with just one point. Try slicing an object using these options.

NOTE

This procedure picks up were the last procedure leaves off. You can start fresh by substituting steps one and two from the Slice by Object procedure for the steps one and three of this procedure.

Practice Procedure for Using SLICE Using the XY Option on Solids

1. Use the UNDO command's Back option remove the work from the last procedure.

2. Turn on the Midpoint running object snap.

3. Use the UNDO command's Mark option to place an Undo mark.

4. Type **slice** and press **Enter** to activate the SLICE command.

5. Select all of the objects by typing **all** and pressing **Enter**.

6. Press **Enter** to end the selection process.

7. Type **xy** and press **Enter** to activate the XY option.

8. Select the object at the point P1 as shown in Figure 8.34.

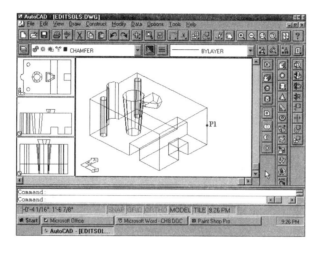

FIGURE 8.34 SLICE using the XY option practice reference.

9. Type **b** and press **Enter** to leave both sides.

10. Select the top of the original object using the MOVE command, and reposition the top up using the Relative coordinate @0,0,4.

11. Use the supplied ZOOMALL routine to view the results.

The results are shown in Figure 8.35. The cutting plane was created parallel *to* the XY plane at the point you selected. The YZ option uses a cutting plane parallel to the Y and Z axes of the current UCS. Try using the YZ option.

This procedure picks up where the last procedure leaves off. Do the last procedure before continuing.

N O T E

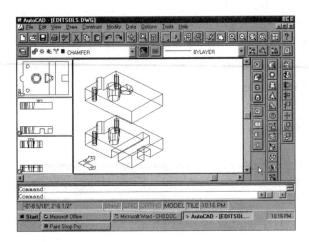

FIGURE 8.35 SLICE using the XY option practice results.

Practice Procedure for Using SLICE Using the YZ Option on Solids

1. Type **slice** and press **Enter** to activate the SLICE command.
2. Select all of the objects by typing **all** and pressing **Enter**.
3. Press **Enter** to end the selection process.
4. Type **yz** and press **Enter** to activate the YZ option.
5. Select the object at the point P1 as shown in Figure 8.36.

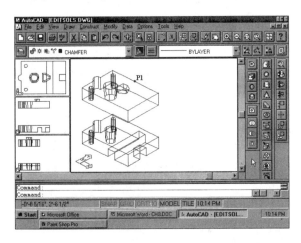

FIGURE 8.36 SLICE using the YZ option practice reference.

6. Type **b** and press **Enter** to leave both sides.

7. Select the original objects on the right side using the MOVE command, and reposition them using the Polar coordinate @4<0.

8. Use the supplied ZOOMALL routine to view the results.

The results are shown in Figure 8.37. The cutting plane was created parallel to the YZ plane at the point you selected. The ZX option uses a cutting plane parallel to the Z and X axes of the current UCS to slice all objects selected that intersect with the cutting plane. Try using the ZX option on the remaining objects.

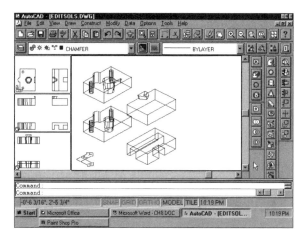

FIGURE 8.37 SLICE using the YZ option practice results.

This procedure picks up where the last two procedures leave off. Do the last two procedures before continuing.

N O T E

Practice Procedure for Using SLICE Using the ZX Option on Solids

1. Type **slice** and press **Enter** to activate the SLICE command.

2. Select all of the objects by typing **all** and pressing **Enter**.

3. Press **Enter** to end the selection process.

4. Type **zx** and press **Enter** to activate the ZX option.

5. Select the object at the point P1 as shown in Figure 8.38.

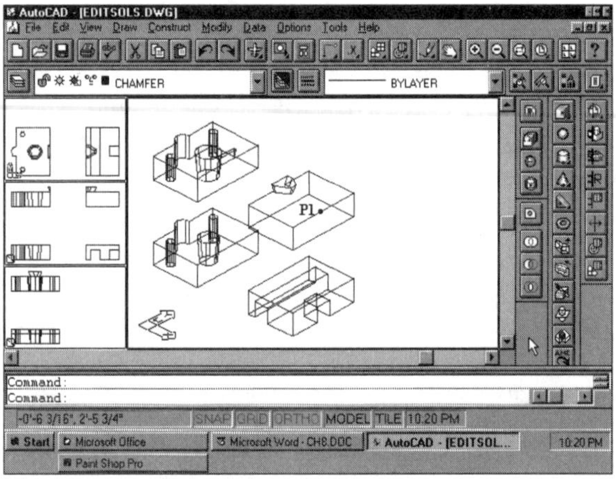

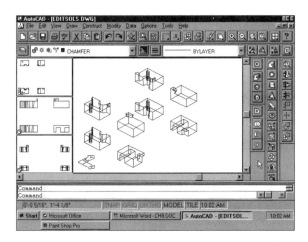

FIGURE 8.38 SLICE using the ZX option practice reference.

6. Type **b** and press **Enter** to leave both sides.

7. Select all of the original objects on the front using the MOVE command, and reposition them using the Polar coordinate @10<270.

254

8. Use the supplied ZOOMALL routine to view the results.

The results are shown in Figure 8.39. The cutting plane was created parallel to the ZX plane at the point you selected.

FIGURE 8.39 SLICE using the ZX option practice results.

The 3Points Option

This option aligns the cutting plane through all three specified points. This method is handy with running object snaps and it is easier for many users because they do not have to figure out the perpendicular point to the cutting plane. Try placing a 3-point cutting plane using the 3point option.

Practice Procedure for Using the SLICE 3Points Option on Solids

1. Open the drawing *Editsols*, make the layer CHAMFER current (you need to thaw it first) and freeze the layers EXTRUDE-PATH, FILLET, HVAC, INTERSECT, INTERSECTION, REGION, REVOLVE, SOLIDS and SURFACE. Restore the viewport configuration called 3D4R-CHAMFER. The results are shown in Figure 8.40.

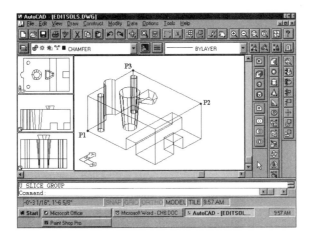

FIGURE 8.40 SLICE using the 3Points option practice reference.

2. Make sure that the running Endpoint object snap is on.

3. Type **slice** and press **Enter** to activate the SLICE command.

4. Select all of the objects by typing **all** and pressing **Enter**.

5. Press **Enter** to end the selection process.

6. Type **3p** and press **Enter** to activate the 3Points option.

7. Select the object at the points P1, P2, and P3 as shown in Figure 8.40.

8. Type **b** and press **Enter** to leave both sides.

9. Select the top of the original object using the MOVE command, and reposition it using the Relative coordinate @0,0,8.

10. Use the supplied ZOOMALL routine to view the results.

The results are shown in Figure 8.41. Notice the cutting plane intersected each point selected.

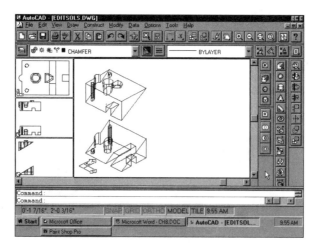

FIGURE 8.41 SLICE using the 3Points option practice results.

When AutoCAD cuts a single solid into more than two objects, one solid is created from the objects on one side of the plane and another solid is created from the objects on the other side. This rule holds true for all of the options. It does not matter how you defined the cutting plane; it always behaves in this fashion. Try slicing an object into more than two objects.

Practice Procedure for Using SLICE to Create Multiple Single Objects

1. Open the drawing *Editsols*, make the layer HVAC current (you need to thaw it first) and freeze the layers CHAMFER, EXTRUDE-PATH, FILLET, INTERSECT, INTERSECTION, REGION, REVOLVE, SOLIDS and SURFACE. Restore the viewport configuration called 3D4R-HVAC. The results are shown in Figure 8.42.

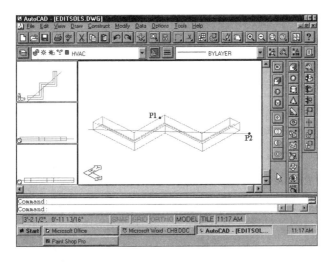

FIGURE 8.42 SLICE multiple single objects practice reference.

2. Type **slice** and press **Enter** to activate the SLICE command.

3. Select the object at the point P1 as shown in Figure 8.42.

4. Press **Enter** to end the selection process.

5. Type **o** and press **Enter** to activate the Object option.

6. Select the cutting plane object at the point P2 as shown in Figure 8.42.

7. Type **b** and press **Enter** to exit the command and leave both sides of the object.

8. Select the front of the original object using the MOVE command, and reposition using the Polar coordinate @8<315.

9. Use the supplied ZOOMALL routine to view the results.

The results are shown in Figure 8.43. Notice that the object was cut into two pieces; each piece remains connected as one solid even though the parts in the piece do not physically touch each other.

The SLICE command and its many options make creating details or examining the internal structure of a complex solid simple. This command becomes a valuable tool in your 3D arsenal of tools. You can also create a profile of a section of your object using the SECTION command.

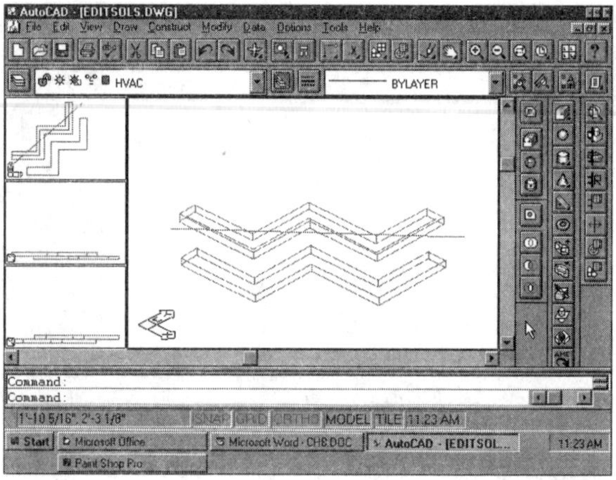

FIGURE 8.43 SLICE multiple single objects practice results.

The SECTION Command

This command creates a profile region of your object on the plane you select. This command uses the same options as the SLICE command but instead of cutting the object into pieces, it leaves a profile region of the solid on the cutting plane. The region can be manipulated using any of the tools covered earlier in this book. Try creating a section using the SECTION command.

Practice Procedure for Using the SECTION Command

1. Open the drawing *Editsols*, make the layer CHAMFER current (you need to thaw it first) and freeze the layers EXTRUDE-PATH, FILLET, HVAC, INTERSECT, INTERSECTION, REGION, REVOLVE, SOLIDS and SURFACE. Restore the viewport configuration called 3D4R-CHAMFER. The results are shown in Figure 8.44.

2. Turn off all running object snaps.

3. Type **section** and press **Enter** to activate the SECTION command.

4. Select all of the objects by typing **all** and pressing **Enter**.

5. Press **Enter** to end the selection process.

6. Type **zx** and press **Enter** to activate the ZX option.

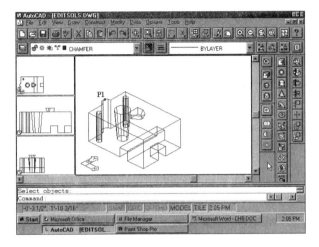

FIGURE 8.44 SECTION first practice reference.

7. Select the object at the point P1 as shown in Figure 8.44.

8. Use the Midpoint object snap to select the region at the point P2 (as shown in Figure 8.45) and, with the MOVE command, reposition it using the Polar coordinate @8<90.

9. Use the supplied ZOOMALL routine to view the results.

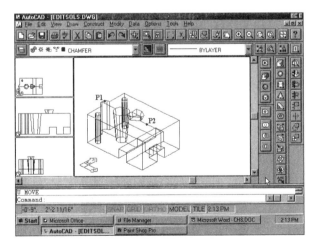

FIGURE 8.45 SECTION second practice reference.

The results are shown in Figure 8.46. The profile is one region that can be used for any purpose where a region can normally be used.

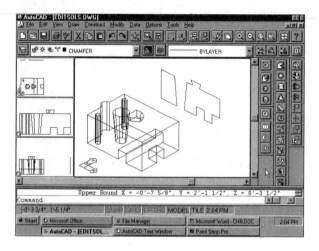

FIGURE 8.46 SECTION practice results.

All of this command's options behave exactly like the options covered for the SLICE command.

NOTE

THE INTERFERE COMMAND

This command creates a solid of the area that intersects between two or more solids. Unlike the INTERSECT command, this command does not delete the areas of the solids that don't intersect. This command does not work on regions. Try creating an interference section between two solids.

Practice Procedure for Using the INTERFERE Command

1. Open the drawing *Editsols*, make the layer INTERSECT current (you need to thaw it first) and freeze the layers CHAMFER, EXTRUDE-PATH, FILLET,

HVAC, INTERSECTION, REGION, REVOLVE, SOLIDS and SURFACE. Restore the viewport configuration called 3D4R-INTERSECT. The results are shown in Figure 8.47.

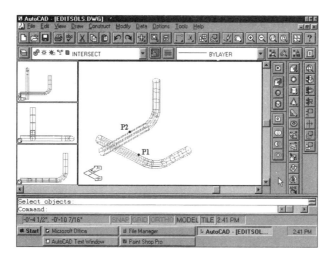

FIGURE 8.47 INTERFERE practice reference.

2. Type **interfere** and press **Enter** to activate the INTERFERE command.

3. Select the object at the point P1 as shown in Figure 8.47.

4. Press **Enter** to end the selection of the first set of objects.

5. Select the object at the point P2 as shown in Figure 8.47.

6. Press **Enter** to end the selection of the second set of objects.

7. Type **y** and press **Enter** to create the interference solid.

8. Using the MOVE command's Last option, reposition the interference object using the Polar coordinate @4<60.

9. Use the supplied ZOOMALL routine to view the results.

The results are shown in Figure 8.48. This command is useful for creating complex shapes or for checking piping or HVAC interferences.

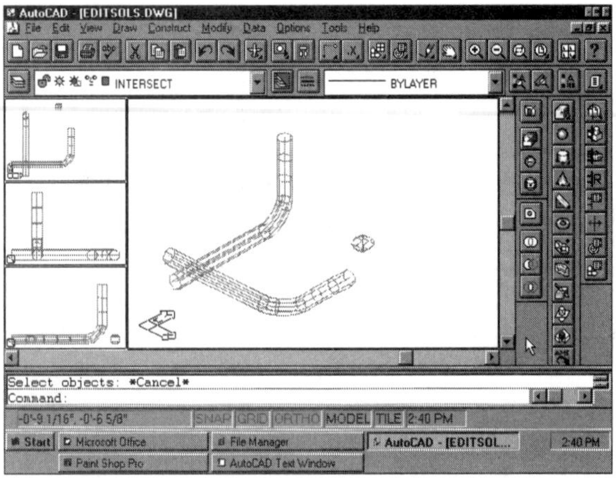

FIGURE 8.48 INTERFERE practice results.

THE AMECONVERT COMMAND

Prior to Release 13, solids were created and modified by an AutoCAD package called the Advanced Modeling Extension (AME). This method of working with solids was abandoned in Release 13 in favor of a more sophisticated method of creating and manipulating solids called ACIS solids. The AMECONVERT command is used to convert the old AME regions or solids (from Release 2 or 2.1) into ACIS solids. The new ACIS method has an increased accuracy over the old AME method. This can cause some problems when certain AME conditions are present. Some examples are:

- When two different shapes are sufficiently close to each other to be considered in the same plane, the ACIS modeler may interpret these surfaces as being slightly offset. This is most apparent when aligned features such as fillets, chamfers, and through-holes are present in the model.

- Holes can be interpreted as being slightly less wide than the solid. Typically, the length of the remaining solid material is the difference between the tolerance of the previous modeler and that of the new modeler.

- Updated fillets or chamfers are occasionally placed slightly below the surface, creating a hole through the solid, leaving the original shape unaltered.

- Fillets or chamfers can be drawn slightly above the original surface, creating an uneven transition between the solid and the fillet or chamfer.

The bottom line to using this command is that you might not always get what you want or need. Sometimes you will need to just re-create the object. Try using the AMECONVERT command on some AME solids.

Practice Procedure for Using the AMECONVERT Command

1. Open the drawing *Ame*.
2. Use the LIST command on any of the objects to see what they are.
3. Type **ameconvert** and press **Enter** to activate the command.
4. Select all of the objects.
5. Press **Enter** to end the selection process and start the conversion.
6. Use the LIST command on any of the objects to see what they are.

The first listing tells you that the object is a block. That is because the old AME method of creating solids actually created anonymous blocks and attached information to them. The second listing, after the conversion, tells you that the object is now a solid. This is because the new ACIS solids are internal objects in AutoCAD just like lines or circles.

THE SLICE, SECTION, INTERFERE, AND AMECONVERT COMMANDS MENU LOCATIONS

These commands all reside on the *Solids* toolbar and the *Draw* pull-down menu's *Solids* cascade item, as shown in Figure 8.49.

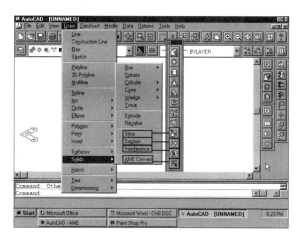

FIGURE 8.49 Menu locations.

In Conclusion

In this chapter, you practiced using all of the available commands for editing regions and solids. The command set for editing is extensive, and all of the options provide the necessary tools to manipulate any solid or region. In the next chapter, modeling issues are discussed and examples of dimensioning in 3D are presented.

CHAPTER NINE

Managing Modeling Issues

In this chapter, many of the issues surrounding 3D modeling are explored. Modeling is the next generation of drafting. Drafting a blueprint represents a plan to create an object. Modeling an object is the process of actually creating the object in your computer. You build the object in the computer and study it in an environment as complex as you wish to make. This has certain advantages that a drafting blueprint cannot match. The biggest advantage is the ability to see exactly how the real object looks and behaves in relation to other objects or the environment. As computers get more powerful and the software to design models more flexible, the ability to create complex real-world objects and environments gets closer. Simple objects like molds, die casts, piping, HVAC, and a host of others can be created and examined using the current state of computer development.

More complex information through modeling is becoming available at a continually increasing rate. Statistical analysis programs have progressed from programs that allow you to punch in numbers to newer programs that allow you to create a model, assign it the necessary properties, query the object, adjust the object, and create a tool path, Stereolithography, or statistical analysis output for the physical object. The CAD environment is growing at such a rate that many users have trouble keeping up with the new hardware, software, and design techniques. The end result is a loss of production instead of an increase in production. This need not be the case, when users and managers have clear and reasonable expectations for the model.

Expectations of Managers and Users

The expectations of the user and the manager have a lot to do with whether a modeling project is successful or not. Some guidelines need to be set forth and followed. The following list is, in many cases, nothing more than common sense, but all too often managers and users fly in the face of the guidelines. Some of the guidelines are general in nature, not specific to modeling. Things to be aware of are:

- Just because the architect or engineer has a computer and AutoCAD doesn't mean that they can design with it.

  Training is a prerequisite to using the AutoCAD software, especially using the 3D modeling features. Training can be broadly interpreted as including self-teaching aids such as this book. Learning to use the AutoCAD software in this way is difficult for most people and requires more experimentation than a structured class. Not all people can teach themselves with only a book.

- Just because a user has received training doesn't mean they are able to produce production drawings as fast as on the board right away.

  Experience has shown that an average user takes about six weeks to learn AutoCAD, and about two years to be proficient. That is assuming that the user is working with the software on a daily basis. Third party add-on products can increase productivity, but they require more training and experience.

- Whether it is a drafting or a modeling project, it is unreasonable to assume that since a computer is involved, the project gets done sooner.

  A good example of this is the actual process of building a model plane. Before modern technology, a person had to hand-build the parts, paint them, and assemble them. Now you can purchase the basic model, use air brush technology to paint the parts, and use new faster drying glues to assemble them. The process takes almost as long as the old process because you spend more time on the detail making a better model. You don't have to create the whole body of the plane, but you might want to remove the windows and give them a special treatment. The air brush speeds up your production during the painting phase, but minor flaws that were acceptable in the past are adjusted because it is so much easier now with the air brush. The result is that the modeling project takes almost as long now as it did before the new technology. The same is true of drafting or modeling on a computer. You might not spend as much time during the initial phase of construction, but you will spend more time on revising the details. The end result is a better model with more detail, but the time required to create it remains about the same.

- Modeling an object on a computer is faster than building the actual object or a physical model of the object.

    Yes, it is. However, the computer is not a magic wand that the user just waves and the model is built. The tools for designing a 3D model in CAD are getting better all the time (better can be defined as more flexible while intuitive to use). The set of tools specific to 3D design is limited but adequate at this time. Third-party software that works inside AutoCAD is helping to increase productivity at a cost of more training and longer learning curves. The computer allows much greater detail and more revisions per project, so the manager should expect a higher quality product for the investment but not necessarily at a savings of time (as described in the first guideline).

- Building a model saves cost in production.

    In the manufacturing industry, where one die casting or mold can cost more than $20,000, build a model of the part as a solid and refine it on the computer as many time as necessary before actually producing the part. Mistakes are eliminated before the object is created, saving production costs.

- Building a model does not solve all problems before production.

    A time comes during the design phase when you must release the design for production. It is possible to design an object that works according to the CAD system's rules, but the object cannot be produced due to limitations of the production machinery. As much as you try to take this into consideration as you design, it is easy to miss something. It is possible to build objects on a computer that cannot physically exist in real space.

- Build the model to fit the need.

    Define your desired use of the model and then choose the best method to create it. A house elevation need not be created with solids, or with great detail, if the desired picture is a long shot. A cam shaft is a good candidate for using solids because you can use the mass properties as a guide for your design. Sometimes the model is used to augment the drafting design, other times it is used as the drafting design. Not all production needs to be in the form of 3D models.

Some of the greatest misunderstandings occur between management and the designer when the design expectations aren't defined before the process begins. The guidelines presented here should help you define your needs better and meet them with less frustration.

When and What to Model

AutoCAD is used for so many different applications, it would be impossible to list all of them and define when it is appropriate to create a model and when it is not. The expectations guidelines listed above go a long way toward making the decision of when to model. Generally, you model an object to provide statistical analysis information, graphical output, verify an assembly, check interferences, create tool paths, or create Stereolithography output. The following sections reviews a few broad examples.

ARCHITECTURAL MODELS

Elevations are a prime candidate for a combination of solids and surfaces. Try a simple office front elevation, as shown in Figure 9.1.

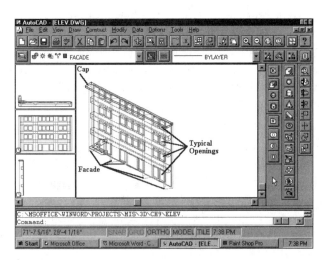

FIGURE 9.1 Front elevation practice reference.

Practice Procedure for Creating a Front Elevation

1. Open the drawing *Elev*.

2. Use the SUBTRACT command to remove all the openings from the front facade.

3. Use the UNION command to create one solid out of all of the parts of the facade.

4. Thaw the BODY layer.

5. Use the DDMODIFY command to place the facade on the FACADE layer (if necessary).

6. Use the supplied HIDEALL routine to view the results.

7. Save the drawing as *Elevx*.

The results are shown in Figure 9.2. This procedure's basic shapes were created in about 20 minutes; the editing steps can be done in less than 10 minutes. This is only a sketch so the shapes are only approximately the correct size (it takes longer using detailed dimensions). The front facade was created using solid boxes and pline triangles converted to regions and then converted to extruded solids. The body of the building was created by placing a surface primitive, exploding it, and changing the front face to all invisible edges. The point of the procedure is that you can quickly create a picture to get the feel of how the building looks by combining solids, surfaces, and construction techniques. You can use detail or just approximate the dimensions depending on your desired results.

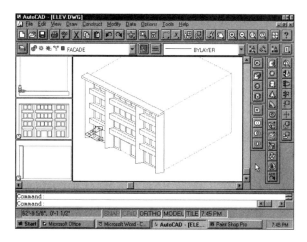

FIGURE 9.2 Front elevation practice results.

Multiple objects on multiple layers can cause AutoCAD to select a (seemingly) random layer for the resulting object. Sometimes you need to change the resulting objects layer by hand.

N O T E

MANUFACTURING MODELS

Building a mold part can be easy using basic primitives and solids editing commands. Try creating a mold part, shown in Figure 9.3.

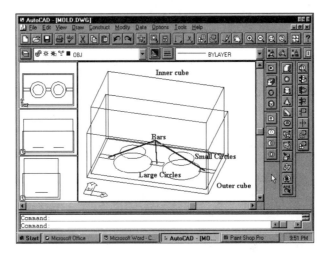

FIGURE 9.3 Mold part practice reference.

Practice Procedure for Creating a Mold Part

1. Open the drawing *Mold*.
2. Subtract the inner cube from the outer cube.
3. Fillet (radius .25) all vertical edges on the cubes (inner and outer).
4. Extrude the two large circles 2 units with a taper of zero.

5. Extrude the two small circles 1.5 units with a taper of -5.

6. Fillet (radius .25) each bottom of the inner circles.

7. Subtract the two small circles from the two large circles.

8. Extrude the three bar sections, in the middle, 1.75 units with a taper of zero.

9. Union the bars, circles, and the outer shell.

10. Use the supplied SHADEALL routine to view the results.

11. Save the drawing as *Moldx*.

The results are shown in Figure 9.4. The basic objects in the part are circle regions, closed polylines for the bars, and solid boxes for the body. The order in which you edit the objects is important. You need to be careful because the rules for subtracting, creating unions, extruding, or any of the other editing commands can leave the wrong results. Practice and experience are the only answers to this problem.

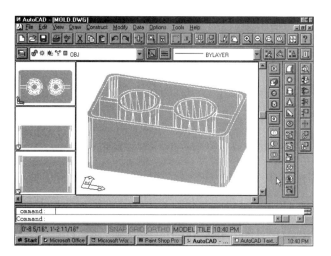

FIGURE 9.4 Mold part practice result.

The last practice procedure created a mold part. You can create the mold itself by placing the results of the last procedure inside a solid box and then slicing the box. Try creating the mold from the mold part.

Practice Procedure for Creating a Mold

1. In the *Mold* drawing using the mold part created in the last procedure, thaw the layer SHELL.

2. Use the supplied ZOOMALL routine to view the object.

3. Subtract the mold part from the solid box, as shown in Figure 9.5.

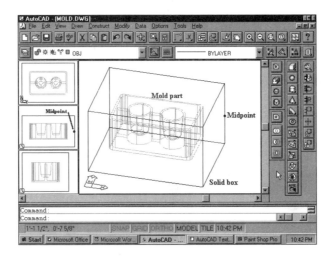

FIGURE 9.5 Mold practice reference.

4. Use the SLICE command to slice the box on the XY axis at the middle of the box (leaving both sides), as shown in Figure 9.5.

5. Move the top of the mold using the Polar coordinate @5<90.

6. Use the supplied ZOOMALL routine to position your views.

7. Use the supplied HIDEALL routine to view your results.

8. Save the results under the filename *Moldxx*.

The result is shown in Figure 9.6. This technique makes creating molds easy. The stages from the basic objects to the final mold are all simple and quick. You have all the advantages of ACIS solids for exporting the final geometry. Many third-party products can use Stereolithography code, exported from the ACIS solid in AutoCAD, to create a prototype part.

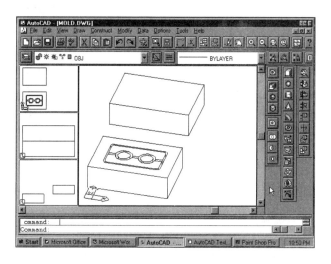

FIGURE 9.6 Mold practice result.

ENGINEERING MODEL

Creating a solid model for running statistical analysis purposes is becoming more common. AutoCAD has provided an export command that allows you to transfer the ACIS solid information into a file format that analysis programs can understand. The command for exporting data for many statistical analysis programs, ACISOUT, is discussed later in this chapter. Try creating a beam for later statistical analysis.

Practice Procedure for Creating a Beam

1. Open the drawing *Beam*.
2. Extrude the eight holes, as shown in Figure 9.7, negative 2 units with no taper.

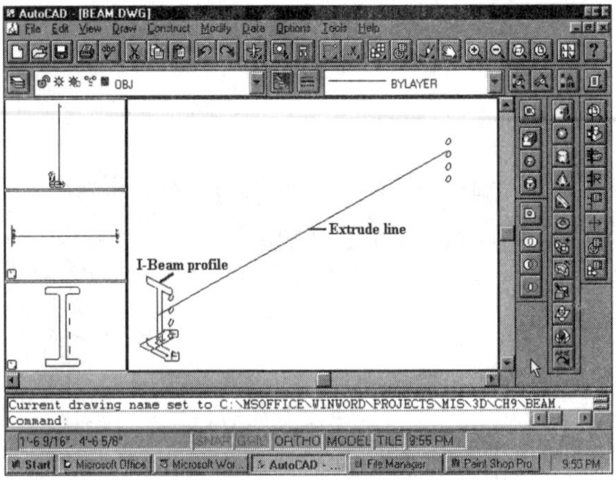

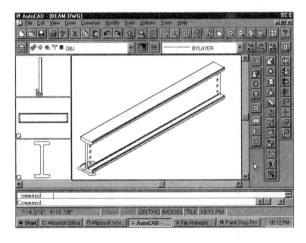

FIGURE 9.7 Engineering practice reference.

3. Extrude the I-Beam profile, as shown in Figure 9.7, along the path line.

4. Subtract the eight holes from the extruded beam.

5. Use the supplied HIDEALL routine to see the results.

6. Save the drawing as *Beamx*.

The results are shown in Figure 9.8. This solid can now be exported to a file format compatible with many statistical analysis programs.

FIGURE 9.8 Engineering practice results.

WHEN AND WHAT TO MODEL WRAP-UP

What to model is easy; "anything you want" is the answer. *When* to model is the hard question. Your desired results drive this question. As shown by the above practice procedures, you can use precise dimensions or approximate the dimensions to create your model. Model an object when you want to:

- Create a 3D rendering of the object.
- Check for interferences.
- Run statistical analysis programs on the model.
- Verify that an assembly fits together.
- Create Stereolithography or tool path output.

Your desired results also drive the detail and complexity of the model. Checking an assembly of parts demands that the parts are modeled to precise dimensions. A front elevation of a building does not need great detail unless you are rendering a close-up of some feature of the elevation. Each situation for modeling demands that you define what output you want before you do your model. When you ignore this simple guideline, the results are often less than you expect.

Staging Model Elements

Staging model elements can be viewed from two different perspectives. The first is the organization of the objects as assemblies, or subassemblies, into libraries. The second is the visual organization of the model for output.

LIBRARIES OF ASSEMBLIES

Modeling is an enhancement of the drafting procedure. You model objects when there is a benefit. All work does not need to be modeled. Occasionally, you come across a project that needs to have all phases modeled. In that circumstance, build a library of model parts just as you would build a library of 2D parts. Organize the library around the final assemblies and proceed just as you would in a 2D drafting environment. An example is a call from the marketing department requesting models built of the whole line of products for inclusion in a brochure. This kind of project needs to have the parts modeled separately and assembled into the final products for creating the images. The marketing people might not be as concerned with precision as they are with the model looking good and being proportional to the other parts in the brochure. Decisions about how to build the library are based on how many parts, how much detail, and how many man-hours to put into the project.

VISUAL ORGANIZATION OF THE MODEL

The final output, or what the model is being used for, is a major factor in how to stage your model. Questions like "How many views of the final model do I need?" or "Is this a still render or animation of the model?" need to be defined before the creation of the model. Answering these questions leads you into not just how to model (surfaces or solids) but how to set up the model. When the possibility exists that the desired results could change (80% of the time), you need to build the model flexible (say in subassemblies). When you are shooting for close up shots of the model, you need to have great detail in the model. Some users create a non-detailed model and a detailed model. This gives them the flexibility they need for the final visualization.

Dimensioning in 3D

There are several schools of thought on this subject. They range from "never dimension in 3D" to "everything in 3D must be dimensioned." Both are on the extreme side. Dimension in 3D when you need to. There are many methods of dimensioning in the 3D environment with many variations. This book reviews two methods. They are dimensioning in 3D model space and dimensioning in Paperspace.

3D DIMENSIONING IN MODEL SPACE

Actual dimensioning in 3D space is no different than 2D space dimensioning. The extra factor to consider is the Z axis. Use the User Coordinate System (UCS) command to place your working plane on the part of the object you wish to dimension and place the dimension. The problem with 3D dimensioning in model space is the viewing angle and the amount of dimensions needed to describe the part. By placing dimensions using the UCS working plane, you limit your view of the object to viewing from the third or fourth quadrants. Viewing from the first or second quadrants makes the dimensions appear upside down (as shown in Figure 9.9). Complex parts can have many extra dimensions that would normally appear in different views if the part were not modeled. This can clutter the screen and make the dimensions hard to read. Try placing some dimensions using the UCS working plane.

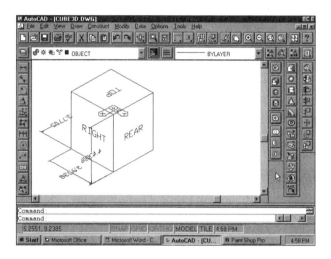

FIGURE 9.9 3D dimensions from the first quadrant.

Practice Procedure for Placing Dimensions Using the UCS Command

1. Open the *Cube3D* drawing and make the layer DIM-1 the current layer.

2. Activate the **Dimension** toolbar and dock it on the left side of the screen, if necessary.

3. Select the Linear dimension button to activate the command.

4. Press **Enter** to select the cube line.

5. Select the cube line at the point P1, as shown in Figure 9.10.

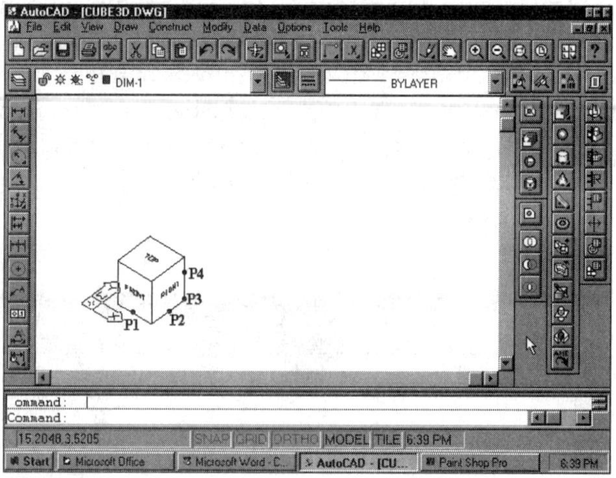

FIGURE 9.10 3D dimensions practice reference.

6. Select a point to place the dimension, as shown in Figure 9.10.

7. Press **Enter** twice to reactive the linear command and the select object option.

8. Select the cube line at the point P2 as shown in Figure 9.10.

9. Select a point to place the dimension as shown in Figure 9.10.

10. Restore the named UCS called FRONT and set the UCS origin to the end point P3 as shown in Figure 9.10.

11. Select the Linear dimension button to activate the command.

12. Press **Enter** to select the cube line.

13. Select the cube line at the point P4 as shown in Figure 9.10.

14. Select a point to place the dimension as shown in Figure 9.10.

15. Set the UCS back to World and zoom in closer to the object.

The results are shown in Figure 9.11. This method works as long as you view the cube from the third or fourth quadrant. There is no way to make the dimensions "automatic." Some users place dimensions on different layers in different views and use layer control to display the correct dimensions. There is no politically correct way to approach dimensioning in the 3D environment. Creativity and getting the job done is the answer more often than not.

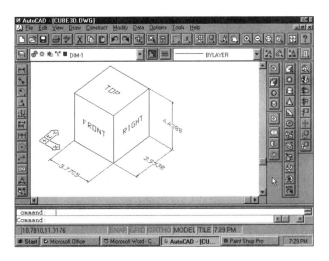

FIGURE 9.11 3D dimensions practice results.

3D DIMENSIONING IN PAPERSPACE

Autodesk has maintained that dimensioning should be done in Paperspace since Paperspace was introduced in Release 11. Most users do not use the Paperspace feature of dimension styles because a change on the part in model space then necessitates the need to move to Paperspace and change the dimension. The technique of placing dimensions in Paperspace is not much different than placing them in model space. The Scale to Paperspace option is turned on in the *Cube3D* drawing's 3D dimstyle. Try placing some dimensions in Paperspace on a 3D model.

Practice Procedure for Placing Dimension on 3D Models in Paperspace

1. Open the *Cube3D* drawing and make the layer DIM-2 the current layer.

2. Activate Paperspace and use the ZOOMALL and HIDEALL routines to see the viewports.

3. Turn on the running Endpoint object snap.

4. Select the **Linear** dimension toolbar button.

5. Select the points P1 and P2 as shown in Figure 9.12, and select a dimension line location.

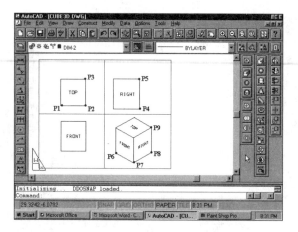

FIGURE 9.12 3D dimensions in Paperspace practice reference.

6. Repeat steps 4 and 5 for the points P2 and P3, and the points P4 and P5.

7. Select the **Align** dimension toolbar button.

8. Select the points P6 and P7, as shown in Figure 9.12, use the Text option to enter the correct text (3.7705), and select a dimension line location.

9. Repeat steps 7 and 8 for the points P7 and P8 (3.9538), and the points P8 and P9 (4.4388).

The results are shown in Figure 9.13. The ISO view needs the Align option with text even though it has a zoom factor of 1xp, the same as the other Viewports.

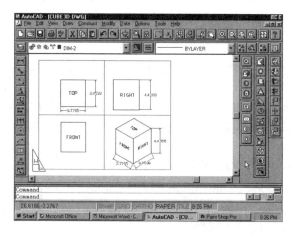

FIGURE 9.13 3D dimensions in Paperspace practice results.

The two methods shown in this section represent a small portion of the methods you can use to place dimensions in 3D space. Some users combine the two techniques, placing dimensions on separate layers in model space and using the VPLAYER control to display only those dimensions that are desired in Paperspace. Whatever method you develop, the use of dimensions in 3D modeling can be accomplished with a little creativity and some skill.

Export File Formats

Plotting to paper is not always the only output result you want from your drawings. Sometimes you need to transfer your drawing to another CAD system or to a different medium, such as images in raster format. AutoCAD has always had many output formats for your geometry. These output formats are provided because Autodesk recognizes that the AutoCAD program cannot be everything to everyone. Third-party add-on applications have been a part of the Autodesk plan since early in the company's creation. Certain output formats have been around for a long time. Porting your geometry to another CAD system is accomplished using the DXFOUT command. Creating a DXB format file has been a technique available for some time. Slide file image format has been available for many releases now.

AutoCAD Release 13 has brought about many additions of output file formats due in part to the ACIS solids core geometry and the need for more vector-to-raster output from a CAD product. Visualization of an object can be just as important as creating the object when it comes to selling an idea. AutoCAD now has a wealth of raster output formats and several invaluable industry standard outputs for the ACIS solids.

NOTE The Initial Graphics Exchange Specification (IGES) format has been discontinued in Release 13. The format is still supported for those who need it as an add-on module.

CAD Output Formats

AutoCAD supports the Data eXchange Format (DXF) for outputting your geometry to other CAD systems. This format has become the default industry output format for CAD file transfer from one CAD system to another.

DXFOUT

This command creates an ASCII file containing the definition of all the geometry in the drawing and the tables of information pertaining to that geometry. Tables include layers, linetypes, shapes, and blocks. This information can then be transferred to other CAD systems and imported into them. Many CAD systems are only able to transfer about 80% of the information in the DXF file into their system. This is because the other CAD systems must write the import routines to change the AutoCAD data into their format and some AutoCAD object types do not translate well into other CAD systems. When you use this command to give AutoCAD information to other CAD systems, remember that simple is best. Complex objects might not transfer well to the other system. Many users explode their complex objects into primitives before creating the output file. This technique creates some headaches in the other CAD system (objects are no longer associated) but it usually allows a higher percentage of the information to get into the other CAD system. Try creating an output file using the DXFOUT command.

Practice Procedure for Using the DXFOUT Command

1. Open the drawing called *Wedge*.

2. Type **dxfout** and press **Enter** to activate the DXFOUT command.

3. When your FILEDIA system variable is set to one (the default), a dialogue box appears, as shown in Figure 9.14. Accept the default name WEDGE by selecting **OK**.

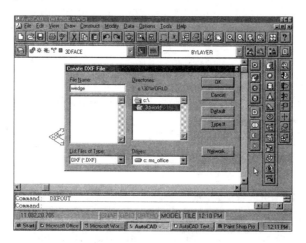

FIGURE 9.14 DXFOUT dialogue box.

4. Press **Enter** to accept the default 6 decimal place precision.

You can review the results by using any ASCII text editor to open the file named WEDGE.DXF. The file is located in the same directory as the drawing (3DWORLD in this case). A partial look at the resulting file is shown in Figure 9.15. The file contains headers for the tables and object definitions in a standard format. Other CAD software packages have the format available to them for creating their import routines. The accuracy of the import of the information is the responsibility of the CAD software vendor who writes the import routine.

```
LINE
   5
  28
 100
AcDbEntity
   8
  10
  62
      4
 100
AcDbLine
  10
9.891741
  20
2.248244
  30
0.0
  11
10.157596
  21
2.248244
  31
0.0
```

FIGURE 9.15 DXFOUT output file practice (partial) results.

In step 4 of the last practice procedure, you selected the default of 6 decimal place precision (you can have up to 16 place accuracy). The command also allows you to create an output file of only the objects in your drawing (no table information) by using the Objects option. The Binary option allows you to create a smaller, more compact, binary version of the output file. Some CAD systems do not have the ability to read a binary DXF output file.

TIP You can sometimes correct a problem with a corrupt file by using the DXFOUT command to create an ASCII version of the drawing and then (in a new drawing file) use the DXFIN command to import the ASCII file. AutoCAD only writes out the good data from the corrupt drawing into the ASCII file. You can lose some geometry but not lose the whole drawing.

The DXF file format is not backward compatible with earlier versions of AutoCAD. You cannot use it to take Release 13 geometry back to Release 10. The process is possible, with limited success, by using a combination of techniques. They are:

- Use the SAVEASR 12 command in the Release 13 drawing to save the drawing to Release 12 format (AutoCAD translates unique 13 geometry to 12 geometry).

- Use Release 12 to create a DXF file from the drawing.

- Use the Release 12 supplemental command DXFIX (as described in the Release 12 Extras manual) to translate the DXF file to Release 10 format.

Transferring information from one CAD system to another or to an earlier version of AutoCAD can be complex and frustrating. Simple is always best when trying to do these processes.

DXB

The Data eXchange Binary format is not a command but a file format. You can create this output format using the PLOT command. The format is useful for taking text and transforming it into line segments. The cube used in the early chapters of this book had text on it that was created in this fashion. Since text shows through surfaces using the HIDE command, the text for the faces of the cube were converted into line segments and brought into the cube drawing (using the DXBIN command). Then the ROTATE3D command was used to place the text onto the faces of the cube. Other users have used this technique whenever they wanted to take text, or other objects, and transform them into line segments for transferring to other mediums or to other CAD systems. Before you can create a DXB output file, you must configure a plotting device to output to that format. Add a plotting configuration for DXB output files.

Practice Procedure for Adding a DXB Output File Configuration

1. In AutoCAD, type **config** and press **Enter** to enter the configuration area.

2. At the main configuration screen (you need to press extra **Enter** keys to get to it), type **5** and press **Enter** to access the plotting configuration menu.

3. Type **1** (one) and press **Enter** at the Plot configuration menu to add a new plotter configuration.

4. You need to select the **AutoCAD file output formats (pre 4.1) – by Autodesk, Inc** menu item from the available plotters menu, by typing the associated number to the left of the item (**2** in my case).

5. You need to select the **AutoCAD DXB file** menu item from the supported models menu, by typing the associated number to the left of the item (**2** in my case again).

6. Press **Enter** to accept all defaults until you get to the `Enter a description for this plotter:` prompt.

7. Type **DXB output file** and press **Enter** to continue.

8. Exit the plotter configuration menu by pressing **Enter**.

9. Exit the configuration menu by pressing **Enter**.

10. Accept the changes by pressing **Enter**.

You now have a new plotter configuration that allows you to plot to a DXB output file format.

Try creating a DXB output file format.

Practice Procedure for Creating DXB Output

1. In a new drawing, in standard ISO view, place the text DXB (large enough to see).

2. Type **plot** and press **Enter** to activate the PLOT command.

3. Select the `Device and Default Selection...` button to select the output configuration.

4. Select the **DXB output file** configuration as shown in Figure 9.16.

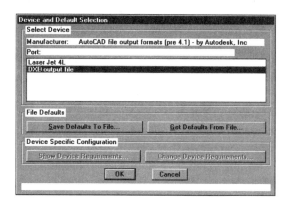

FIGURE 9.16 DXB output file (PLOT dialogue box) practice reference.

285

5. Select **OK** to exit the dialogue box.

6. Select **OK** to plot the current settings to the DXB output file.

7. Start a new drawing without saving the contents of this drawing and set your view to plan view.

8. Use the DXBIN command to select the *Unnamed.DXB* file.

9. Use the supplied routine ZOOMALL to view the results.

The results should appear similar to those shown in Figure 9.17. While you can use views other than plan view to create your DXB files, you should stick to plan view when you create the file. Objects, more so than text, get distorted by this technique. Better to create the file in plan view and then rotate the imported geometry to the necessary plane afterwards.

286

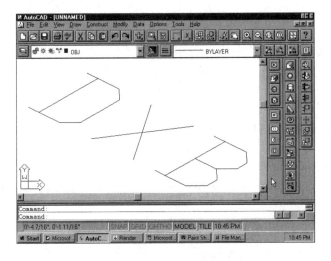

FIGURE 9.17 DXB output file practice results.

IMAGE OUTPUT FILE FORMATS

AutoCAD has had the slide output for many releases now. Raster image output file formats have been added in recent releases to augment AutoCAD's own proprietary slide format. TIFF, GIF, and PostScript output formats were added to allow you to output your wireframe, hidden, shaded, or rendered objects to those industry standards. Release 13 for Windows has added the BMP and WMF output formats to allow you a richer choice in raster output formats.

MSLIDE

This command enables you to create a raster output file format in AutoCAD's own native slide format. Slides are used in menus to visualize choices. Slides are also used to create rudimentary slide shows for presentations. AutoCAD uses the VSLIDE command to view a slide inside a drawing. Slide shows are made by creating a script that automatically shows each slide you create in the order you chose. Try creating the slides for a slide show and running the supplied script to view them.

Practice Procedure for Creating Slides for a Slide Show

1. Open the *Wedge* drawing.
2. Restore the view called ISO and use the supplied routine HIDEALL.
3. Type **mslide** and press **Enter** to activate the MSLIDE (make slide) command.
4. Name the slide **ISO** in the filename edit box and select **OK**.
5. Restore the view called NEISO and use the supplied routine HIDEALL.
6. Type **mslide** and press **Enter** to activate the MSLIDE (make slide) command.
7. Name the slide **NEISO** in the filename edit box and select **OK**.
8. Restore the view called SEISO and use the supplied routine HIDEALL.
9. Type **mslide** and press **Enter** to activate the MSLIDE (make slide) command.
10. Name the slide SEISO in the filename edit box and select **OK**.
11. Restore the view called SWISO and use the supplied routine HIDEALL.
12. Type **mslide** and press **Enter** to activate the MSLIDE (make slide) command.
13. Name the slide **SWISO** in the filename edit box and select **OK**.
14. Type **script** and press **Enter**.
15. Select the script from your 3DWORLD directory called SHOW(.SCR).

The script is an ASCII text file designed to show the slides you created (the names must be exactly the same). You can exit the script by using the **Escape** key. This example used preset views to create the slides. You can create slide show scripts that are much more elaborate for displaying a concept using a 3D model.

Third-party shareware programs exist that allow you to view, create libraries, and create script shows without AutoCAD (you do need AutoCAD to create the original slides). This is handy for presentations where the client does not have AutoCAD but a computer is available. Autodesk publishes a third-party software list, or you can browse around on bulletin boards like CompuServe to find them.

TIP

PSOUT

This format, Encapsulated PostScript (EPS), is not new to Release 13. It is an industry standard and AutoCAD writes out the image information upon request. This format is aimed at filled fonts and printers that can handle PostScript fonts quickly. Certain types of objects (filled polylines and others) appear solid in the output file when the file is viewed or printed. Try creating a PostScript output file using the PSOUT command.

Practice Procedure for Creating an Encapsulated PostScript File

1. Open the drawing *Elevx* (you saved it from an earlier practice procedure).
2. Use the supplied HIDEALL routine to view the elevations.
3. Make sure that the large ISO Viewport is active.
4. Type **psout** and press **Enter** to activate the command.
5. Select **OK** to accept the default name ELEVX.
6. Press **Enter** to accept the default for each of the next five prompts.

To view the results, you can start a new drawing and use the PSIN command to insert the created image (ELEVX.EPS) into your drawing. The image is not hidden as was your screen view. This is because the PSOUT command interprets the objects as they are created and writes them to the output file. Solids and surfaces appear as wireframes in this format.

See page 534 of the AutoCAD User's Guide for more detailed information on what and how objects translate to this format.

NOTE

BMPOUT

This command allows you to create a BitMaP output image. The BMP file format is common to the Windows platform and is a true raster image format. The resulting output file is dependent on the current screen resolution and color palette. This format is used extensively for the creation of toolbar button images in Windows and AutoCAD. Try creating a bitmap output file.

Practice Procedure for Creating a Bitmap File

1. Open the drawing Elevx (you saved it from an earlier practice procedure).
2. Use the supplied HIDEALL routine to view the elevations.
3. Make sure that the large ISO viewport is active.
4. Type **bmpout** and press **Enter** to activate the command.
5. Select **OK** to accept the default name ELEVX.
6. Type **all** and press **Enter** to select all objects in the drawing.
7. Press **Enter** to exit the selection process and the command.

You can view the result by opening the ELEVX.BMP file in the Windows Paintbrush program. The image is raster and the hidden lines stayed hidden. You can add text to the image and then use the image in a toolbar button or print it to a color printer.

WMFOUT

The Windows Metafile output format is new to Release 13 for Windows. This raster format is used by many Windows products in much the same way as the BMP format is used. The procedure for creating this raster image output file format is the same as the BMP procedure and is not presented here.

SOLIDS OUTPUT FILE FORMAT

The new ACIS solids have two output file formats for different types of disciplines. Solids are also output in the previous file formats, but these formats are specifically for the solids. The strength of ACIS solids is the ability to export the information into statistical analysis programs or into a file format that can be used for Stereolithography prototyping.

STLOUT

This command extracts the solid information into STereoLithography format. Stereolithography is a relatively cheap way of creating a prototype part by layering the part using lasers and the information from ACIS solids. Try creating an output file in the Stereolithography format.

Practice Procedure for Creating a Stereolithography Output File

1. Open the drawing *Moldx* (you saved it from an earlier practice procedure).

2. Use the supplied HIDEALL routine to view the elevations.

3. Make sure that the large ISO viewport is active.

4. Type **stlout** and press **Enter** to activate the command.

5. Type **all** and press **Enter** to select all objects in the drawing.

6. Press **Enter** to exit the selection process and the command.

7. Select **OK** to accept the default name MOLDX.

8. Type **n** and press **Enter** to create a binary STL output file.

A sample of the resulting output file is shown in Figure 9.18.

```
solid AutoCAD
    facet normal 0.0000000e+000 0.0000000e+000 1.0000000e+000
        outer loop
            vertex 7.0802648e+000 1.0408740e+001 1.2500000e-001
            vertex 7.0471009e+000 1.0535881e+001 1.2500000e-001
            vertex 6.5261209e+000 1.0535881e+001 1.2500000e-001
        endloop
    endfacet
    facet normal 0.0000000e+000 0.0000000e+000 1.0000000e+000
        outer loop
            vertex 7.0802648e+000 1.0408740e+001 1.2500000e-001
            vertex 6.5261209e+000 1.0535881e+001 1.2500000e-001
            vertex 6.4929570e+000 1.0408740e+001 1.2500000e-001
        endloop
    endfacet
    facet normal 0.0000000e+000 0.0000000e+000 1.0000000e+000
        outer loop
            vertex 5.0802648e+000 1.0408740e+001 1.2500000e-001
            vertex 5.0471009e+000 1.0535881e+001 1.2500000e-001
            vertex 4.4116109e+000 1.0535881e+001 1.2500000e-001
        endloop
    endfacet
    facet normal 0.0000000e+000 0.0000000e+000 1.0000000e+000
```

FIGURE 9.18 STL output file sample.

TIP

The FACETRES (facet resolution) system variable controls the fineness of the mesh information that is written to the STL output file. The higher the setting, the finer the mesh.

ACISOUT

The SAT file format is used to transfer ACIS solids information that can be used in other programs, including statistical analysis programs and other CAD programs. Try creating an output file in the SAT format using the ACISOUT command.

Practice Procedure for Creating and Using a SAT Output File

1. Open the drawing *Moldx* (you saved it from an earlier practice procedure).

2. Type **acisout** and press **Enter** to activate the command.

3. Type **all** and press **Enter** to select all objects in the drawing.

4. Press **Enter** to exit the selection process and the command.

5. Select **OK** to accept the default name MOLDX.

6. Erase all of the geometry in the drawing.

7. Use the ACISIN command to import the MOLDX.SAT file you just created.

The result in your drawing is the solid object is imported at the exact same spot it was exported. A sample of the resulting output file is shown in Figure 9.19.

```
105  1179  1  0
body $1 $2 $-1 $-1 #
f_body-lwd-attrib $-1 $3 $-1 $0 #
lump $4 $-1 $5 $0 #
ref_vt-lwd-attrib $-1 $-1 $1 $0 $6 $7 #
ref_vt-lwd-attrib $-1 $-1 $-1 $2 $6 $7 #
shell $8 $-1 $-1 $9 $2 #
refinement $-1 0 0 0 0 0.042868714779615402 0 0 0 2 #
vertex_template $-1 3 0 1 8 #
ref_vt-lwd-attrib $-1 $-1 $-1 $5 $6 $7 #
face $10 $11 $12 $5 $-1 $13 forward single #
color-adesk-attrib $-1 $14 $-1 $9 256 #
face $15 $16 $17 $5 $-1 $18 forward single #
loop $-1 $-1 $19 $9 #
cone-surface $-1 4.6616109069601865 11.035880889345503 1 0 0 1 -0.17677669529
fface-lwd-attrib $-1 $20 $10 $9 #
fface-lwd-attrib $-1 $21 $-1 $11 #
face $22 $23 $24 $5 $-1 $25 forward single #
loop $-1 $-1 $26 $11 #
plane-surface $-1 4.4116109069601865 10.660880889345503 1.625 1 0 0 0 0 -1 0
coedge $27 $28 $29 $30 $31 0 $12 $-1 #
ref_vt-lwd-attrib $-1 $-1 $14 $9 $6 $-1 #
```

FIGURE 9.19 SAT output file sample.

SURFACES OUTPUT FILE FORMATS

AutoCAD has the ability to export and import the surfaces of a 3D model to and from a 3D Studio file format. Solids have surfaces placed on them automatically before the export, but the best results are with surfaces defined with one of the mesh or surface commands.

3DSOUT

This command allows you to export surfaces (and solids surfaces) into a 3D Studio surface mesh output file format. Try exporting to a 3D Studio file format using the 3DSOUT command.

Practice Procedure for Creating a 3D Studio Output File

1. Open the drawing *Moldx* (you saved it from an earlier practice procedure).

2. Type **3dsout** and press **Enter** to activate the command.

3. Select the mold object and press **Enter** to end the object selection process.

4. Select **OK** to accept the default name MOLDX.

5. Select **OK** to accept the defaults of the file export options dialogue box as shown in Figure 9.20. Be very patient, this could take a while and it sometimes looks like the system is hung (it isn't!).

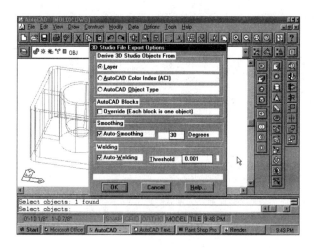

FIGURE 9.20 3D Studio File Export options.

6. Erase all of the geometry in the drawing.

7. Use the 3DSIN command to import the MOLDX.3DS file you just created.

The object that gets imported back into your file is a polyline mesh. That is because the 3DSOUT command places a temporary mesh on the solid and exports that mesh.

 This is a great method for converting a solid to a surface mesh.

NOTE

EXPORT COMMANDS MENU LOCATIONS

Most of the commands discussed in this section are available in an export dialogue box activated by selecting the *Export...* menu item from the *Files* pull-down menu. The Files pull-down is shown in Figure 9.21 and the Export dialogue box is shown in Figure 9.22.

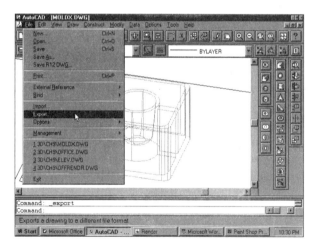

FIGURE 9.21 *File* pull-down menu with *Export...* menu item.

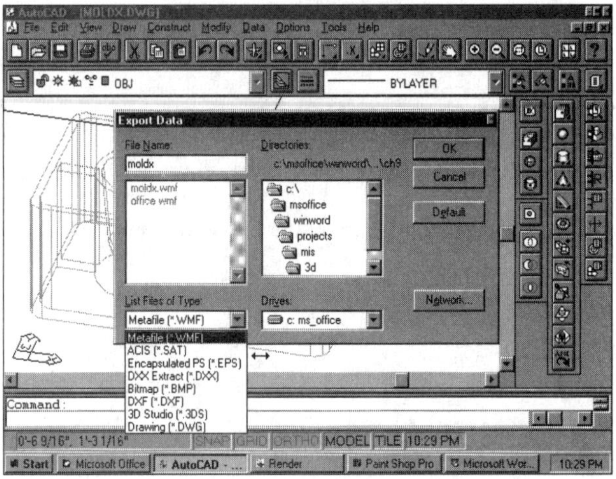

FIGURE 9.22 Export Data dialogue box.

The EPS selection in the Export data dialogue box forces all of the default options automatically.

N O T E

EXPORT FILE FORMATS WRAP-UP

The many export commands in AutoCAD allow you to transfer data (solids or surfaces) between programs (CAD or others). The way you design your 3D models is dictated by the way you want to use the end results. AutoCAD has given you the necessary tools for transferring your data.

Hardware Requirements

Writing about hardware requirements is always difficult when the hardware changes every 6 months and books or magazine articles have a time lag of nearly the same time span. A general rule of thumb when dealing with CAD software, or raster software, is to always have the biggest and fastest hardware available at the time. This is difficult because the usefulness of hardware in the CAD field is about 2 years, while the depreciation of the hardware is usually figured over three years or more. Many companies adapt a trickle-down process for their hardware. The CAD department gets the latest and greatest and the other departments get the older hardware which, in most cases, has a useful life span of several more years doing non–CAD-related work. The cost of hardware seems high until you start to track how much lost productivity is generated by slow hardware. Most companies do not want to get into the benchmarking business, but you can usually estimate how long it takes to finish a process, and measure that time on two machines. The difference in time between the same process completed on two different machines is the loss of productivity for that one process. Multiply that number by the employee's salary and how many times a day, a week, or a month the process is done and you have a number by which to gauge your decisions. Often, you can justify the higher cost of newer hardware using these types of figures. When that doesn't work, you can fall back on the old saw "but our competition is doing it." This is not as lame as you might think. In the business world of today, as in the one of yesterday, the company that invests in high technology and has a good product usually is successful. You must spend money to make money. Just do not spend more than you need to!

Today's AutoCAD software runs on a combination of CPU speed, hard drive space, and available memory. You can think of this as the brain, the short-term memory, and the long-term memory. The fastest brain in the world isn't very good if it cannot remember anything. AutoCAD and the other high-end programs of today are engineered to take full advantage of the brain's speed (CPU), the short-term memory (RAM), and the long-term memory (disk storage). The trick is to have a machine that has the most but costs the least. Remember, 3D modeling pushes your machine to the limits.

Currently the Pentium 120 and 133 MHz are the high end PC platforms. However, many of the older 486 computer platforms are still in use. You can leverage your 486 computers by upgrading them to more memory, faster CPUs, and more hard drive space. This process increases the length of use of the machine while allowing you to keep your upgrade costs down. When purchasing a new machine, go with the biggest, fastest machine because it will be out of date in 6 months, old technology in 18 months, and a boat anchor in 3 years. The new machine must be designed to upgrade, so you can increase these times to a reasonable length.

Autodesk gives you minimum requirements for CPU, RAM, and hard drive capacity. Remember, minimum means that this is the very least the program needs to run. Autodesk never suggests that you can be productive with those numbers. 3D modeling is the high end of design, so it needs the high end of hardware configuration. Even recommended requirements are on the low end for 3D modeling.

There are several different machine configurations that lend themselves to 3D modeling in AutoCAD Release 13. These configurations include:

- Low end is the 486 66 MHz machine. This machine should have a minimum of 24 Mb of RAM and a hard disk capacity of 540 Mb (stand-alone or networked). When using the Windows 3.x platform, add another 8 Mb of RAM and another 100 Mb of disk storage. This is because Windows needs the additional RAM and a permanent swap file of 64 Mb (or more) on the hard drive for AutoCAD.

- High end (in the PC market) is the Pentium 133 MHz machine. This machine should have a minimum of 64 Mb of RAM and a hard disk capacity of 1 gigabyte (stand-alone or networked).

The current PCs are running at a maximum of 133 MHz. By the time this book is published both the low- and high-end machines could very well be one or more notches higher. When entering the world of modeling, you step into the next level of complexity for hardware and software. You are no longer concerned with just a drawing and maybe some BOM takeoffs. You must consider how the model is to be used. When it is the engine for statistical analysis, you need more computing power for both the modeler (AutoCAD) and the analysis program. When the model is the engine for a still image or a walk-through, you need the horse power to generate the model and create the rendered image or animation. The price is high but the results are often worth it when the model gets your company a multimillion dollar job or saves hundreds of thousands of dollars in production cost because an error is found in the computer model. Modeling is like high stakes poker. You need to bring a large investment to the table in the hopes that you will take larger winnings home.

Software Availability

This book concentrates on the core commands and techniques used to create a 3D model in AutoCAD. There are currently many other products (created by both Autodesk and other companies) that enhance the native abilities of the AutoCAD 3D modeling environment. The mechanical discipline has the Designer and AutoSurf products by Autodesk. To enhance still images, Autodesk has supplied AutoVision for higher quality renderings inside AutoCAD. Autodesk supplies the Animator Pro, Animator Studio, 3D Studio, and 3D Max products for creating animations from objects built in those packages or, in the case of 3D Studio and 3D Max, objects built inside AutoCAD. Third-party companies have built programs that take information from ACIS solids to run statistical analysis computations, create tool paths, and use Stereolithography code. These are but a few examples of the hundreds of programs that use AutoCAD directly or indirectly as a data source. Autodesk has a resource guide that lists many of the known products and where to find them; contact your authorized AutoCAD dealer for information on how to get a copy of the guide.

Prototypes

Managing prototype drawings for 3D modeling is no different than managing prototype drawing for 2D drafting. You do need to add the necessary viewport configuration, views, layers, and other tools for 3D, but all of the rules remain the same. Prototype drawings for the 3D modeling environment are covered in detail in Chapter 12.

In Conclusion

Managing modeling issues cover a broad range of subjects, as shown in this chapter. You were introduced to the expectation guidelines for modeling along with some of the reasons you should model and examples of what you should model. Export commands, hardware requirements, and software availability were covered. In the next chapter, the basics of rendering are explored. The commands and tools, along with various techniques, are introduced.

CHAPTER TEN

Rendering

Using rendered images to sell a project, visualize a concept, or enhance a finished project has become more common as the tools for creating the images become more flexible and accessible. AutoCAD Release 13 has more core rendering capability than any previous release of the software. You can now place point, spot, or distant lights. The materials that are accepted have expanded and the ability to use a materials library has been added. Even with this new enhanced ability, rendering in the AutoCAD package using just the core commands is severely limited. To get high quality renderings that are photo-realistic, you need to add a separate package like the AutoVision package or some other third party software. The core commands are good enough to give you a simple rendering that gives the feel for the part or structure. The rendering seldom approaches the realism you can get from the more sophisticated packages. The rendering chapters in this book are focused on the commands and tools used to get simple renderings while covering some of the basic tips and tricks to creating a good-looking rendering. There are currently books on the market that cover the theory behind lighting, the use of scenes, color, materials, and all of the other rendering-related subjects in much more depth than a mere two chapters can cover. These chapters are meant to get you up and started creating simple renderings using the AutoCAD core commands.

Setting up for Rendering

Two of the very first items you need to consider when moving into the realm of rendering are resolution and color palettes. These terms are the foundation to rendering and they need to be understood before you can even start to create good looking images.

Resolution is the density of pixels or dots that form the screen or paper image. A pixel is the basic square or dot that is used to form the screen or paper image. A computer's screen resolution is measured as a matrix of square rows and columns. A screen with a resolution of 1024 by 768 has a matrix of pixels that measures 1024 pixels across the horizontal axis and 768 pixels across the vertical axis. The higher the number for the two axis, the better diagonal lines look on the screen. The same is true for a plotted sheet of paper. Printers and plotters are measured in dots per inch (DPI), but the concept is the same. A printer that has a resolution of 300 DPI does not print a diagonal line a well as a printer that has a DPI of 600. The diagonal line appears jagged on the 300 DPI printer when compared to the diagonal line printed on the 600 DPI machine.

The color palette is the number of colors your device allows shown. The smaller the palette, the less blending of colors allowed. The blending of colors is what makes realism in the image. Most things in life are not simply black or white, red or green. The shading between the two extremes is what makes for depth and definition of an object. Two of the three primary colors of light are red and green. When you have a small color palette that only allows 16 colors, there is no room to create all of the various blending that constitutes the shades of color that appear between red and green. Without the shades between red and green, you can not get an image that has depth or the subtle definition of a rounded object. The image appears cartoonish (or flat), because cartoons have traditionally used a small limited–color palette.

NOTE The difference between light's red, green, and blue (RGB) primary colors and paint's red, yellow, and blue (RYB) primary color is part of the reason an image can look good on the screen but not good on paper. Another consideration is the matchup of color between the two mediums. Red in light medium (computer screen) can look very different from red on paper because of issues like saturation, hue, and luminosity.

Many people think that resolution is the key to getting a better looking rendered image. They think that the higher the resolution of the output (to screen or paper) the better the image. This is not the case. Color is the key to a more realistic image. You can have a lower resolution but a larger color palette and get a better looking image than with a high resolution but a small color palette. The result might have slightly more jagged diagonal lines, but it looks more realistic because of the depth (gradation) of color. The down side to a larger color palette is the additional time it takes to create a rendering. The computer must analyze the object, all of the lights effect on the object, and the color of the lights and the object (or material on the object). The more colors available, the longer it takes to find the correct shade of the color needed. Considerations such as the complexity of the object, how many lights to use, color of the object (or material used on the object), and color of the lights are some of the many things you need to consider as you set up your object for rendering. The gradation between colors shows up even in gray scale gradation. Figures 10.1 and 10.2 show the difference between 16 color and 256 color palettes on the AutoCAD color wheel.

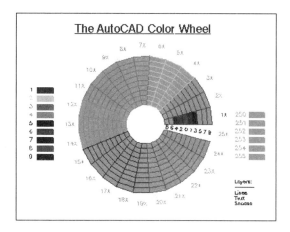

FIGURE 10.1 16–color palette.

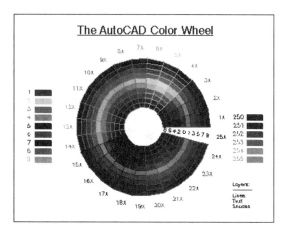

FIGURE 10.2 True 32-bit color.

Figures 10.3 and 10.4 show a few examples (in gray scale) of how color palettes can effect the gradation or depth of a simple object like a cube.

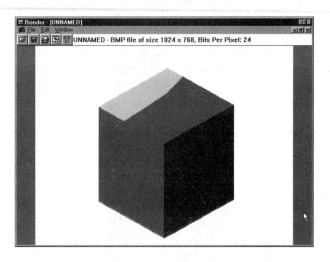

FIGURE 10.3 16–color rendered cube.

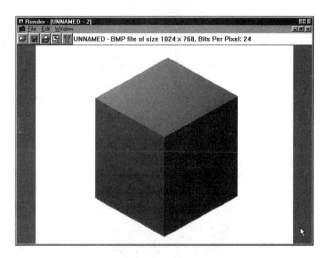

FIGURE 10.4 True 32–bit color rendered cube.

Notice that the true 32–bit color rendered cube has better definition due to the blending of the color (gray scale in this image).

Video Setup

You need a video card that can handle a minimum of 65,536 colors (true 32-bit color) to create any kind of realistic looking rendered image. Windows Setup is where you select your video driver. The images created for this book are generated on a Matrox PCI video card with 2Mb of memory. The card's driver is set to true 32-bit color (the highest possible) and a resolution of 800 by 600 (the highest possible at the true 32-bit color setting). The card has higher resolution available but at the cost of color. True 32-bit color allows 65,536 colors. Each video card has instructions on how to install the card and connect the video driver. A general review of adjusting your video driver in Windows 3.x or Windows 95 is warranted.

Windows 3.x

You can change your display driver from the Control Panel, which is located in the Main folder of the program manager. The steps are outlined here and shown in Figure 10.5.

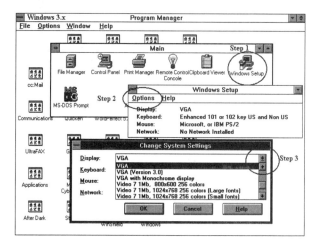

FIGURE 10.5 Windows 3.x video driver interface.

1. In your Main folder, activate the **Windows Setup** by double-clicking on the icon.

2. Select Change System Settings… from the *Options* pull-down menu.

3. Select the **Display** list from the Change System Settings dialogue box and select your device driver.

Windows 3.x needs to restart when you select a driver that changes the resolution or color palette to a higher setting.

Windows 95

You can change your display driver from the Control Panel, which is located in the Settings choice of the Start menu. The steps are outlined here and shown in Figure 10.6.

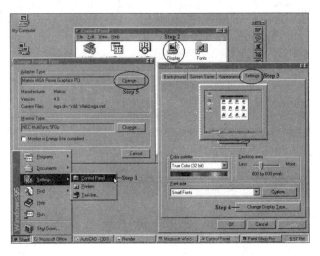

FIGURE 10.6 Windows 95 video driver interface.

1. Activate the **Control Panel** from the Settings item of the Start menu.

2. Double-click on the **Display** icon of the Control Panel to activate the Display Properties dialogue box.

3. Select the **Settings** tab of the Display Properties dialogue box.

4. Select the Change Display Type... button to activate the Change Display Type dialogue box.

5. Select the Change... button.

6. Use the Show compatible devices or Show all devices radio button to view your choices and select the driver that you need, as shown in Figure 10.7 (the Have Disk... button is for drivers not on the list).

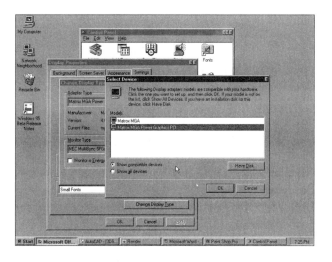

FIGURE 10.7 Select device dialogue box.

Windows 95 needs to reboot when you select a driver that changes the resolution or color palette to a higher setting.

Take the time to install or update your video driver to a minimum of 65536 colors and a resolution of 800 by 680 so that any practice exercises you do will appear the same as those in the book (yours are color while the book only shows grayscale).

HARDWARE REQUIREMENTS

The thing to remember in any discussion of hardware or software is that both are out of date as soon you buy them—especially hardware. The high-end hardware requirements for doing 3D modeling in AutoCAD are the low- to medium-end requirements for rendering. The video card defined above is high-end for AutoCAD production but low-end for a high-quality rendering. A card capable of 16 million colors at a resolution of 1280 by 1024 or more is desirable for creation of a high-end rendering. You need a CPU capable of crunching the huge amount of data a rendering entails. A Pentium 120 or 133 are about as fast as you can get on the PC platform at the time this book is written. The examples of renderings shown in these chapters are done on a Pentium 90 with 32 Mb of random access memory (RAM) and a hard drive capacity of 1 GB. This configuration is not high-end for production rendering. A machine set up for production rendering should have 64 Mb or more of memory (RAM) and 2 GB or more of disk storage. Raster images take much more space to store than the typical CAD file, and they are much more memory-intensive to produce.

Rendering Commands and Tools

The rest of this chapter is dedicated to the core commands and tools that AutoCAD contains. The various dialogue boxes and their usage are covered and some techniques are explored for creating realistic-looking images.

THE RENDER COMMAND

This command is used to create rendered images of an object. There are many tools on the Render dialogue box, as shown in Figure 10.8, for controlling the creation of an image. They include:

- the Rendering Type poplist that allows you to select from various rendering types of software you might have installed. AutoVision appears on the list when it is installed.

- the Scene to Render list that allows you to select a scene you have saved to render. Scenes are discussed later in this chapter.

- the Screen Palette poplist that allows you to select a palette type when you have a noncontinuous render driver installed.

- the Destination poplist and the More Options... button that allows you to select a target destination.

- the Render Options area and the More Options... button that allow you to define a render quality for the image and to control the various techniques that can be applied to the image.

- the Render Scene button that allows you to render the current scene or a saved scene.

- the Render Objects button that allows you to render selected objects from a scene.

Each button controls a facet of the rendering process and is examined in detail in the following section.

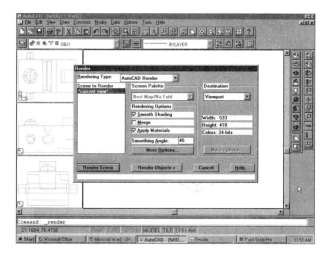

FIGURE 10.8 Render dialogue box.

The Render Scene Button

This button activates the RENDER command on the active Viewport. All of the other dialogue settings are applied to render the scene. Try rendering a scene using the RENDER command.

Practice Procedure for Rendering a Scene

1. In the *Widget* drawing, activate the RENDER command by typing **render** and pressing **Enter**.

2. Select the **Render Scene** button.

The results are shown in Figure 10.9. This object has no lights or material assigned but the image is still lighted and appears the same color as the object's color. Lights, scenes, and materials are covered later in this chapter and the next chapter.

AutoCAD automatically assigns a spotlight from the viewpoint aimed at the object whenever you do not specify a light source in a scene.

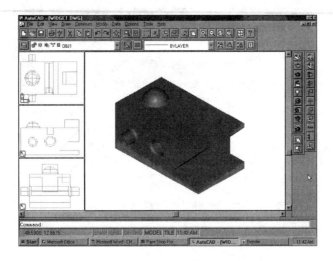

FIGURE 10.9 Render Scene practice procedure results.

The Render Objects Button

This button allows you to select objects from the scene to have rendered. This is good for quick snap shots to test how a light is affecting an object. Place a solid sphere next to the widget and use the **Render Object** button to render just the sphere from the scene.

Practice Procedure for Using the Render Objects Button

1. In the *Widget* drawing, add a sphere near the widget as shown in Figure 10.10.
2. Activate the RENDER command by typing **render** and pressing **Enter**.
3. Select the **Render Objects<** button.
4. Select the sphere and press **Enter** to return to the Render dialogue box.

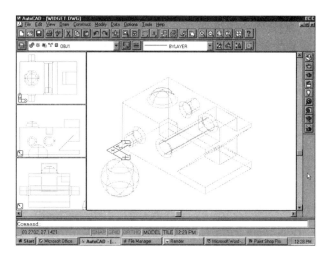

FIGURE 10.10 Render Objects practice procedure reference.

The results are shown in Figure 10.11. The widget is ignored while the selected sphere is rendered.

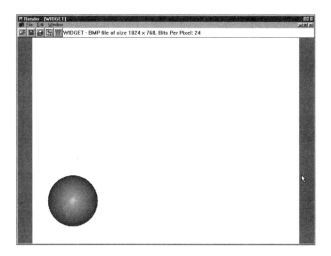

FIGURE 10.11 Render Objects practice procedure results.

The Render Type Poplist

This list is used when you have other rendering software installed. AutoVision (the next step up in rendering software from Autodesk) is commonly used and selected from this list when installed.

The Scene to Render List Box

This list box lists all of the currently saved scenes for rendering. Scenes are covered later in this chapter. The WIDGET drawing has no saved scenes at this time.

The Screen Palette Poplist

This poplist controls the available colors when rendering an image using a 256-color rendering driver. There are three options available when not using a continuous color rendering driver:

- **Best Map/No Fold** calculates the best colors based on the available colors of the driver and creates a separate color map. It does not fold the AutoCAD colors into colors 1 through 8.

- **Best Map/Fold** creates a color map folding the colors from 9 through 256 into the first 8 primary colors.
- **Fixed ACAD Map** uses the AutoCAD 256 color map to produce low-quality renderings.

These three options are only available for Viewport rendering with a noncontinuous render driver.

NOTE

The Destination Poplist and More Options Button

This area is used to control the output of your rendering. You can send your rendering to any one of the following places:

- To the active viewport.
- To a Render window.
- To a defined hard copy device.
- To a file in any one of a dozen different standard raster formats.

The **More Options...** button allows you to configure your file output to the desired format, resolution, color format, and several other options for generating a raster image in the form you need. The File Output Configuration dialogue box called by the **More Options...** button is shown in Figure 10.12.

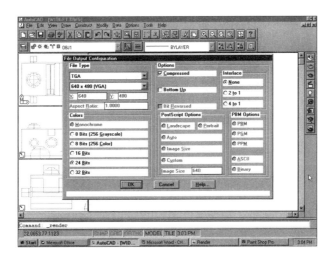

FIGURE 10.12 File Output Configuration dialogue box.

NOTE The chosen file type in this dialogue box controls which options are available. The Portable Bit Map options are only available when exporting to the PBM format, the Postscript options for the postscript output, and interlace for the GIF and TIF formats.

Change the Destination to the Render Window and render the widget again.

Practice Procedure for Changing the Destination and Rendering a Scene

1. In the *Widget* drawing, erase the sphere you created earlier.
2. Activate the RENDER command by typing render and pressing **Enter**.
3. Select the **Destination** poplist and pick the **Render Window** item.
4. Select the **Render Scene** button.

The results are shown in Figure 10.13 along with the Options dialogue box for the Render window. You can control the resolution of the output and then use the

File pull-down menu to save the rendered image to a bitmap (BMP) file. This is handy for sending out high resolution images to a printing service.

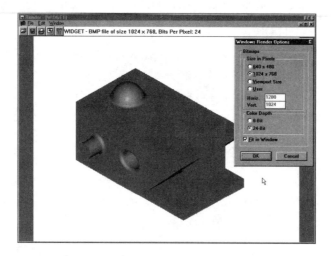

FIGURE 10.13 Render Scene to a render window practice procedure results.

The higher the resolution, the longer the render takes.

N O T E

The Rendering Options and More Options Buttons

The **Rendering Options** area controls the smoothing of faces (and the degree at which a smooth takes place), the merging of a changed image into an existing image, and the use of materials that are applied to the object. The **More Options...** button in the area allows you to change the render quality (Gouraud or Phong) and the face controls. The more faces the rendering has to consider, the longer it takes.

Changing to Phong rendering can speed up the rendering process with little loss of resolution on many objects. This technique is good for quick checks of the rendering.

T I P

RENDER PREFERENCES

This dialogue box, shown in Figure 10.14, is where you set up your defaults for rendering. The command to activate the dialogue box is RPREF. You can adjust settings like:

- Rendering Type
- Screen Palette
- Destination
- Rendering Options
- Rendering Procedure
- Lights
- Rendering Configuration (devices)

All of these can be set dynamically as you do your renderings, but this is the area where the defaults are locked in.

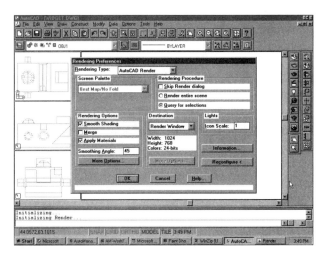

FIGURE 10.14 Render Preferences dialogue box.

TIP

Once you set up this dialogue box, you should turn on the **Skip Render Dialog** toggle to by pass the Render dialogue box each time you render a view. This saves time because you usually do not have to change any of the basic settings as you render but only want to adjust lights and views.

Change the lights setting for use later in this chapter.

Practice Procedure for Adjusting the Render Preferences

1. In the *Widget* drawing, activate the RPREF command by typing **rpref** and pressing **Enter**.

2. Select the **Lights Icon Scale:** edit box and change the number to **25**.

3. Select **OK** and exit the preferences dialogue box.

When you enter lights into the scene later, their size will be correct for viewing in relation to this object.

RENDER STATISTICS

This command, STATS, gives you the information on the last rendering as shown in Figure 10.15. Items tracked are:

- The scene name.
- The last rendering type.
- How long the render took.
- How many total faces in the scene.
- How many triangles in the scene.

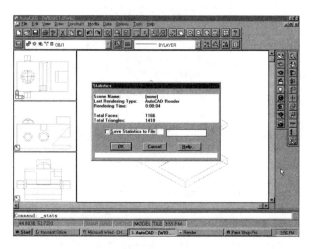

FIGURE 10.15 Render Statistics dialogue box.

The dialogue box also allows you to save the information to an ASCII text file for later reference.

LIGHTS

AutoCAD has four different light sources available in the AutoCAD software. They include:

- **The Point light** to create a light source similar to the sun, spreading the light in all directions.

- The Distant light to create a light source that shines in one direction and does not have a cone. A "real world" laser is an example of this kind of light source, because the light beams are parallel and they do not diminish over distance.

- **The Spotlight** that shines in one direction but spreads out as it leaves the light source creating a cone effect.

- **The Ambient light** is the general background light that exists everywhere in nature. Starlight or reflective light add to the general ambient light in a scene. A room with all the doors and windows closed still has some light that trickles in from under the blinds or through the door cracks. That light is the ambient light of that room.

The point light and the spotlight can emit a light that falls off in a mathematical relationship called *attenuation*. The attenuation settings are as follows:

- **None** turns off the attenuation and makes objects far from the light appear as bright as objects close to the light.

- **Inverse Linear** uses the value of half the extent's distance (the distance from the minimum lower-left coordinates to the maximum upper-right coordinates) to calculate the light intensity.

- **Inverse Square** takes half the square of the extent's distance as the light intensity.

Each method has its application in various situations. The flexibility of the settings in conjunction with the types of lights available allow you to create most real–world lighting effects.

One serious drawback to creating a photo-realistic rendering using the core rendering commands is the lack of shadow cast by the lights.

NOTE

All lights in AutoCAD can be assigned a color. Colored lights change the overall scene by adding to the color of the object or material on the object. Before adjusting color in your lights, you need to practice how to create and modify a light. The lights in the next few practice procedures have no color assigned.

Place all lights on their own lights layer for better control.

TIP

The Lights Dialogue Box

This dialogue box is used to control the creation, removal, and modification of all light types, along with the color and intensity of the light. The dialogue box is shown in Figure 10.16.

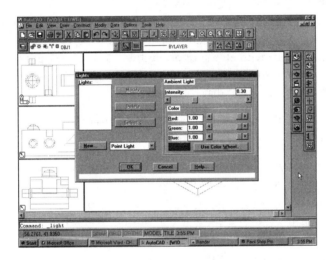

FIGURE 10.16 Lights dialogue box.

The various buttons on the dialogue box are:

- The **Modify...** button allows you to set the intensity and the color for the light, to position the light in 3D space, and to change the name of the light.

- The **Delete** button allows you to remove an unwanted light.

- The **Select<** button allows you to select an existing light for modification or information.

- The **New...** button allows you to create a new light of the type listed in the poplist next to the button. The dialogue box is the same as the Modify button dialogue box and allows you to control all the same functions of the light.

- The **Ambient light intensity** slider bar allows you to control how much ambient light is in the scene.

- The **Color** slider bars allow you to assign a color to the ambient light in the scene.

- The **Use Color Wheel...** button allows you to use another dialogue box to assign the color to the ambient light.

The dialogue boxes that some of the above buttons call are covered in detail in the following section.

The Point Light

This light can be viewed as an extension of ambient light. The light is omni-directional and the intensity does fall off over a distance. The sun and moon are "real world" point lights (even though the moon is only reflecting light from the sun). This is a light that washes over a scene, covering all of the objects in the scene. Place a point light in a scene and render the scene.

Practice Procedure for Creating a Point Light

1. In the *Widget* drawing, type **light** to activate the LIGHT command.
2. Select the **New...** button to begin the creation process in the New Point Light dialogue box, shown in Figure 10.17.
3. Type **sun** in the Light Name edit box.
4. Select the **Modify<** button to position the light in 3D space.
5. Use the .XY filter to select the point P1 as shown in Figure 10.17.
6. Select the P2 point as the Z axis point as shown in Figure 10.17.
7. Set the Intensity to **15.00** and select **OK** to exit the New Point Light dialogue box.
8. Select **OK** to exit the LIGHT command dialogue box.
9. Make the large ISO Viewport the active Viewport and use the RENDER command to render the scene.

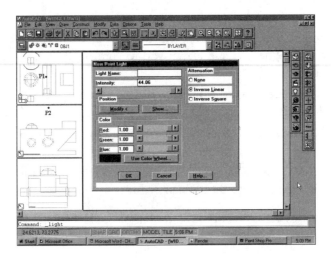

FIGURE 10.17 New Point Light dialogue box.

The results of the point light placement are shown in Figure 10.18, and the results of the rendering using the sun are shown in Figure 10.19.

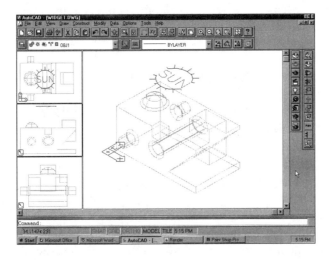

FIGURE 10.18 Sun Point Light practice procedure results.

NOTE

The light icon saying SUN is the proper size because you set the lights icon scale to 25 in preferences earlier.

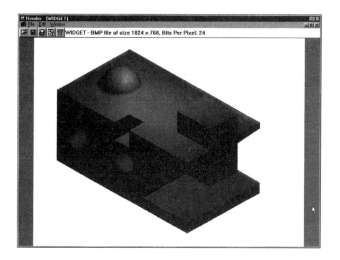

FIGURE 10.19 Sun Point Light render results.

319

NOTE

You can use the **Modify** button for the highlighted light in the Light dialogue box to change intensity settings for a light or the lights color. More often than not, you must experiment with the intensity by adjusting it and rendering the scene a few times to find a good setting.

The Distant Light

This light source is the laser light inside the computer. The beam it throws does not drop off in intensity as distance is increased between the light and the object, and the beam does not form a cone (spread out). The light is unidirectional, which means that you must aim it at a target location from a source location. The dialogue box for creating and controlling the distant light is shown in Figure 10.20. Using the UCS to place the light is one of the quickest techniques. Add a laser distant light to the widget scene.

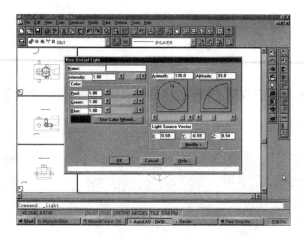

FIGURE 10.20 New Distant light dialogue box.

Practice Procedure for Creating a Distant Light

1. In the *Widget* drawing, use the ZOOMALL supplied routine and then use the ZOOM .5x scale option in each of the small viewports. Leave the large viewport the active viewport.

2. Adjust the UCS to the position shown in Figure 10.21. The origin is approximately the center of the hole by the point P1 (.XY) with the Z axis shown as point P2. The UCS is rotated on the X axis by 90 degrees.

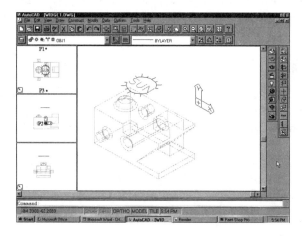

FIGURE 10.21 New Distant light practice procedure reference.

3. Type **light** to activate the LIGHT command.

4. Select the **Distant light** poplist item from the **New...** poplist (currently it is set to **Point Light**).

5. Select the **New...** button to begin the creation process in the New Distant light dialogue box, shown in Figure 10.20.

6. Type **laser1** in the Light Name edit box.

7. Select the **Modify<** button to position the light in 3D space.

8. Use the .Z filter to position the target of the light at the point P3 and select the point P2 (for the XY part of the target point), as shown in Figure 10.21.

9. Type **0,0,0** for the source of the light.

10. Select **OK** to exit the New Distant light dialogue box and **OK** to exit the Light dialogue box.

11. Use the supplied ZOOMALL routine to adjust the Viewports.

12. Use the VPOINT command to rotate the view to 45 degrees in the XY plane and 33 degrees from the XY plane and use the ZOOM Window option to get in close to the object as shown in Figure 10.22.

13. Use the RENDER command to render the scene.

321

The results of the light placement are shown in Figure 10.22 and the results of the rendering are shown in Figure 10.23.

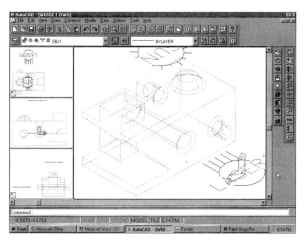

FIGURE 10.22 New Distant light practice procedure results.

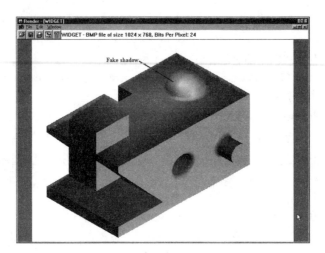

FIGURE 10.23 New Distant light rendering results.

The rendering has what appears to be a shadow on the globe top. You can sometimes fake shadows using the distant light with the point light. This technique is difficult to reproduce consistently.

N O T E

The Spotlight

The spotlight in the computer behaves the same as a spotlight in the real world. It has a cone because it spreads out over distances, and the intensity drops off as the light is moved further away from the object. Spotlights are best placed in pairs at intersecting angles from each other. One technique is to place one intense spotlight above the object along the line of view with a second weaker intensity spotlight on the same face but on the other end of the object and underneath the object. This technique creates a nice contrast. Another technique is to place the same types of spotlights over and under the object but at diagonal corners from each other. Some people like to use three lights and mix these settings. The rule of thumb for lighting is to keep the amount of lights down, always have one spotlight stronger than the rest, and keep the lights at angles from each other. This creates depth in the image.

The spotlight has two extra settings to control the cone effect. They are called the hotspot and falloff. The *hotspot* is the circular area of the highest intensity light inside the cone. The *falloff* is the area of light outside the hotspot that gradually gets weaker as it moves to the outside of the cone. The hotspot setting can never be larger than the falloff setting. Try creating some spotlights.

Practice Procedure for Creating a Spotlight

1. In the *Widget* drawing, use the VPOINT command to rotate the view to 315 degrees *in* the XY plane and 33 degrees *from* the XY plane. Use the ZOOM Window option to get in close to the object in the large Viewport, as shown in Figure 10.25.

2. Use the ZOOMALL supplied routine and then use the ZOOM .5x scale option in each of the small viewports and leave the large viewport the active viewport.

3. Type **light** to activate the LIGHT command.

4. Select the **Spotlight** poplist item from the **New...** poplist (currently it is set to **Distant** light).

5. Select the **New...** button to begin the creation process in the New Spotlight dialogue box, shown in Figure 10.24.

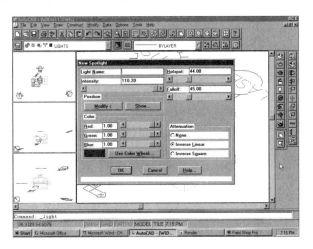

FIGURE 10.24 New Spotlight dialogue box.

6. Type **spot1** in the Light Name edit box.

7. Select the **Modify<** button to position the light in 3D space.

8. Select the point P1, shown in Figure 10.25, as the target point for the spotlight.

9. Use the .XY filter to position the source of the light at the point P2 and select the point P3 (for the Z part of the source point), as shown in Figure 10.25.

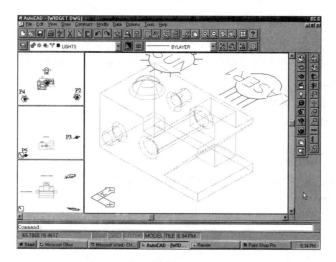

FIGURE 10.25 New Spotlight practice procedure reference.

10. Select the **OK** button to exit the New Spotlight dialogue box.

11. Do steps 4 through 9 to create another spotlight called spot2. Make the position of the light (step 8) correspond to the target point P1 and the source points P4 and P5. Set the intensity of the SPOT2 spotlight to 52.00.

12. After creating the second light in step 10, select **OK** to exit the Light dialogue box.

13. Use the supplied ZOOMALL routine to adjust the viewports.

14. Adjust the large viewport to a close up view.

15. Use the RENDER command to render the scene.

The results of the spotlights placement are shown in Figure 10.26, and the results of the rendering are shown in Figure 10.27.

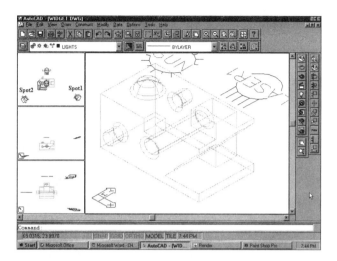

FIGURE 10.26 New Spotlight practice procedure results.

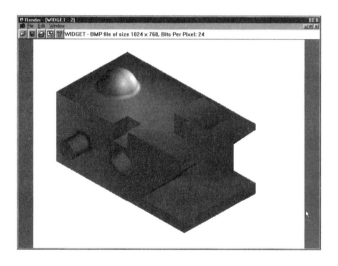

FIGURE 10.27 New Spotlight rendering results.

The position of the lights is critical to the creation of a good-looking image. It takes a lot of practice and experimentation to get good at placing lights. All of the lights created in this section were given no color. When you add color to the mix, it gets even tougher to create a realistic-looking image.

Colored Lights

Adding color to your lights has several effects on the final image. You can use complementary color on two opposing lights to create highlights on the object. The color also affects the color of the object. It takes a lot of study to be able to blend colored light effectively with the material on an object or the color of the object to create the image you desire. Adjusting existing lights color is accomplished by using the Modify light dialogue box, the Color dialogue box, and/or the Select a Color dialogue box:

- The **Modify** dialogue box allows you to use slider bars on the individual RGB (Red, Green, and Blue) colors to blend a color or use the **Use Color Wheel...** button to access the Color dialogue box.

- In the **Color** dialogue box you can use the RGB system or the HLB (Hue, Luminance, and Brightness) system to set the color, or you can use the **Select from ACI...** button to access the Select a Color dialogue box to select the color.

- The **Select a Color** dialogue box allows you to select from the standard AutoCAD color chart.

Understanding color mixing and the effect it has on your objects is more complex than this book has the space to explain. Use the **Modify** button on the Light dialogue box to adjust the color of the existing lights you created earlier in this chapter. Try adjusting the light color.

Practice Procedure for Adjusting the Color of Lights

1. In the *Widget* drawing, use the ZOOMALL supplied routine and then use the ZOOM .5x scale option in each of the small viewports and zoom in close on the object in the large Viewport (this is the position of the last practice procedure).

2. Type **light** to activate the LIGHT command.

3. Select the **SPOT1** lights item and use the **Modify** button to activate the Modify spotlight dialogue box.

4.   Select the **Use Color Wheel...** button to access the Color dialogue box shown in Figure 10.28.

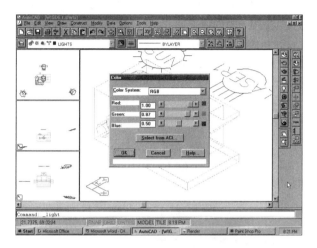

FIGURE 10.28 Color dialogue box.

5.   Use the **Select from ACI...** button to access the Select a Color dialogue box.

6.   Set the **Color:** edit box to **41** or select the circled square as shown in Figure 10.29.

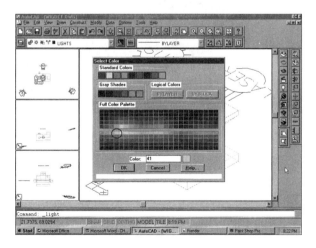

FIGURE 10.29 Select color dialogue box for practice reference.

327

7. Select **OK** on the last three dialogue boxes to get back to the Lights dialogue box.

8. Select the **SPOT2** lights item and use the **Modify** button to activate the Modify spotlight dialogue box.

9. Repeat steps 4 through 7, giving the color 151 for the color in step 6.

10. Select the **LASER1** lights item and use the **Modify** button to activate the Modify spotlight dialogue box.

11. Set the Intensity to **zero** and select **OK** to exit the Modify Distant Light dialogue box.

12. Select **OK** to exit the Lights dialogue box.

13. Use the RENDER command to render the scene.

The results of the adjusted color on the lights are shown in Figure 10.30 (in gray scale). Notice that your color adds a highlight effect to the object.

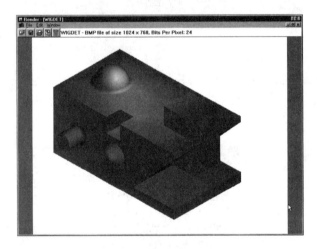

FIGURE 10.30 Lights color adjustment practice procedure results.

This image actually has three colored lights: the two you adjusted and the SUN point light which is still a white light. Change the sun light to the color 41 and render the image again.

Practice Procedure for Adjusting the Color of the Sun Light

1. Type **light** to activate the LIGHT command.

2. Select the **SUN** lights item and use the Modify button to activate the Modify Point light dialogue box.

3. Select the **Use Color Wheel...** button to access the Color dialogue box, shown in Figure 10.28.

4. Use the **Select from ACI...** button to access the Select a Color dialogue box.

5. Set the **Color:** edit box to **41** or select the circled square as shown in Figure 10.29.

6. Select **OK** on the last three dialogue boxes to get back to the Lights dialogue box.

7. Select **OK** to exit the Lights dialogue box.

8. Use the RENDER command to render the scene.

The results of the adjusted color on the sun is shown in Figure 10.31 (in gray scale). Notice that adding the same color to the sun as you used for the hot spotlight creates a wash on the top of the object while the highlight remains on the front.

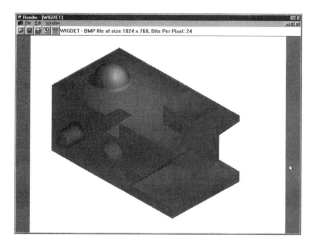

FIGURE 10.31 Sun light color adjustment practice procedure results.

Ambient Light

You can use the ambient light color to wash away some of the highlight to give a matte finish look to your object.

Too much intensity on the ambient light can cause the image to wash away and look flat.

TIP

Wash your image using the light blue highlight color you used for the weak spotlight (spot2).

Practice Procedure for Adjusting the Color of the Sun Light

1. Type **light** to activate the LIGHT command.
2. Select the **Use Color Wheel...** button (from the Lights dialogue box in the Ambient Light Color area) to access the Color dialogue box shown in Figure 10.28.
3. Use the **Select from ACI...** button to access the Select a Color dialogue box.
4. Set the **Color:** edit box to **151** as shown in Figure 10.29.
5. Select **OK** on the last two dialogue boxes to get back to the Lights dialogue box.
6. Select **OK** to exit the Lights dialogue box.
7. Use the RENDER command to render the scene.

The results of the adjusted ambient light color is shown in Figure 10.32 (in grayscale). Notice that adding the weak spotlight color to the ambient background light creates a subtle wash on the object, while the highlight on the front and the hot spot remains.

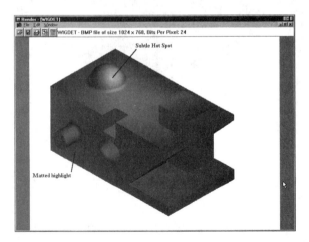

FIGURE 10.32 Ambient light color adjustment practice procedure results.

SCENES

Scenes are handy for experimenting with lighting. You can turn off a light by setting its intensity to zero (like you did to the laser light). This technique is awkward and hard to keep track of in complex scenes. Scenes save the lights and view. You can also set a scene to use the current view with or without lights. This flexibility makes scenes very useful.

Several techniques are available for using scenes to control and experiment with your image. One technique is to set a scene for each light and then use the scene to activate lights by adding or removing lights from the scene. Another technique is to use one light for one scene, and then activate each scene to adjust the intensity and color of the light. Then add all of the lights to one final scene to view the results. Many more variations on these techniques exist. You can experiment with scenes to control your production of rendered images. Scenes are created, modified, and removed by using the SCENE command and the Scene dialogue box (shown in Figure 10.33). The dialogue box has a **New...** button to create a new scene, a **Modify...** button to make changes to an existing scene, and a **Delete** button to remove an existing scene. Try creating several scenes using lights with the Scenes dialogue box.

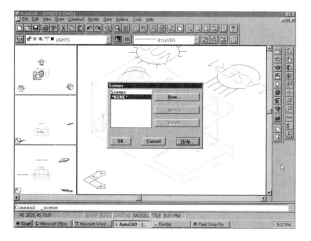

FIGURE 10.33 Scene dialogue box.

Practice Procedure for Creating Scenes

   1.   Type **scene** to activate the SCENE command.

2. Select the **New...** button to activate the New Scene dialogue box, shown in Figure 10.34.

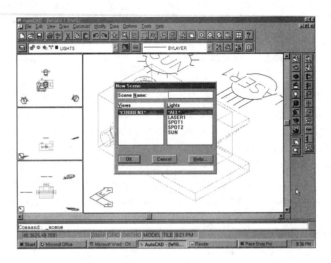

FIGURE 10.34 New Scene dialogue box.

332

3. Give the scene the name **ALL** and select the **ALL lights** item from the Lights list box.

4. Select **OK** to exit the New Scene dialogue box.

5. Create a scene for each light (using the light's name) by repeating steps 2 through 4 until all are created.

6. Create a scene named **Front** using the two spotlights (select both from the Lights list box).

The final result in the Scene dialogue box is shown in Figure 10.35.

TIP

The list of scenes adds the new scene name to the top of the list. There is no sorting the names or shifting of the names. Many people create the scenes in the reverse order of how they want them to appear so that they appear in the correct order. The most-used scene should be near the top of the list.

Practice using the scenes.

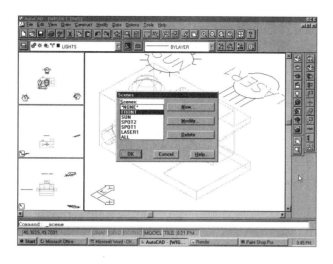

FIGURE 10.35 Creating scene results.

Practice Procedure for Using the Named Scenes to Render

1. Use the RENDER command to activate the Render dialogue box.

2. Select the desired scene name from the Scene to Render list box.

3. Select the **Render Scene** button.

4. Repeat steps 1 through 3 for each scene and view the results each time.

As you see which scenes work, you can experiment by adding a light or removing a light from a scene. This technique for experimenting with the lighting shaves time from your production time.

The LASER1 light was left with a setting of zero in the last procedure. By changing the intensity of that light along with the other lights, you create a complex scene.

NOTE

RENDERING COMMANDS AND TOOLS MENU LOCATIONS

The Rendering commands and tools are found on the *Render* menu item of the *Tools* pull-down menu and on the *Render* toolbar, as shown in Figure 10.36.

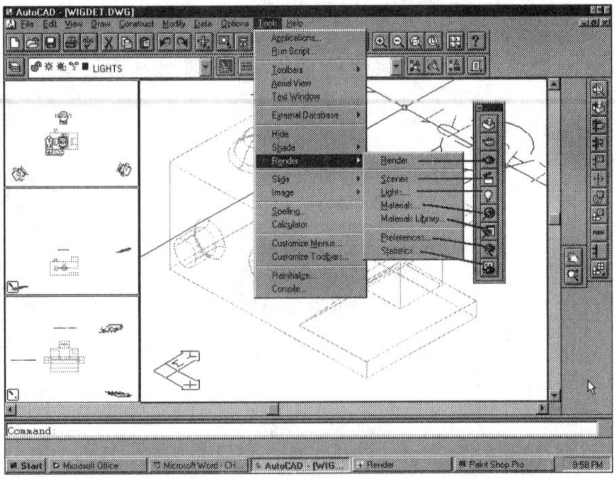

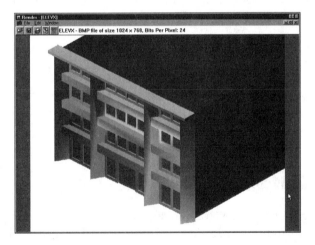

FIGURE 10.36 Render commands and tools menu locations.

Chapter Exercise

334

You saved an elevation drawing from a practice procedure in Chapter 9 called ELEVX. Use that drawing to place lights and scenes and render the results. Using the simple standard setting covered in this chapter, the image in Figure 10.37 was created.

FIGURE 10.37 Rendered image of the elevation drawing.

In Conclusion

In this chapter, you had the opportunity to practice the rendering commands and tools available in the AutoCAD software. Techniques for placing lights and assigning colors to the lights were covered. The equipment needed to produce realistic renderings was discussed. The material covered in this chapter and the next chapter is only the first step toward creating realistic-looking renderings. Subjects like color, light, and staging need to be examined and practiced before you can successfully create complex images. In the next chapter, you are introduced to the material commands and tools used to assign materials to your objects.

CHAPTER ELEVEN

Rendering Materials

The last piece of the rendering puzzle in AutoCAD is the use of materials. A material is used by the rendering command to change the look of an object. In the real world, a material like cloth is used to change the color and look (texture) of an object. Materials in AutoCAD are used the same way. You can assign a metallic-looking material to your object, a hard shiny plastic-looking material, or a flat-matte finish material. Materials can have any of the colors of the palette. The use of materials in AutoCAD is severely limited when compared to other rendering packages. You are not given tools like texture mapping or opacity maps. These are features that are found in higher-end products like AutoVision or 3D Studio. Despite this limitation, materials enhance the image and give you a better looking product.

Controlling Materials

AutoCAD has two commands for controlling materials. The first command is the RMAT command for attaching and detaching materials to an object. The second is the MATLIB command for creating materials and managing them in a library. The materials library serves the same function for materials as a block library serves for blocks. It is used to organize the materials into one file that contains all the materials used in a drawing or project.

THE MATERIALS LIBRARY

The MATLIB command activates a dialogue box for manipulating material libraries. The dialogue box is shown in Figure 11.1. AutoCAD ships with a material library called RENDER.MLI that contains many materials ready for use.

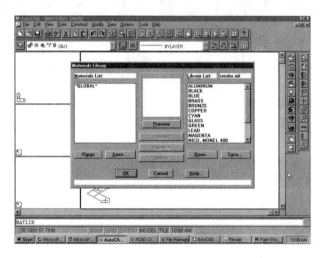

FIGURE 11.1 Materials library dialogue box.

The dialogue box consists of three working areas. The left area is the Materials List and it contains a list of those materials selected from the library for use in your drawing. The right area is the Library List that contains a list of all of the materials available in the current library. The center area is a Preview area for testing how a material looks. Each area has a set of buttons underneath it that allow you to control some facet of the area above. The buttons include:

- The **Purge** button to remove any unused materials from the Material List area.

- The **Save** button to save the list of materials in the Materials List area to a file of your choice.

- The **Open** button to access any material library file and place it into the Library List area.

- The **Preview** button for viewing the current material. This button is only active when one material is selected in either of the list areas. Selecting two materials or more disables the button.

- The **Import** button to place any highlighted materials in the Library List area into the Materials List area.

- The **Export** button to place any highlighted materials in the Materials List area into the Library List area.

- The **Delete** button to remove any materials that are highlighted in either List area.

Practice the various dialogue box functions.

Practice Procedure for the Materials Library Dialogue Box:

1. Open the drawing *Material*.

2. Type **matlib** and press **Enter** to activate the materials library dialogue box, shown in Figure 11.1.

3. Select the **LEAD** material from the Library List area.

4. Select **Preview** in the Preview area.

The result is shown in Figure 11.2. You can preview any one item from either the Library List or the Materials List.

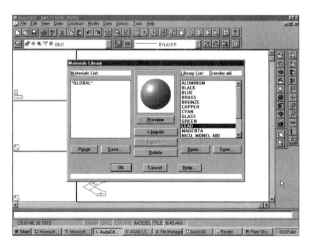

FIGURE 11.2 Materials library preview.

The Open Button

This button allows you to attach a variety of material libraries. This book ships with a customized materials library for use in this chapter. Attach that library using the materials library dialogue box.

Practice Procedure for Using Alternate Material Libraries:

1. In the *Material* drawing, type **matlib** to activate the materials library if you are not already in the dialogue box.

2. Select the **Open...** button to activate the Library File input dialogue box, as shown in Figure 11.3, for selecting a library.

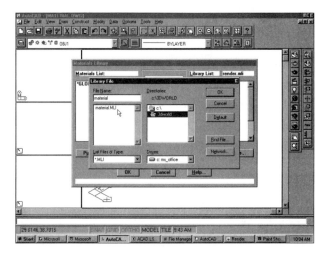

FIGURE 11.3 Library File input dialogue box.

3. Select the library **MATERIAL** from the 3DWORLD directory as shown in Figure 11.3 (double click select the **OK**).

You now have all of the materials in the library available for importing into your drawing.

The Import Button

None of the materials in the library are available for use in your drawing until you select them from the Library List area and use the Import button to place them in the Materials List area. Place some materials into the Materials List area.

Practice Procedure for Importing Materials into the Materials List Area

1. Do the last practice procedure before continuing.

2. Select the material items BLUE GRASS, BRASS, CHECKER OPACITY, DARK WOOD TILE, and GLASS from the Library List area, as shown in Figure 11.4.

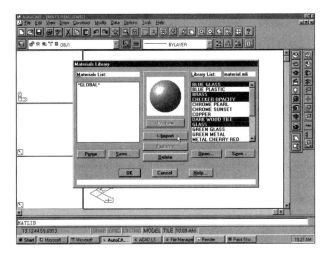

FIGURE 11.4 Import practice reference.

3. Select the **<-Import** button to copy their definitions into the Materials List area.

The results are shown in Figure 11.5. The materials in the Materials List area are now available for your use in the drawing.

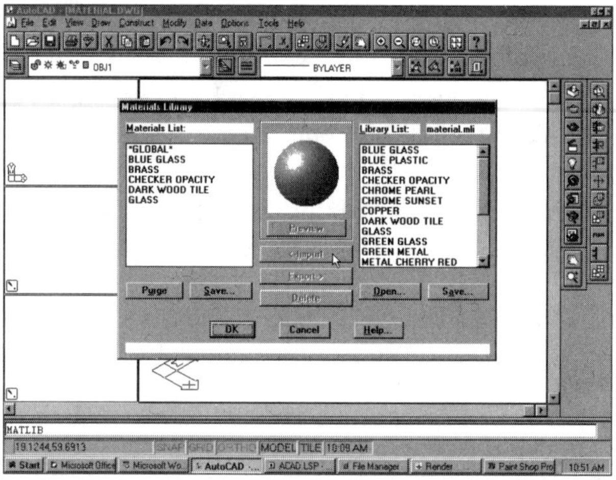

FIGURE 11.5 Import practice results.

The Save Button for the Material List

Once you have selected the materials for use in your drawing, you can save those materials into their own library. Some people do not like to do this because it takes additional file management and disk space, but when you name the new material library the same as the drawing, management of the files is not hard. The advantage to this method is that you are not carrying around a large library of all materials for all projects, and you can customize individual materials for an object and it has no effect on the original global library. Save the current materials to their own library.

Practice Procedure for Saving Materials in the Materials List Area to a File

1. Complete the last practice procedure before continuing.

2. Select the **Save...** button under the Materials List area on the left of the dialogue box.

3. Give the library file the name *WIDGET* in your 3DWORLD directory, as shown in Figure 11.6 (because these materials are to be used on the widget object), and select **OK**.

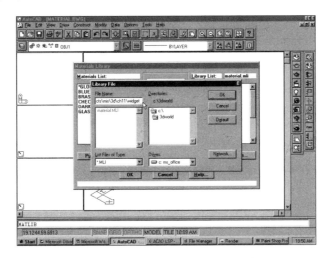

FIGURE 11.6 Save library file.

The materials are now saved to a library file for future use.

The Open Button

Attach the appropriate library file to the drawing using the **Open** button of the Materials Library.

Practice Procedure for Opening a New Materials Library File

1. Complete the last practice procedure before continuing.

2. Select the **Open...** button under the Library List area of the Materials Library dialogue box.

3. Select the **WIDGET** library from your 3DWORLD directory, as shown in Figure 11.7.

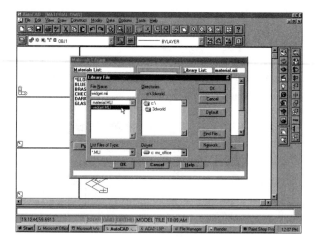

FIGURE 11.7 Open a library file.

The results are shown in Figure 11.8.

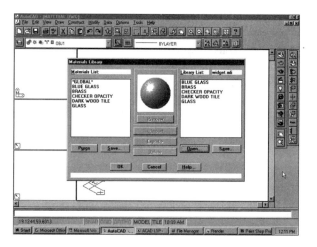

FIGURE 11.8 Open a library file practice results.

The Delete Button

The **Delete** button on the Materials Library dialogue box removes unwanted materials from the Material List. Remove a material using this button.

Practice Procedure for Removing a Material from the Materials List

1. Complete the last practice procedure before continuing.

2. Select the **BRASS** material from the Materials List area, of the Materials Library dialogue box, as shown in Figure 11.9.

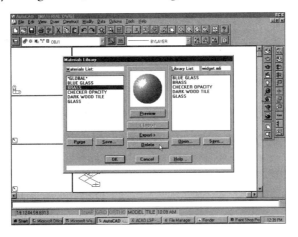

FIGURE 11.9 Removing a material from the Material List reference.

3. Select the **Delete** button under the Preview area.

The results are shown in Figure 11.10. Notice that the material is still in the Library List area.

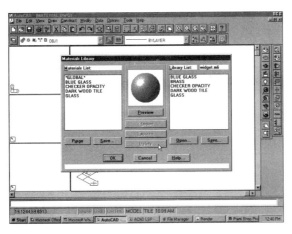

FIGURE 11.10 Removing a material from the Materials List results.

The Export Button

The **Export->** button takes an existing material in the Materials List and places it into the current library. You can place a new material into the library or replace an existing one. The Reconcile Exported Material Names dialogue box, shown in Figure 11.11, allows you to change the name of the exported material to a new name when the name already exists in the library.

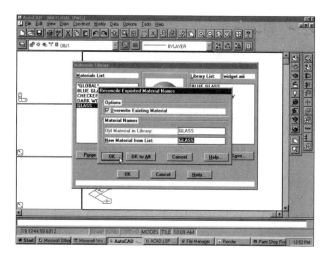

FIGURE 11.11 The Reconcile Exported Material Names dialogue box.

Replace an existing material using the **Export->** button.

Practice Procedure for Replacing a Material in the Library

1. Complete the last practice procedure before continuing.

2. Select the **GLASS** material from the Materials List area of the Materials Library dialogue box, as shown in Figure 11.12.

3. Select the **Export->** button under the Preview area as shown in Figure 11.12.

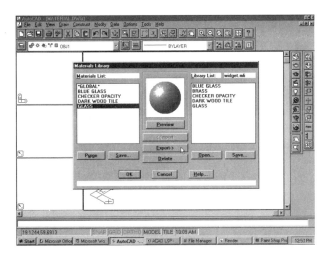

FIGURE 11.12 Export practice procedure reference.

4. Select **OK**, as shown in Figure 11.11, to accept the current name and replace the existing material definition in the library with the new definition.

5. Select **OK** on the Materials Library dialogue box to exit the dialogue box.

347

The Save Button for the Library List

The next step after exporting a material (new or modified) to the library is to save the library with the new definition out to a library file. You can use the same library file name or create a new library file (sort of a revision library). The **Save...** button under the Library List area is used to do the save. Since the material that was exported was not changed, it is not necessary to save the file at this time. The **Save...** button for the current library file behaves exactly the same as the **Save...** button for the Materials List area.

The last step of the above practice procedure exits the Material Library dialogue box and ends your examination of the features of the box. The drawing materials are now set up for working with the objects. Before moving to the placement of materials on objects and the various options, one last materials library feature is examined.

Using 3D Studio Material Libraries

Autodesk has made the materials library structure for AutoCAD the same as the materials library structure for 3DStudio. This allows you to use the 3DStudio material libraries in AutoCAD drawings. There are limitations on some of the material types that are allowed in 3DStudio, but not in AutoCAD. The main limitation is the lack of texture mapping in AutoCAD. Any material that has a texture map attached shows up as a black material. Materials containing bump maps or reflection maps look similar to the 3DStudio materials when applied in AutoCAD. Figure 11.13 shows four types of material mapping in 3DStudio, the same materials look similar in AutoCAD.

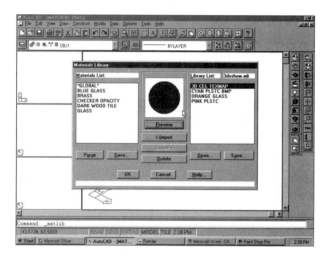

FIGURE 11.13 3DStudio materials library in 3DStudio.

Try viewing the same materials in AutoCAD.

Practice Procedure for Viewing 3DStudio Materials in a 3DStudio Library

1. In the Material drawing, type **matlib** and press **Enter** to activate the MATLIB command.

2. Select the **Open...** button and chose the **3DSSHOW** materials library from your 3DWORLD directory.

3. View all of the materials in the library one at a time by using the **Preview** button as shown in Figure 11.14.

All of the materials appear similar to the ones shown in Figure 11.13 (3DStudio) except the 3D CEL TEXMAP material. That material has a texture map as part of its definition. It appears black in AutoCAD materials preview since AutoCAD does not support texture maps in materials.

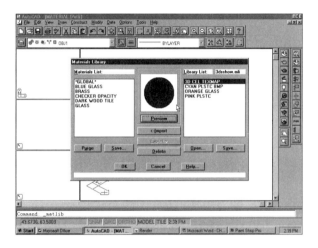

FIGURE 11.14 3DStudio materials library in AutoCAD.

MATERIALS PROPERTIES

The RMAT command activates the Materials dialogue box shown in Figure 11.15. This dialogue box allows you to manipulate materials in the following manner:

- You can modify a material's properties (color and color attributes).
- You can duplicate an existing material (giving it a new name).
- You can create a new material from scratch.
- You can access the Materials Library dialogue box.
- You can control the attachment of materials to objects.

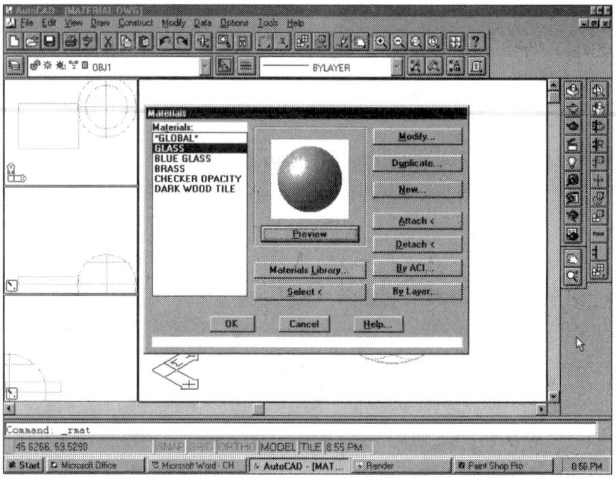

FIGURE 11.15 Materials dialogue box.

Modify a Material's Properties

The **Modify** button activates the Modify Standard Material dialogue box, shown in Figure 11.16. This dialogue box allows you to control the color attributes of the material and to assign a color to the material (the material's properties). Color attributes are as follows:

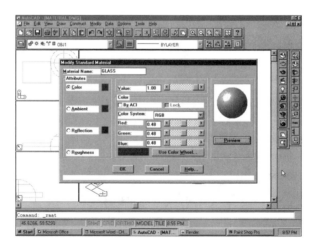

FIGURE 11.16 Modify Standard Material dialogue box.

- The **Color** is the general hue assigned to the whole object.

- The **Ambient colo**r is the shaded color on a sphere, as shown in Figure 11.17.

- The **Reflection color** is the highlight color on a sphere, as shown in Figure 11.17.

- The **Roughness** controls how large an area the Reflective color occupies on a sphere.

NOTE

The sphere shown in the dialogue box is not an object. Objects with curved surfaces best show the effect of ambient and reflective light. The color effects assigned affect all objects but they are more evident on objects, like spheres or cylinders.

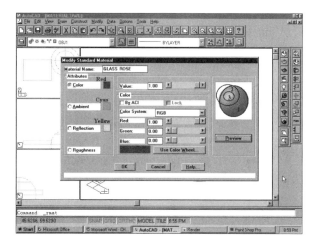

FIGURE 11.17 Color attribute example.

Try manipulating a material's property using the Modify dialogue box button.

NOTE

Before proceeding, use the MATLIB command to highlight all of the materials in the Materials List and delete them. Then attach the WIDGET library and import the GLASS material.

Practice Procedure for Modifying a Material's Properties

1. In the Materials dialogue box, highlight the GLASS material and select the **Modify...** button.

2. In the Modify Standard Material dialogue box, select the **Use Color Wheel...** button.

3. In the Color dialogue box, select the **Select from ACI...** button.

4. In the Select Color dialogue box, select the color **RED** and select **OK** until you are back at the Modify Standard Material dialogue box.

5. Select the **Ambient Attribute** and assign the color CYAN to it by repeating steps 2 through 4.

6. Select the Reflection Attribute and assign the color YELLOW to it by doing steps 2 through 4.

7. Change the name of the material to GLASS ROSE.

8. Use the **Preview** button to view your work and select **OK** to save the work and exit to the Materials dialogue box.

The results are shown in Figure 11.17. Circle #1 is the ambient color assigned to a sphere with the material. Circle #2 shows the area of the sphere that lets the color show. Circle #3 shows the area of the sphere that is the reflection. The reflection area is controlled by the Roughness button. You can select the Roughness button and use the Value slider above the color area to assign the degree of reflection on the sphere. The higher the value, the larger the reflection area. Try adjusting the reflection area.

Practice Procedure for Adjusting the Reflection Size

1. In the Modify Standard Material dialogue box (where you left off in the last procedure), select the **Roughness** button.

2. Use the Value slider bar to set the roughness to **1.0**.

3. Use the **Preview** button to view your work.

The results are shown in Figure 11.18. Notice that the yellow reflection area is now larger than the default reflection area shown in Figure 11.17. The Value slider bar works for each of the attribute buttons. The value selected is assigned to whichever button is active at the time.

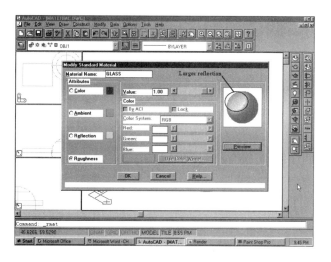

FIGURE 11.18 Reflection size adjustment results.

Duplicate a Material's Properties

The **Duplicate...** button allows you to copy an existing material, giving it a new name and making any adjustments to the new material you desire. Make a copy of the new GLASS ROSE material created in the last practice procedure.

Practice Procedure for Modifying a Material's Properties

1. In the Materials dialogue box, highlight the GLASS ROSE material and select the **Duplicate...** button.

2. In the New Standard Material dialogue box, change the material name to **GLASS BLUE**.

3. Set the Blue slider value to **1.0** and the Red slider value to **0.0**.

4. Use the Preview button in the New Standard Material dialogue box to view your changes. The sphere should look blue with a turquoise ambient color (cyan) and a light green highlight (yellow).

5. Select **OK** to exit to the Materials dialogue box.

The new material is created from the original and you have changed the color properties and the name. The last method of creating a material is the method of creating a new material from scratch.

Create a New Material Property

The **New...** button allows you to create a new material from scratch. The button activates the New Standard Material dialogue box (the same one that the **Duplicate...** button uses). The dialogue box has no color assigned to any of the attributes and no name is present in the Material Name edit box. Try creating a new material.

Practice Procedure for Creating a New Material

1. In the Materials dialogue box, select the **New...** button.

2. In the New Standard Material dialogue box, make the material name **GLASS YELLOW**.

3. Turn off the Color By ACI (AutoCAD Color Index).

4. Set the **Red** and **Green** slider values to **1.0**. This sets the color to yellow for all three color attributes.

5. Select the Ambient attribute and turn **off** the **Lock** button (and then turn **off** the **By ACI** button). By default, the three attributes are locked into the same color unless you turn off this button. Turning the Lock button off turns on the By ACI button. That is why you must also turn it off after turning off the Lock button.

6. Set the **Red** slider value to **1.0**, the **Green** slider value to **0.5**, and the **Blue** slider value to **1.0**.

7. Select the Reflection attribute and turn off the **Lock** button and the **By ACI** button.

8. Set the **Red** slider value to **0.5**, the **Green** slider value to **1.0**, and the **Blue** slider value to **1.0.**

9. Use the **Preview** button in the New Standard Material dialogue box to view your new material. The sphere should look yellow with a turquoise ambient color (cyan) and a light green highlight (yellow).

10. Select **OK** to exit to the Materials dialogue box.

The resulting materials list contains the modified GLASS ROSE material along with the duplicate GLASS BLUE material (with changes) and the new GLASS YELLOW material, as shown in Figure 11.19.

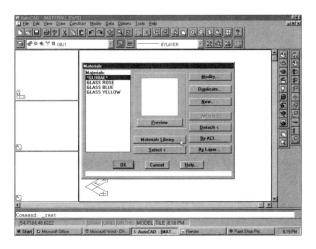

FIGURE 11.19 Modify, Duplicate, and New practice results.

NOTE

Before continuing, use the **Materials Library...** button on the Material dialogue box to attach the WIDGET library and import all of the materials (including the GLASS material again). Use the **Save...** button under the Material List area to save your materials to a file called TEST.MLI. Use the **OK** button to exit the Materials Library and the **OK** button in the Materials dialogue box to exit and save the changes.

ATTACHING MATERIALS TO OBJECTS

To attach a material to an object, you must select the desired material from the Material list in the Materials dialogue box and then choose the method button for the attachment. The Materials dialogue box (called by the RMAT command) contains several method buttons used for attaching a material to an object (or detaching it from and object):

▪ The **Attach <** button allows you to assign a material to objects by directly selecting them from the screen.

- The **Detach** < button allows you to remove the assignment of a material on objects by directly selecting them from the screen.

- The **By ACI...** button allows you to assign a material to objects by using the AutoCAD Color Index (ACI).

- The **By Layer...** button allows you to assign a material to objects by the layer the objects are on.

- The **Select** < button allows you to select an object to find out the material currently assigned to the object.

The following sections builds upon the work done in the previous section. You need to be in the MATERIAL drawing with the materials from the TEST library created earlier imported. Before proceeding with the attaching materials to object section, you need to have these steps done and you need to create two objects in the MATERIAL drawing for testing purposes.

Practice Procedure for Creating Test Objects

- In the MATERIAL drawing, create a solid sphere and a solid box as shown in Figure 11.20 (dimensions are not important).

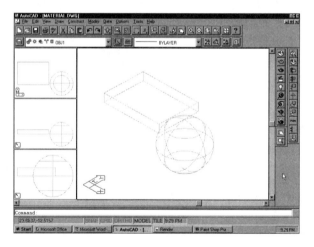

FIGURE 11.20 Test objects reference.

The Attach < Button

This attachment method button allows you to attach one material to one or more objects. Try attaching a material to the two objects using this method.

Practice Procedure for Attaching a Material

1. In the Materials dialogue box, with the TEST library attached and all of its materials imported, select the **GLASS ROSE** material in the Materials list on the left of the dialogue box.

2. Select the **Attach <** button.

3. Use a crossing box (or select one at a time) to **select both objects**.

4. Press **Enter** to exit the selection process.

5. Select **OK** to exit the Materials dialogue box.

6. Use the **RENDER** command to render the scene.

The results appear similar to those shown in Figure 11.21. The rendering is using a scene defined earlier for expediency sake.

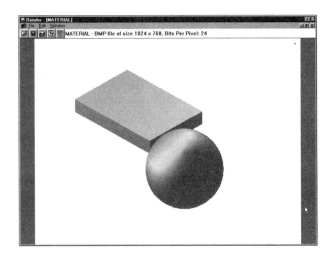

FIGURE 11.21 Attaching a material results.

The Detach < Button

Use the **DETACH** < button to remove materials from objects. Try removing the materials you just assigned in the last procedure.

Practice Procedure for Detaching a Material

1. In the Materials dialogue box, with the TEST library attached and all of its materials imported, select the **Detach** < button.
2. Use a crossing box (or select one at a time) to select both objects.
3. Press **Enter** to exit the selection process.
4. Select **OK** to exit the Materials dialogue box.
5. Use the **RENDER** command to render the scene.

The results appear similar to those shown in Figure 11.22. The color material is removed and the objects appear gray. Ambient and reflective light is missing because the object no longer has any material associated with it.

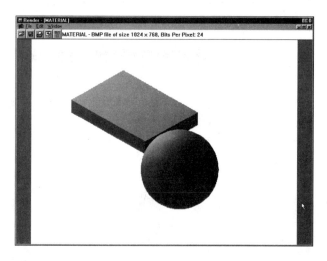

FIGURE 11.22 Detaching a material results.

The By ACI... Button

This button assigns the material by the AutoCAD Color Index. The object's color (whether by layer association or assignment) controls the material assignment.

When a color of 2 is assigned by using the ACI, all objects associated with that color are assigned the material. Try using the By ACI button to assign a material.

Practice Procedure for Attaching a Material Using the ACI... Button

1. In the Materials dialogue box, with the TEST library attached and all of its materials imported, select the **GLASS BLUE** material from the Material List.

2. Select the **ACI...** button.

3. Select item **9** in the Select ACI listbox in the Attach by AutoCAD Color Index dialogue box.

4. Select the **Attach >** button, as shown in Figure 11.23.

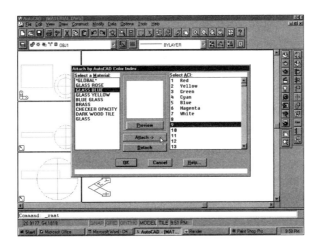

FIGURE 11.23 Attach by AutoCAD Color Index dialogue box.

5. Select **OK** to exit the Attach by AutoCAD Color Index dialogue box.

6. Select **OK** to exit the Materials dialogue box.

7. Use the **RENDER** command to render the scene.

8. Detach the material from both objects before continuing.

The results appear similar to those shown in Figure 11.24. The color of the objects are now the glass blue material. The Select ACI dialogue box allows you to quickly assign or remove any material to an object.

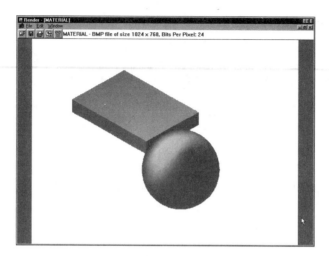

FIGURE 11.24 Detaching a material practice rendering results.

The By Layer... Button

This button allows you to attach a material to an object by the assigned layer name. Try assigning a material via the layer name.

Practice Procedure for Attaching a Material Using the By Layer... Button

1. In the Materials dialogue box, with the TEST library attached and all of its materials imported, change the solid box to the SOLID layer.
2. Select the **GLASS YELLOW** material from the Material List.
3. Select the **By Layer...** button.
4. Select the layer name **OBJ1** from the Select Layer listbox in the Attach by Layer dialogue box.
5. Select the **Attach >** button, as shown in Figure 11.25.
6. Select **OK** to exit the Attach by Layer dialogue box.
7. Select **OK** to exit the Materials dialogue box.
8. Use the **RENDER** command to render the scene.
9. Detach the material from the object before continuing.

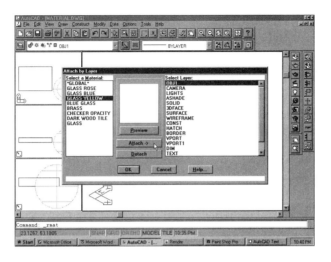

FIGURE 11.25 Attach by Layer dialogue box.

The results appear similar to those shown in Figure 11.26. The color of the object on the OBJ1 layer is now the glass yellow material while the object on the SOLID layer does not have a material assigned.

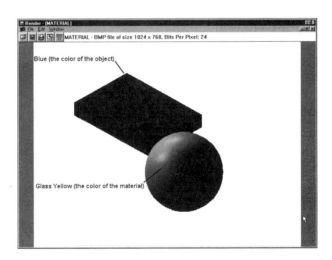

FIGURE 11.26 Assign a material by layer results.

RENDER MATERIALS COMMANDS MENU LOCATIONS

The rendering materials commands are found on the **Render** menu item of the **Tools** pull-down menu and on the **Render** toolbar as shown in Figure 11.27.

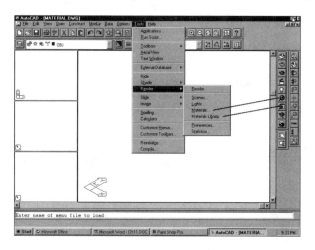

FIGURE 11.27 Render materials commands menu locations.

ASSIGNING A MATERIAL TO A PART

Assigning a material to a part is the same as many of the practice procedures used to show you the various features of the two materials dialogue boxes. Try placing a typical part into the drawing, attaching the appropriate library, selecting the correct material, and assigning the material to the part.

Practice Procedure for Attaching a Material to a Part

1. In the *Material* drawing, insert the *Widget* drawing at 0,0,0 with a scale factor or 1 and a rotation of 0.
2. Use the supplied ZOOMALL routine to adjust the viewports' views.
3. Use the **MATLIB** command to activate the Materials Library dialogue box.
4. Purge the current Materials List (delete any materials that were attached).
5. Open the WIDGET library and import all of the materials.
6. Select **OK** to exit the materials library dialogue box.

7. Use the **RMAT** command to activate the Materials dialogue box.

8. Attach the CHECKER OPACITY material to the widget object shown in Figure 11.28.

9. Exit the Materials dialogue box and render the scene.

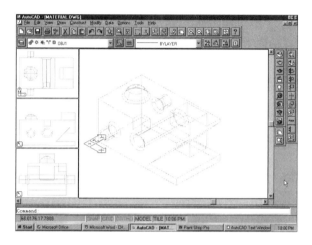

FIGURE 11.28 Attaching material to a part reference.

363

The results are shown in Figure 11.29. The CHECKER OPACITY material creates a rose-colored part. Practice detaching the material and attaching each of the other materials one at a time.

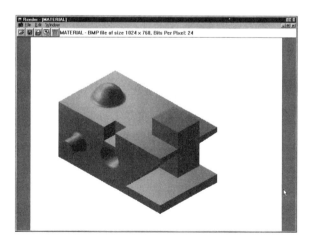

FIGURE 11.29 Attaching material to a part results.

TIP

Turn on the LIGHTS layer and adjust the SPOT2 light to a yellow color, then render the scene with the DARK WOOD TILE material attached. The default scene in the MATERIAL drawing uses the SPOT2 and SPOT3 lights. The resulting render has a nice mellow yellow glow to it.

ASSIGNING MULTIPLE MATERIALS TO MULTIPLE OBJECTS

All of the practice procedures used one material on an object. Architectural models contain multiple objects that need to have vastly different materials attached. Try setting up a simple scene with multiple materials.

TIP

You can delete the palm tree to speed up your rendering speed.

Practice Procedure for Attaching Multiple Materials

1. In the *Arch* drawing, import all of the materials from the ARCH material's library.

2. Use the Materials dialogue box to attach the materials shown in Figure 11.30 to the appropriate object (see the materials table below for reference).

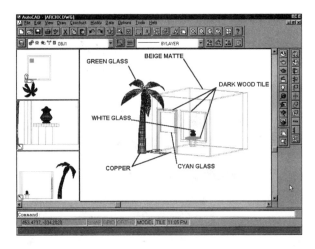

FIGURE 11.30 Multiple material attachment reference.

3. Exit the Material's dialogue box.

4. Restore the view called CLOSEUP and render the scene.

The results are shown in Figure 11.31. This drawing has the lights already set up along with the scenes. All of the settings were adjusted to get a quick image of how the building would look. The vase and palm tree are 3D surface meshes created in 3DStudio and imported into the AutoCAD drawing. This method of creating a quick image to get a feel for the structure is used extensively by professionals. Once the scene is selected, you can then proceed to play with the lights and adjust the materials to get a more realistic-looking image.

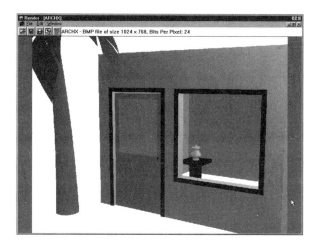

FIGURE 11.31 Multiple material attachment results.

TABLE 11.1 Materials Table.

Material	Associated Object
Beige Matte	Walls
Copper	Door and tree trunk
Cyan Glass	Door's Window
Dark Wood Tile	Trim around door and window, and vase table
Green Glass	Palm leaves
White Glass	Vase

In Conclusion

This chapter has taken you through all the tools and commands for manipulating materials in an AutoCAD drawing. The images that you can create with these tools and commands vary from simple to complex, depending on how much time you want to spend on the details of the relationship between materials, lights and view angles. In the next chapter, prototype drawings and toolbar customizing are examined. These two subjects can increase your productivity dramatically in 3D modeling.

CHAPTER TWELVE

3D Prototypes and Toolbars Equal Productivity

Productivity is generally measured as the amount of time it takes to complete a task. Simple tasks that only take five or ten minutes can be trimmed back to a couple of minutes by customizing your system. Productivity in 3D modeling is measured the same as in 2D drafting. The same tools used to increase productivity in 2D drafting are used to increase productivity in 3D modeling. Setting up your prototype drawing and creating customized toolbars for 3D go a long way towards increasing your productivity in 3D modeling.

3D Prototype

The prototype drawing allows you to begin your design process without having to set up your drawing environment every time you create a new drawing. Standard tools that are preset include:

- Named Views
- Named Viewports
- Layers
- Linetypes
- Named User Coordinate Systems

- Lighting
- Scenes

This section covers all but the layers. Layers in 3D modeling need to be setup just as layers in 2D drafting. The layer standards you choose need to reflect your company's work habits. Some extra layers need to be added for modeling, but they reflect your needs and only you can determine what layer names you need. The subjects covered in this section are generic in nature. The names used reflect general settings that are found in all disciplines of drawing. Add any discipline-specific settings to your prototype that you feel will benefit you and your users.

Settings that are used a high percentage of the time by many users are candidates for inclusion in your prototype drawing.

TIP

This section takes you through the creation of a 3D prototype drawing similar to the one supplied on the companion disk.

SET UP USER COORDINATE SYSTEMS

The UCS is used for controlling display, drawing, and editing your geometry. You can save a lot of time during production by setting up several generic named UCS in your prototype. The supplied 3DPROTO prototype drawing contains the most typical saved UCS. Here, you create those typical named UCS in your own 3D prototype drawing.

Determining Your UCS Needs

The supplied prototype drawing on the companion disk is based on an Architectural building footprint of 450 feet by 250 feet (limits set to 500' by 300'). The 3D prototype created in this section is based on a model part of 45 inches by 25 inches (limits set to 50 by 30). The UCS is positioned to the various planes of your object for quick positioning. You can then move the UCS to any origin on the plane that you need by using the UCS Origin option. Start the prototype creation by defining some standard User Coordinate Systems. Setup your new prototype drawing before continuing.

Practice Procedure for Creating a New 3D Prototype Drawing

1. Start a new drawing called *3Dseed* (use your 2D prototype drawing, not 3DPROTO).

2. Set your view to an ISO view of 315 degrees *in* the XY plane and 33 degrees *from* the XY plane in a single Viewport.

3. Set your limits to 0,0 and 50,30 and turn on your grid.

4. Create a solid box using the corner option at 0,0,0 with the dimensions 45 x 30 x 20 (XYZ) inside the limits and ZOOM Extents.

5. Save the prototype drawing 3DSEED.

Now you can start the process of adding your settings.

Practice Procedure for Creating Standard UCS in Your 3D Prototype

1. Use the UCS command to set the UCS to World and create a named UCS called PLAN.

2. Set the origin of the UCS to the point P1 as shown in Figure 12.1 and rotate the UCS 90 degrees on the X axis.

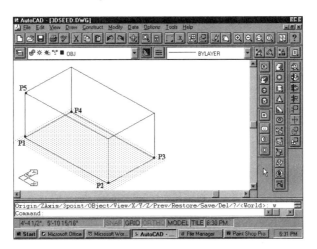

FIGURE 12.1 UCS creation practice reference.

3. Use the UCS command to create a named UCS called FRONT.

4. Use the UCS command to rotate the FRONT UCS around the Y axis 90 degrees and set the UCS origin to the point P2, as shown in Figure 12.1.

5. Use the UCS command to create a named UCS called RSIDE.

6. Use the UCS command to rotate the RSIDE UCS around the Y axis 90 degrees and set the UCS origin to the point P3, as shown in Figure 12.1.

7. Use the UCS command to create a named UCS called REAR.

8. Use the UCS command to rotate the REAR UCS around the Y axis 90 degrees and set the UCS origin to the point P4, as shown in Figure 12.1.

9. Use the UCS command to create a named UCS called LSIDE.

10. Use the UCS command to restore the named UCS PLAN and set the origin to the point P5, as shown in Figure 12.1.

11. Use the UCS command to create a named UCS called TOP12. Use the UCS command to rotate the TOP UCS around the Y axis 180 degrees and set the UCS origin to the point P2, as shown in Figure 12.1.

13. Use the UCS command to create a named UCS called BOTTOM.

14. Set the UCS back to the saved UCS called PLAN and save the drawing.

These steps create the basic UCS settings you need to quickly access the various faces of an object, as shown in Figure 12.2. Objects that are a different size than the prototype object can have the UCS changed to their faces by using the saved named UCS and then using the UCS Origin option with an object snap to place the UCS on the face of the object.

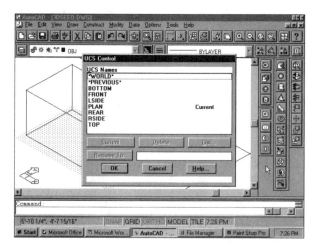

FIGURE 12.2 UCS creation practice results.

When you have sloping faces, you add saved UCS settings for the slopes.

TIP

NOTE

Creating a UCS for the World UCS (PLAN) might seem to be redundant, but the ability to pick the named UCS instead of having to use the UCS command with the World option comes in handy.

SET UP VIEWS

Different views on a large 2D part or buildings are handy in 2D drafting. Views in 3D can dramatically increase your productivity. When you combine the views with multiple viewport configurations, you get a very flexible system for accessing your object from any point of view.

Determining Your View Needs

Setting up four standard ISO views and views for the faces of the object allows you to quickly jump around your object. These standard views are based on your prototype object. That is why the object should be the largest object of the typical part or building you design. Restoring the views and then using the ZOOM or PAN command to refine the image increases your productivity. Create the basic ISO views in the prototype drawing.

Practice Procedure for Creating Basic ISO Views in Your 3D Prototype

1. In your *3Dseed* drawing, use the VPOINT command to setup an ISO view with a rotation of 45 degrees *in* the XY plane and 33 degrees *from* the XY plane.

2. Use the supplied ZOOMALL routine to position your view and use the VIEW command to save the image as ISO1 (for the first quadrant).

3. Use the VPOINT command to setup an ISO view with a rotation of 135 degrees *in* the XY plane and 33 degrees *from* the XY plane.

4. Use the supplied ZOOMALL routine to position your view and use the VIEW command to save the image as ISO2 (for the second quadrant).

5. Use the VPOINT command to setup an ISO view with a rotation of 225 degrees *in* the XY plane and 33 degrees *from* the XY plane.

6. Use the supplied ZOOMALL routine to position your view and use the VIEW command to save the image as ISO3 (for the third quadrant).

7. Use the VPOINT command to setup an ISO view with a rotation of 315 degrees *in* the XY plane and 33 degrees *from* the XY plane.

8. Use the supplied ZOOMALL routine to position your view and use the VIEW command to save the image as ISO4 (for the fourth quadrant).

9. Save your *3Dseed* drawing.

The resulting view names for the ISO views are shown in Figure 12.3.

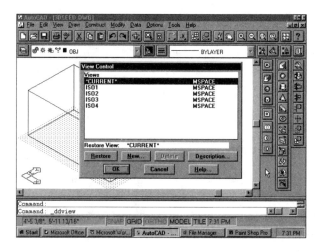

FIGURE 12.3 ISO views creation practice results.

Standard face views come in handy along with the ISO views. Create the standard face views.

Practice Procedure for Creating Basic ISO Views in Your 3D Prototype

1. In your *3Dseed* drawing, use the UCS command to restore the PLAN UCS.

2. Use the PLAN command and the supplied ZOOMALL routine to position the view, and use the VIEW command to save the view called PLAN.

3. Use the UCS command to restore the FRONT UCS.

4. Use the PLAN command and the supplied ZOOMALL routine to position the view, and use the VIEW command to save the view called FRONT.

5. Use the UCS command to restore the RSIDE UCS.

6. Use the PLAN command and the supplied ZOOMALL routine to position the view, and use the VIEW command to save the view called RSIDE.

7. Use the UCS command to restore the REAR UCS.

8. Use the PLAN command and the supplied ZOOMALL routine to position the view, and use the VIEW command to save the view called REAR.

9. Use the UCS command to restore the LSIDE UCS.

10. Use the PLAN command and the supplied ZOOMALL routine to position the view, and use the VIEW command to save the view called LSIDE.

11. Use the UCS command to restore the BOTTOM UCS.

12. Use the PLAN command and the supplied ZOOMALL routine to position the view, and use the VIEW command to save the view called BOTTOM.

13. Restore the World UCS and save the *3Dseed* drawing.

The resulting view names for the standard views are shown in Figure 12.4. They are now available at any time using the DDVIEW command.

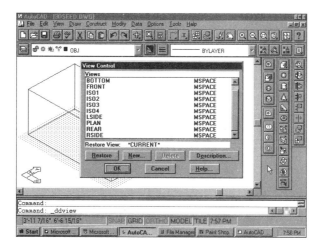

FIGURE 12.4 Standard views creation practice results.

SET UP VIEWPORTS

While viewports are handy in 2D drafting, they are almost mandatory for the design process of 3D modeling. Positioning an object in 3D is made easier by having multiple viewports, showing different views of the object, and point filters. Setting up some generic viewport configurations based upon your discipline's standard object size enables you to increase productivity.

Determining Your Viewport Needs

Architects design the viewports and their views around an average building footprint, while a manufacturer designs the viewports and views around an average part. Viewport configurations remember not only the size and shape of the viewports, but the view that each viewport contains. This enables you to setup some generic viewports with generic views of a typical object that you design. Create some typical viewport configurations for 3D modeling.

Practice Procedure for Creating Typical Viewport Configurations in Your 3D Prototype

1. In your *3Dseed* drawing, restore the ISO4 view (this assumes that you only have one viewport at this time).

2. Use the VIEWPORTS command to create a 2 Vertical Viewport configuration.

3. Use the VIEW command to restore the PLAN view in the left viewport, use the ZOOMALL routine to position the viewports, activate the right viewport, and use the VIEWPORTS command to create a viewport configuration called DOUBLE as shown in Figure 12.5.

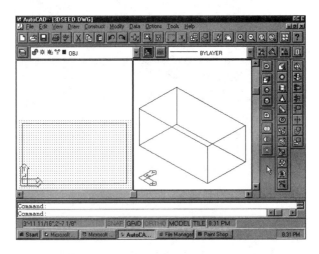

FIGURE 12.5 Viewport DOUBLE configuration creation practice result.

4. Restore the SINGLE viewport configuration.

5. Use the VIEWPORTS command to create a 4 viewport configuration as shown in Figure 12.6.

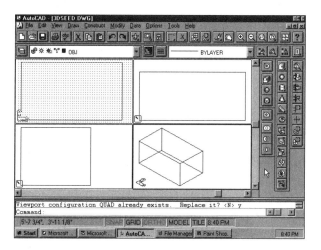

FIGURE 12.6 Viewport QUAD configuration creation practice result.

6. Use the VIEW command to restore the PLAN view in the upper left viewport, restore the FRONT view in the upper right viewport, restore the LSIDE view in the lower left viewport, and restore the ISO4 view in the lower right viewport.

7. Use the ZOOMALL routine to position the viewports, and use the VIEWPORTS command to create a viewport configuration called QUAD as shown in Figure 12.6.

8. Restore the SINGLE viewport configuration with the ISO4 view.

9. Use the VIEWPORTS command to create a 4 viewport configuration as shown in Figure 12.7.

10. Use the VIEW command to restore the PLAN view in the upper left viewport, restore the FRONT view in the middle left Viewport, restore the LSIDE view in the lower left viewport, and restore the ISO4 view in the large right viewport.

11. Use the ZOOMALL routine to position the viewports, and use the VIEWPORTS command to create a viewport configuration called 4R as shown in Figure 12.7.

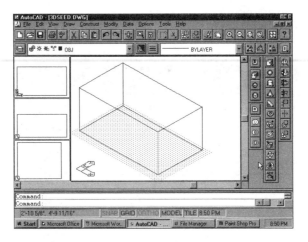

FIGURE 12.7 Viewport 4R configuration creation practice result.

12. Restore the SINGLE Viewport configuration with the ISO4 view and save the *3Dseed* prototype drawing.

These viewport configurations are but a few that can be made for increasing your productivity. As you model in 3D, you will develop your own standards. The supplied DDVPORTS routine, shown in Figure 12.8, allows you to quickly restore named viewports. The saved views came in handy for the creation of the viewport configurations and they are equally handy in production when combined with the viewport configurations.

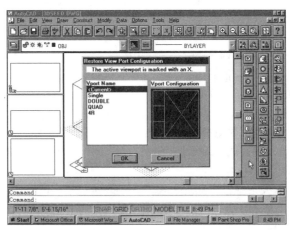

FIGURE 12.8 Viewport configuration DDVPORTS results.

SET UP FOR RENDERING

You can speed up your rendering by presetting your lights, cameras, and scenes in your prototype. This technique gives you standard scenes to render and allows you to experiment with more exotic views for your renderings.

NOTE Set your Lights Icon scale to 25 in your Render preferences dialogue box.

Setup Lights

A standard light setup is two spotlights at diagonally opposed corners slightly above the object, or two spotlights at opposite corners of the same face of the object. You can set up an additional point light as a sun source and turn it on or off as needed. In the prototype, you set up four spotlights (one at each corner of the object) and then you can turn the lights you desire on or off in production by creating scenes. Create the point and spotlight lights in your prototype drawing.

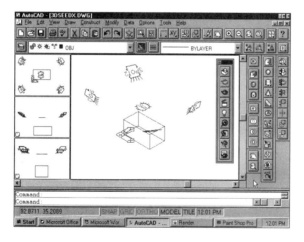

FIGURE 12.9 Lights practice reference.

Practice Procedure for Placing Lights in the Prototype

1. In your *3Dseed* drawing, restore the 4R Viewport configuration and make the LIGHTS layer current (create the layer if necessary).

2. Activate the LIGHT command.

3. Create a Point light called SUN giving it an intensity of 80, a color of 9 on the ACI color wheel, and a position of 22,16,42.

4. Create a spotlight called SPOT1 giving it Inverse Linear with an intensity of 40, a color of 9 on the ACI color wheel, and a position of target in the center of the object and the source at 75,51,50. Set the hotspot to 42 and the falloff to 84.

5. Create a spotlight called SPOT2 giving it Inverse Linear with an intensity of 40, a color of 9 on the ACI color wheel, and a position of target in the center of the object and the source at -30,51,50. Set the hotspot to 42 and the falloff to 84.

6. Create a spotlight called SPOT3 giving it Inverse Linear with an intensity of 60, a color of 9 on the ACI color wheel, and a position of target in the center of the object and the source at -30,-21,50. Set the hotspot to 42 and the falloff to 84.

7. Create a spotlight called SPOT4 giving it Inverse Linear with an intensity of 60, a color of 9 on the ACI color wheel, and a position of target in the center of the object and the source at 75,-21,50. Set the hotspot to 42 and the falloff to 84.

8. Set the ambient light to an intensity of .60 and a color of 9 on the ACI color wheel.

9. Exit the LIGHTS command dialogue box and save your *3Dseed* drawing.

10. Freeze your LIGHTS layer (create and make OBJ the current layer) and use the supplied ZOOMALL routine to position your viewport's views.

11. Thaw your LIGHTS layer.

12. Render your cube to see the lighting results as shown in Figure 12.10.

This setup allows you to have generic lighting around your object. You can set the intensity to zero for any light you wish to turn off in production, or you can set up scenes based on your lighting.

TIP Freezing the layer with the lights on it can cause unpredictable results when editing existing lights (the intensity value does not behave properly). Always thaw the lights layer before editing any lights.

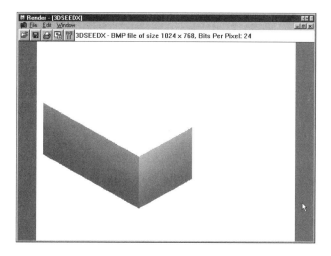

FIGURE 12.10 Lights practice results.

The results with all of the lights turned on is a washed out scene. Setting up scenes to control lights is a common practice and can have many benefits including increasing production speed.

Set Up Scenes

Creating generic scenes using the basic lighting defined above is a subjective task based upon the individual's needs and preferences. Some users prefer to have dramatic lighting while others prefer a more washed (brighter) look. The scenes in this prototype are set up to be as versatile as possible. You can create many more scene variations using just the four lights.

The view name portion of this command is currently shifting the rendered images to the left of the defined view. This is not the behavior you would expect, and it should be corrected in some upcoming release.

NOTE

The saved views can be handy but using the current view in conjunction with the scene is more flexible. Create 10 standard scenes in your 3DSEED prototype drawing.

Use only the CURRENT view in all of the scene creations in the following practice procedure.

NOTE

Practice Procedure for Creating Scenes in the Prototype

1. In your *3Dseed* drawing, restore the 4R Viewport configuration.

2. Activate the SCENE command.

3. Create a new scene called CUR-432 and select the spotlights numbered 4, 3, and 2.

4. Create a new scene called CUR-321 and select the spotlights numbered 3, 2, and 1.

5. Create a new scene called CUR-214 and select the spotlights numbered 2, 1, and 4.

6. Create a new scene called CUR-134 and select the spotlights numbered 1, 3, and 4.

7. Create a new scene called CUR-41 and select the spotlights numbered 4 and 1.

8. Create a new scene called CUR-32 and select the spotlights numbered 3 and 2.

9. Create a new scene called CUR-24 and select the spotlights numbered 2 and 4.

10. Create a new scene called CUR-13 and select the spotlights numbered 1 and 3.

11. Create a new scene called CUR-SUN and select the SUN light.

12. Create a new scene called CUR-ALL and select all of the lights.

13. Exit the SCENE command using **OK** and save your *3Dseed* prototype drawing.

14. Restore the scene called CUR–32, restore the view named ISO3, and render the object. The results are shown in Figure 12.11.

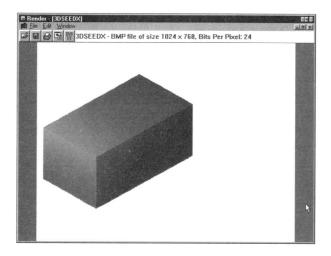

FIGURE 12.11 Scenes practice results with two-light scene.

15. Restore the scene called CUR–321 and render the object. The results are shown in Figure 12.12.

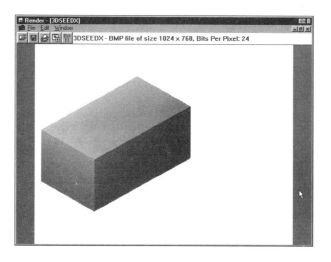

FIGURE 12.12 Scenes practice results with three-light scene.

These basic scenes can be changed during production, but the scenes do not have to be created over again by anyone wishing to render an object.

Customizing 3D Toolbars

Many of the 3D commands and tools are spread out among several different toolbars. Many of the system variables that pertain to 3D are missing from any menu. Organizing your 3D commands and tools into groups of related toolbars increases your productivity. Everything is at your fingertips. Try to keep the tools and commands organized into logical groups.

Creating and Editing Toolbars

AutoCAD Release 13 has given you the necessary tools to create your own toolbars. The tools are intuitive and you do not need to be a programmer to use them. It is necessary that you understand the relationship of the various menu files to avoid losing toolbar changes.

Menu Hierarchy

AutoCAD searches for the menus in a different order than prior to Release 13 (because there are new menu files). The files (for Windows) and their function are:

Filename	Function
XXX.MNC	Compiled menu that is loaded
XXX.MNR	Support bitmap resource menu
XXX.MNS	Source menu (same as .MNU with no comments or headers)
XXX.MNU	ASCII menu for editing

AutoCAD searches for the filename plus the extension in a set order. The search hierarchy order is shown in Figure 12.13.

```
                    ┌──────────── Is there a .MNC file? ────────────┐
                  Yes                                              No
                   │                                               │
     Is it newer than the .MNS file?                   Is there a .MNS file?
         │                        │                      │              │
       Yes                       No                     Yes             No
         │                        │                      │              │
   Load the .MNC file.     Compile the .MNS file.   Is there a .MNU file?
                           Load the .MNC file.          │              │
                                                       Yes             No
                                                        │              │
                                              Create a .MNS file.     Error
                                              Compile the .MNS file.  No load.
                                              Load the .MNC file.
```

FIGURE 12.13 AutoCAD menu search hierarchy.

NOTE

The .MNR file (not shown in Figure 12.13) is created each time a new .MNC file is compiled.

The search hierarchy is important because a new toolbar creation is stored in the .MNS file. That means that any new toolbars created are destroyed when you force the .MNU file to re-create the .MNS file. Autodesk suggests that you move the code that the toolbar creation tools place in the .MNS file to the .MNU file to avoid this problem. Many users feel that this is not a good solution (too much work). They are moving the original .MNU file from the search path or destroying it altogether. Accidents can't happen when the original .MNU file is not around anymore!

PRODUCTIVITY ROUTINES

This book ships with several productivity routines included. They are located on the partial menu called 3DWORLD (a partial menu is a menu that only contains pull-downs and/or toolbars for use with the MENULOAD command). The bitmaps that were used to create the toolbar are also included on the companion disk. This section takes the 3DWORLD partial menu and shows you how to add other tools to the toolbars, or create new toolbars.

TIP

Copy the 3DWORLD.MNS file in the companion directory to 3DWORLD.SAV in case you need to return to the original later.

How to Customize a Toolbar

There are four steps (dialogue boxes) used to customize a toolbar (adding or deleting a button). The first is the activation of the Toolbars dialogue box which lists all available toolbars and has some buttons for customizing. The dialogue box for the toolbars in the 3DWORLD menu is shown in Figure 12.14.

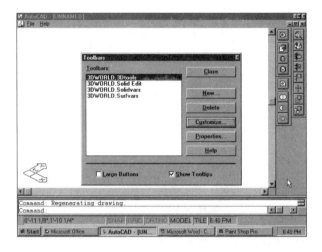

FIGURE 12.14 Toolbars dialogue box.

Attach the 3DWORLD menu as a standalone menu by using the MENU command to attach it instead of the MENULOAD command usually used to attach it.

N O T E

You activate the Toolbars dialogue box by selecting any toolbar button using the right mouse button (the **Enter** button). The dialogue box has several buttons for customizing a toolbar:

- The **New** button for creating new toolbars
- The **Delete** button to remove toolbars
- The **Customizing** button to add or delete buttons from a toolbar
- The **Properties** button to view the help information and the toolbar's alias

The **Properties** button is good for finding out what name the menu is using for a toolbar. You can then use that name with the TOOLBARS command to hide or show the toolbar. The **Delete** button removes the toolbar definition that is currently highlighted. There is no UNDO command for toolbar customizing; once you delete something it is gone for good. The **New** button is discussed later in this section. The **Customizing** button accesses the highlighted toolbar for adding or deleting buttons, using the dialogue box shown in Figure 12.15.

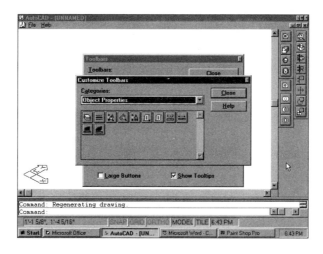

FIGURE 12.15 Customize Toolbars dialogue box.

PLAN

The second step to customizing a toolbar is to access the Custom dialogue box. The PLAN command is used often and is not on any toolbars. Add the PLAN command to the existing toolbar called 3DWORLD.3DTOOLS.

Practice Procedure for Adding a Button to a Toolbar

1. Attach the 3DWORLD menu using the MENU command.

2. Use the right mouse button (the **Enter** button) to activate the Toolbars dialogue box by clicking over any toolbar button.

3. Select the **3DWORLD.3Dtools** toolbar on the Toolbars dialogue box.

4. Select the **Customize...** button on the Toolbars dialogue box.

5. Select the **Custom** item from the Categories: list of the Customize Toolbars dialogue box.

6. Select the blank button and drag it over to the bottom of the toolbar, as shown in Figure 12.16.

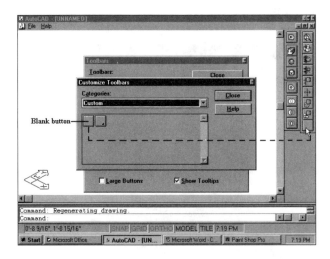

FIGURE 12.16 Customize Toolbars dialogue box Custom item.

The Custom item allows you to take a blank button or a blank flyout button and drag a copy to a toolbar. This new button can then be edited to add the necessary code and bitmap image. You can also choose from any existing button definitions by selecting the corresponding toolbar item from the Category list.

TIP

You can also move or copy any button from any toolbar on the screen (to copy, hold down the **Control** key before you select the button). Just select the button from the toolbar and drag it to the new toolbar.

The third step is to fill out the information about the button and the command associated to the button. This is done by activating the Button Programming dialogue box. The dialogue box is shown in Figure 12.17. The areas for button creation include:

- The Name for the Tool Tips.

- The Help for the status bar.

- The Macro area for supplying the command.

- The Button Icon area that shows what the selected button looks like.

- The Edit button for changing the image on the button.

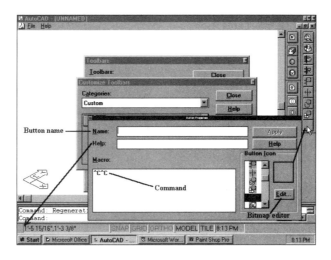

FIGURE 12.17 Button Programming dialogue box.

The command attached to a button can be a core command, system variable, third-party routine, or a DIESEL command. The name and help areas are self-explanatory.

The fourth step to complete the customizing process is to edit the image on the button by selecting the **Edit...** button. This area is designed to allow you to attach an existing bitmap (.BMP file) to your button or design your own button graphic and export it to a file. Finish creating the PLAN button on the toolbar using the third and fourth steps.

Practice Procedure for Finishing the Customizing of the Toolbar

1. Select the new blank button on the 3Dtools toolbar by clicking the right mouse button over the blank button.

2. Type **Plan** into the Name edit box.

3. Type **Change view to the plan view of the current UCS** into the Help edit box.

4. Add **_plan;;** to the ^C^C macro line.

5. Select the **Edit...** button to activate the button image editor.

6. Create the word **Plan** by using the Windows standard tools in AutoCAD for creating icons as shown in Figure 12.18.

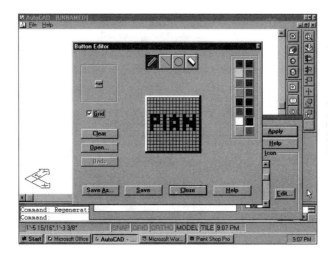

FIGURE 12.18 Button Editor dialogue box.

7. Select the **Save** button and then the **Close** button to exit the editor.

8. Select **Apply** on the Button Programming dialogue box.

9. Close the Button Programming dialogue box by picking the upper left corner minus sign.

10. Select **Close** to exit the Customize Toolbars and Toolbars dialogue boxes.

11. Move the cursor over the new Plan button and see the results of your work as shown in Figure 12.19.

The other variables and commands in this section are for practice purposes and to create the necessary tools you need for increasing your productivity. Feel free to add as many additional items as you want.

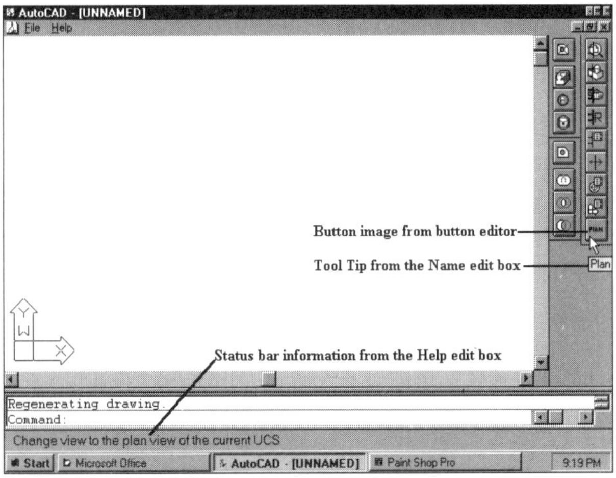

FIGURE 12.19 Customize Toolbars Plan button results.

To many buttons on a toolbar or too many toolbars active at the same time can be confusing to your eye. Find a balance that works for you.

TIP

The steps to add or change an existing button on a toolbar are always the same. They are presented here in a generic form for reference in the remaining practice procedures.

1. Use your right mouse button (the **Enter** button) over any toolbar button to activate the Toolbars dialogue box.

2. Select the **New...** button and give the toolbar a name. (This step is only used when you need to create a totally new toolbar.)

3. Select the **Customize...** button to activate the Customize toolbars dialogue box.

4. Select the **Category** you wish to take a button from or drag a button from an existing toolbar.

5. Activate the Button Programming dialogue box by using your right mouse button over the button you wish to program.

6. Fill out the information in the Button programming dialogue box (Name, Help, and Macro).

7. Change or add a bitmap image to the button by using the Button Editor that is accessed from the **Edit...** button on the programming dialogue box.

8. Apply all changes and close all dialogue boxes to finish.

The above steps are repeated every time you edit a toolbar. The steps are referred to as the basic steps in the following procedures.

VPORTS

The VPORTS command is not on any of the toolbars. You can practice the method of creating a new button by copying an existing button to add this command to the 3DTOOLS toolbar.

Practice Procedure to Copy an Existing Button to a Toolbar

1. Use your right mouse button (the **Enter** button) over any toolbar button to activate the Toolbars dialogue box.

2. Select the **Customize...** button to activate the Customize toolbars dialogue box.

3. Hold down the **Control** key and select the **REGENALL** button and drag the button to the bottom of the same toolbar, as shown in Figure 12.20.

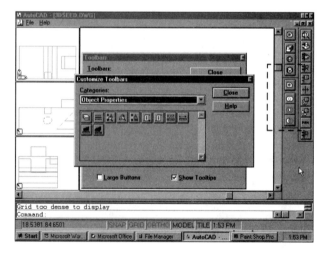

FIGURE 12.20 VPORTS command button copy results.

4. Activate the Button Programming dialogue box by using your right mouse button over the copied button at the bottom of the toolbar.

5. Fill out the information in the Name, Help, and Macro edit boxes as shown in Figure 12.21.

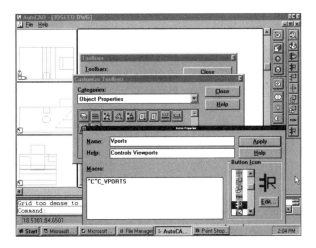

FIGURE 12.21 VPORTS command button programming reference.

6. Edit the button image by selecting the **Edit...** button and making the image appear as shown in Figure 12.22 (erase the whole R).

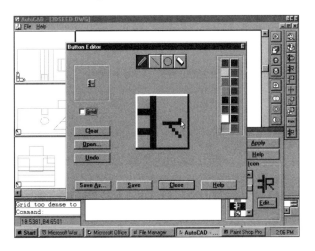

FIGURE 12.22 VPORTS button image.

7. Apply the changes and close the dialogue boxes.

The results are shown in Figure 12.23. Both methods for creating a button (copying from the Category or from an existing button) have their advantages. It is always easier to edit an existing button image and information but sometimes you do not have any existing buttons that come close to the image you want. Either method is appropriate when you have the need to use it.

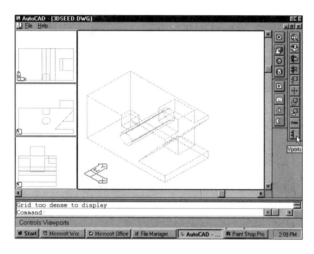

FIGURE 12.23 VPORTS command button results.

UCS

The UCS command and its options are on the Standard toolbar as a flyout menu. Since you do not have either of the AutoCAD menus attached while creating this menu, you must use the Category choice from the Customize dialogue box.

Practice Procedure to Copy a Button from UCS to a Toolbar

1. Use your right mouse button (the **Enter** button) over any toolbar button to activate the Toolbars dialogue box.

2. Select the **Customize...** button to activate the Customize toolbars dialogue box.

3. Select the UCS flyout button from the Standard **Category** and drag it to the bottom of the 3DTOOLS toolbar as shown in Figure 12.24. (You can

do the same from the standard toolbar when you have the AutoCAD menu attached.)

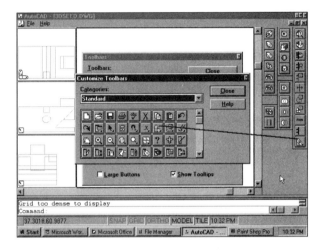

FIGURE 12.24 UCS command button copy results.

The results are shown in Figure 12.25 with the AutoCAD menu attached. The figure shows the results of the UCS flyout when the AutoCAD menu has been attached.

393

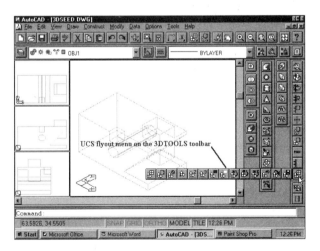

FIGURE 12.25 UCS button result.

The UCS flyout button does not work unless the ACAD or ACADFULL menu is attached. This is true of any flyout button you copy from the ACAD menus to your own toolbars that reside in your own menu.

NOTE

ELEVATION

The ELEVATION command is not on any menu or toolbar. Place this command on a new toolbar.

Practice Procedure to Create a New Toolbar and Place a Button on it

1. Use your right mouse button (the **Enter** button) over any toolbar button to activate the Toolbars dialogue box.

2. Select the **New...** button and give the new toolbar the name LOCATION as shown in Figure 12.26.

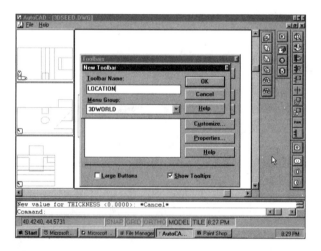

FIGURE 12.26 New Toolbar dialogue box.

3. Select the **Customize...** button to activate the Customize toolbars dialogue box.

4. Drag the **Layer** button from the Object Properties category to the new blank toolbar, as shown in Figure 12.27.

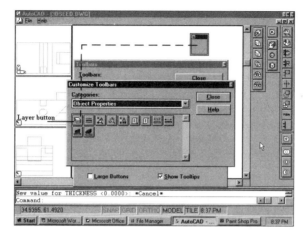

FIGURE 12.27 Layers button to the blank toolbar.

5. Use the right mouse button on the new button of the new toolbar to activate the Button Programming dialogue box.

6. Change the information in the Name, Help, and Macro edit boxes to those shown in Figure 12.28.

395

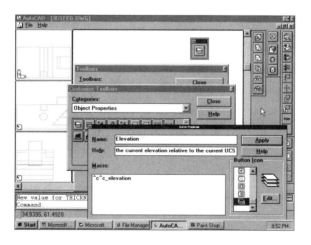

FIGURE 12.28 Button information.

7. Select the **Edit...** button and change the image on the button to the one shown in Figure 12.29.

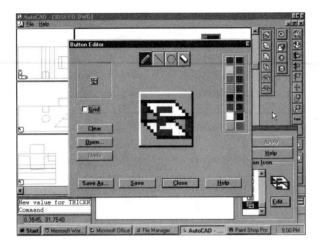

FIGURE 12.29 Button image changes.

8. Apply the image and close all the dialogue boxes.

The results are shown in Figure 12.30. The above procedure is the standard method for creating a new toolbar.

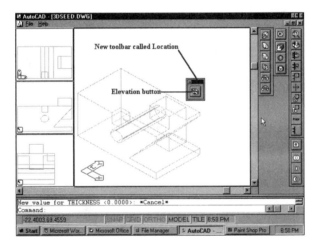

FIGURE 12.30 New toolbar and button results.

NOTE

The help string scrolls to the right when a help string is longer than the edit box length.

THICKNESS

The THICKNESS command is not on any menu or toolbar. Place this command on the new toolbar.

Practice Procedure to Create a New Toolbar and Place a Button on it

1. Use your right mouse button (the **Enter** button) over any toolbar button to activate the Toolbars dialogue box.

2. Select the **Customize...** button to activate the Customize toolbars dialogue box.

3. Drag the **Blank** button from the Custom category to the new Location toolbar with the ELEVATION button on it, as shown in Figure 12.31.

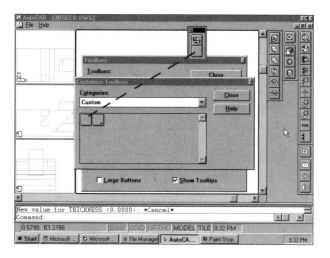

FIGURE 12.31 Blank button to the Location toolbar.

4. Change the information in the Name, Help, and Macro edit boxes to those shown in Figure 12.32.

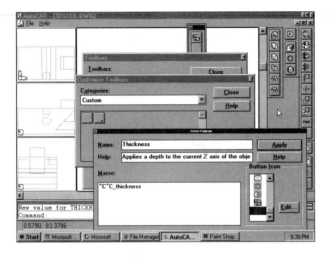

FIGURE 12.32 Button information.

5. Select the **Edit...** button and change the image on the button to the one shown in Figure 12.33.

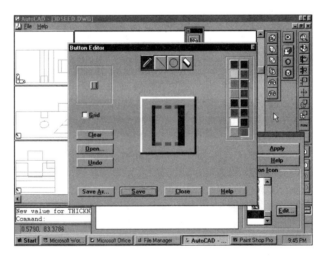

FIGURE 12.33 Button image changes.

6. Apply the image and close all of the dialogue boxes.

The results are shown in Figure 12.34.

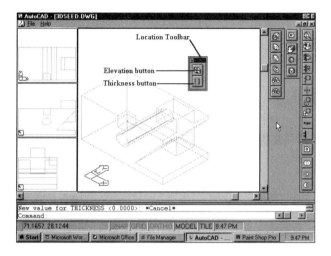

FIGURE 12.34 Thickness button results.

Surface Variables Toolbar

None of the surface variables are on any menus or toolbars. These variables include:

- SPLFRAME
- SURFU
- SURFV
- SURFTYPE
- SURFTAB1
- SURFTAB2

They have all been added to the 3DWORLD menu in a toolbar called 3DWORLD. SURFVARS, as shown in Figure 12.35. Activate the toolbar by typing **toolbar** and the name of the toolbar. Select the show option and the toolbar appears. You can add any other surface button to the toolbar at your own discretion.

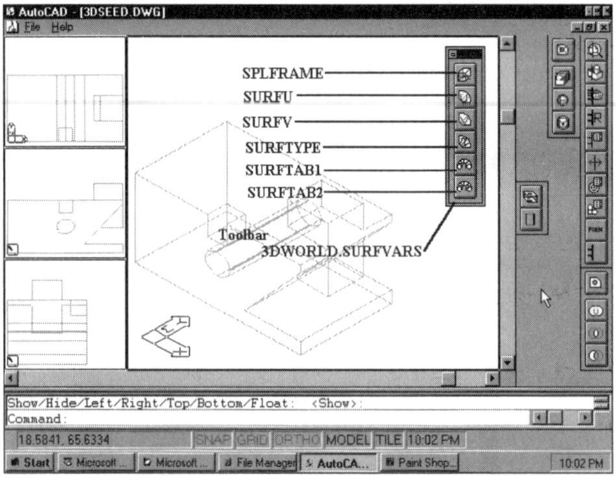

FIGURE 12.35 Surface Variables toolbar.

Region and Solid Variables on a Toolbar

None of the region or solid variables are on any menus or toolbars. These variables include:

- DELOBJ
- ISOLINES
- FACETRES
- DISPSILH

They have all been added to the 3DWORLD menu in a toolbar called 3DWORLD. SOLIDVARS, as shown in Figure 12.36. Activate the toolbar by typing **toolbar** and the name of the toolbar. Select the show option and the toolbar appears. You can add any other surface button to the toolbar at your own discretion.

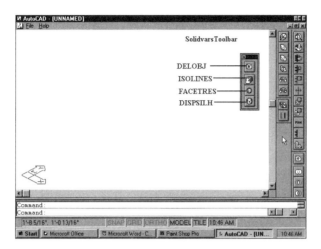

FIGURE 12.36 Solid Variables toolbar.

The 3DTOOLS Toolbar

This toolbar contains the supplied routines from this book and a few AutoCAD core commands. The buttons are:

- ZOOMALL
- HIDEALL
- SHADEALL
- REGENALL
- DDVPORTS
- Swap Viewports
- Named Views
- Named UCS
- PLAN
- VPORTS
- UCS flyout menu

NOTE

You might want to add the supplied routine INTERSEC to this tool-bar or add it to a new surfaces toolbar.

The toolbar is activated using the TOOLBAR command and using the name 3DWORLD.3DTOOLS. The toolbar is shown in Figure 12.37.

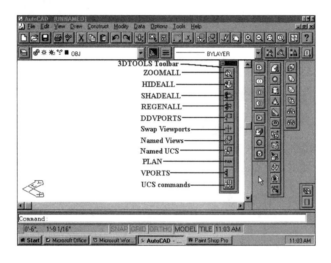

FIGURE 12.37 3DTOOLS toolbar.

The Solid Edit Toolbar

This toolbar contains the commands used to edit solids that are not on the ACAD.SOLIDS toolbar. The commands are on other toolbars, but they have been consolidated onto this toolbar for convenience. The commands include:

- REGION
- UNION
- INTERSECTION
- SUBTRACT

The toolbar is activated using the TOOLBAR command and using the name 3DWORLD.SOLID_EDIT. The toolbar is shown in Figure 12.38.

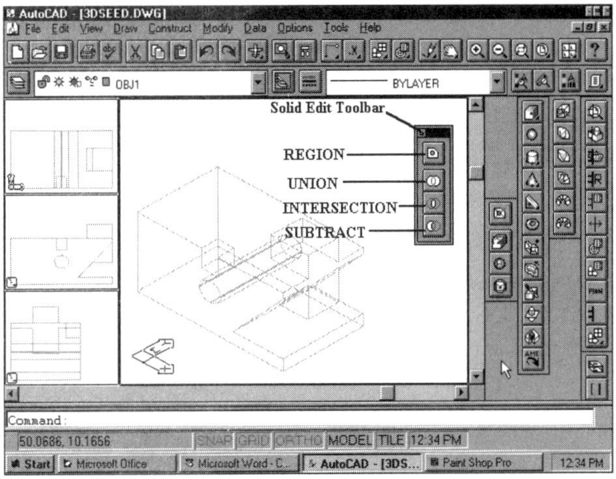

FIGURE 12.38 SOLID_EDIT toolbar.

NOTE

The spacer between the top button and the rest of the buttons on this toolbar can be added by inserting into the .MNS file the line [- - -] between the lines of code for the first two buttons in the ★★SOLID_EDIT toolbar.

403

In Conclusion

This chapter has reviewed two methods for increasing your productivity. 3D prototype drawings with their views, Viewports, lights, scenes, and other tools make starting a new drawing faster and the various toolbars containing the 3D commands and supplied routines. Several methods for creating or modifying a toolbar were introduced. Everything in this chapter is user-friendly and logical. You do not have to be a programmer or CAD guru to implement these simple steps.

GLOSSARY

3D primitive	An internally defined 3D surface object representing a basic shape.
3D solid primitive	An internally defined 3D solid object representing a basic shape.
ACIS solids	The AutoCAD R13 internal solids definition.
AME solids	The AutoCAD R12 solids definition.
angle	The measurement from the point from which two lines or surfaces diverge.
AutoLISP	A mid-level programming language used to create macros and programs to augment the AutoCAD commands. LISP means LISt Processing.
axis	A central line about which positions are referred.
binary format	A format of data storage that is computer compatible. This format cannot be read by the user.
Cartesian plane	The mathematical term used for the XY plane.
coordinate systems	Absolute, relative, polar, cylindrical, and spherical methods of placing geometry.
cylindrical system	Calculates a point using a distance and angle in the XY plane and a distance from the origin point from the XY plane.
dialogue box	Graphical user interface for collecting data.
direction	Any way in which one may face or point.

ECS	The Entity Coordinate System is the internal coordinate system AutoCAD uses on every object to keep track of the object orientation in 3D space.
elevation	Distance measured along the Z axis of the current UCS from zero.
from **the XY plane**	Defining an angle relative to the working plane using the X and Z axis.
hide	Remove lines and surfaces from the view that are covered by surfaces closer to your view.
in **the XY plane**	Defining an angle relative to the working plane using the X and Y axis.
ISO view	An isometric view above your object, generally from 31 to 35 degrees, measured between the X and Z axis.
M direction	Variable direction of a mesh based on the creation of the object, not the X or Y plane.
materials	The definition of properties applied to an object to be used in a render.
N direction	Variable direction of a mesh based on the creation of the object, not the X or Y plane.
palette	The definition of the number of colors allowed on screen or in the output file.
plan view	A view of the current UCS work plane from directly above.
prototype	The original drawing from which other drawings are created.
quadrant	The fourth part of the circumference of a circle; an arc of 90 degrees.
raster format	A file that stores pixel data instead of vector data. GIF, TIF, BMP, WMF, PostScript, and many other raster file formats are supported by AutoCAD.
relative spherical system	Calculates a point using a distance and angle in the XY plane and an angle from the origin point from the XY plane.

render	To rasterize objects into an image.
resolution	A measurement of output density given in the form of horizontal/vertical pixels on the screen or dots per inch for paper output.
right–hand rule	A technique for visualizing the XYZ axis of 3D space.
SAT file format	A file format that is used to transfer ACIS solids information that can be used in other programs, including statistical analysis programs and other CAD programs.
scene	The definition of lights and views to be used during a render.
solids	3D objects that have the characteristics of a solid object.
stereolithography prototype	A relatively cheap way of creating a prototype part by layering the part using lasers and the information from ACIS solids.
surfaces	The skin or exterior of a wireframe area. Wireframe surfaces are defined with 3 or 4 points. Solids define their own surfaces.
system variable	A control switch or value used to change the way a command or the environment behaves.
thickness	The width of an object as measured along either the X or Y axis of the current UCS.
toolbar	A menu interface that contains buttons for command selection. The toolbar can float anywhere on the screen or be docked on the sides, above, or below.
UCS	The User Coordinate System command controls the flat XY (working) plane position. You can change the working plane with this command.
UCSIcon	Controls the display of the User Coordinate System icon.
vector	A point. Angles can be measured between two vectors (points).

WCS   The World Coordinate System is the default XYZ planes inside AutoCAD. This working plane never changes.

wireframe   3D object created using lines, arcs, and circles. No surface or solid features are present.

XY plane   Flat 2D work area that can be rotated in any direction.

XYZ axis   The central lines defining the reference position for 3D space.

XYZ plane   Spherical 3D work area that can be rotated in any direction.

INDEX

3DARRAY, 139
   Rectangular, 139
   Polar, 141
3DFACE, 147, 149, 150, 177, 181
3DMESH, 157, 183
3DPOLY, 80, 82, 109
3D Prototype, 367
3DStudio, 337, 348, 349

A

ACISOUT, 273
ACIS solids, 109, 189, 190, 191
ALIGN, 120
AMECONVERT, 262
AME solids, 59, 109, 191
Assemblies, 275
AutoCAD color wheel, 301
AutoVision, 337

B

Bitmap, 348
Boolean operations, 191
Bump map, 348

C

Cartesian plane, 11, 16
Chamfer, 232, 234
CHPROP, 62
Color palette, 300
Control Panel, 303, 304
Coplanar, 115, 218, 224, 232
Copy, 100
Coons surface patch, 179
Coordinate Systems, 67
   Absolute, 27, 67
   Cylindrical, 67

Polar, 27, 67

Relative, 27, 67

Spherical, 67

D

Data eXchange Binary file
  (DXB), 146

DDVPOINT, 15

DDVIEW, 50, 54

Dialogue boxes

  3DStudio file export, 292

  3D Surface Primitives, 94

  AutoCAD Color Index
    (ACI), 359

  Attach by Layer, 361

  Button Editor, 388

  Button Programming, 387

  Color, 327

  Customize Toolbars, 385

  Define New View, 51

  DDCHPROP, 157

  DDMODIFY, 156

  DDVIEW, 50

  DDVPORTS, 93

  DXFOUT, 282

  Export Data, 294

  File Output Configuration, 311

  Library File, 340

  Lights, 316

  Materials, 350

  Materials library, 338

  Modify Standard Material, 350

  Named UCS, 44

  New Distant Light, 320

  New Point Light, 318

  New Scene, 332

  New Spotlight, 323

  New Toolbar, 394

  Plot, 285

  Preset UCS, 43

  Reconcile Exported Material
    Names, 346

  Render, 307

  Render preferences, 313

  Render Statistic's, 314

  Scenes, 331

  Select Color, 327

  Select device, 305

  Surface Primitives, 94

  Tile Viewport Layout, 57

  Toolbars, 384

  View Control, 51

  Viewpoints Preset, 14

  UCS, 392

DIESEL, 387

Dimensioning, 276

  Model space, 276

Paperspace, 279
DVIEW, 1, 17, 19, 33, 34
   The Camera option, 19, 21, 22
   The Clip option, 29
   The Distance option, 24
   The Hide option, 19
   The Off option, 24, 25
   The Pan option, 27
   The Points option, 25
   The Select objects: prompt, 18
   The specify a point option, 32
   The Target option, 23
   The Twist option, 28
   The Undo option and Exit
     option, 32
   The Zoom option, 24, 27

E

EDGE, 145, 152, 179
EDGESURF, 167, 168, 180, 183
Elevation, 60, 80, 82, 394
Entity Coordinate System (ECS),
  62, 76
Export file formats, 281, 294
   CAD output formats, 281
     DXB, 284
     DXBIN, 284
     DXFOUT, 282

Image output formats, 286
   BMPOUT, 288
   MSLIDE, 287
   PSOUT, 288
   WMFOUT, 289
  Solids output file format, 289
   ACISOUT, 291
   STLOUT, 289
  Surfaces output file formats, 291
   3DSOUT, 292
EXTEND, 115, 116
Extrude, 201, 217, 227, 229

F

FILLET, 112, 232, 233
Filter, 194

G

Geometric Calculator, 68
Gradation, 301

H

Hardware, 294
Hidden line removal, 63, 97
HIDE, 6, 145, 148
HIDEALL, 91, 111

I

Interfere, 260
Interference, 201
Intersec, 222
Intersect, 217, 221, 240
Intersection, 201, 217
ISO view, 71, 95, 98, 102, 371, 372

L

Layer Control, 103
Libraries, 275
Libraries of Assemblies, 275
Lights, 315, 377
LIST, 60, 61

M

Mass property, 201
  MASSPROP, 217, 224, 236
    Area, 224
    Bounding box, 224, 225
    Centroid, 224, 225
    Mass, 225
    Moments of inertia, 225
    Perimeter, 224
    Principal moments and directions about a centroid, 225
    Products of inertia, 225
    Radii of gyration, 225
    Volume, 225
Materials library, 338
MATLIB, 337, 338, 351
Menu, 384
  Locations
    3DAarray, 144
    3Dface, 151
    3Dmesh, 159
    3DSurfvars, 168
    3D Surface Primitives, 94, 162
    Align, 123
    DDView, 52
    DELOBJ, 194
    Edge, 154
    Edgesurf, 180
    Elevation, 61
    Export Commands, 293
    Extrude, 231
    Hide, 147
    MASSPROP, 226
    Mirror3D, 138
    Pan, 47
    PEDIT, 187
    Plan, 39
    Pface, 160
    Point Filters, 66
    Rendering, 333

Render Materials, 362

Revsurf, 171

Rotate3D, 129

Rulesurf, 178

Slice, Section, Interfere, AMECONVERT, 263

Solid, 182

Solid Primitives, 214

Subtract, Union, Intersection, 223

Thickness, 64

UCS, 42, 80

VPOINT, 13

VPORTS, 56

Zoom, 48

Menuload, xiii, xiv, 117, 383

Menu search hierarchy, 382

Meshes, 154, 157, 160, 163, 184, 365

MIRROR3D, 129, 131

Last option, 135

Plane by Object, 131

View option, 135

The 3points option, 138

The XY, YZ, and ZX options, 136

Zaxis option, 133

Modeling, 265

Architectural, 268, 364

Engineering, 273

Expectations, 266

Manufacturing, 270

Mechanical, 273

Staging, 275

Visual Organization, 276

P

PAN, 45, 52, 102

PEDIT, 157, 164, 166, 183, 184

Desmooth, 186

Edit vertex, 184

Mclose, 186

Nclose, 187

Smooth surface, 186

PFACE, 154, 160

PLAN, 1, 2, 34, 35, 40, 58

World, 36

UCS, 37, 38

PLINE, 109

Point filters, 64

Polygon mesh, 160

primitive shapes, 85, 160

Creating a 3D Sphere with the AI_SPHERE command, 91

Creating a Wedge with the AI_WEDGE command, 89

The 3D Box AI_BOX command, 86

413

The 3D Cone using
AI_CONE, 91
The 3D Dish created by the
AI_DISH command, 94
The 3D Dome AI_DOME
command, 90
The 3D Torus using the
AI_TORUS command, 92
The Pyramid AI_PYRAMID
command, 87
PROJMODE, 115, 116, 120
Productivity routines, 383
Prototypes, 297

R

RECTANG, 82
Redraw, 58
REDRAWALL, 58
Reflection map, 147
REGEN, 147
REGENALL, 58, 147, 401
Region modeler, 191, 215, 218,
223, 232
Rendering, 299, 306, 377
Hardware requirements, 305
RENDER command, 181
Resolution, 300
REVOLVE, 217
REVSURF, 167, 168, 170, 183

RGB, 300
right-hand rule, 10, 78
RMAT, 337, 349, 355
ROTATE3D, 123, 125, 127
RULESURF, 174, 176
RYB, 300

S

Scenes, 331, 379
Section, 217, 258
SHADEALL, 158, 162, 238,
271, 401
Slice, 201, 217, 242
<3points>, 255
By Object, 243
View, 248
XY, 250
YZ, 250
Zaxis, 245
ZX, 250
Software, 296
SOLID command, 181
SOLIDS, 200
Box, 201
Cylinder, 205
Cone, 206
Sphere, 204
Torus, 211
Wedge, 209

Solid primitives, 200
Stereolithography apparatus
    format, 265
STRETCH, 112, 113
Subassemblies, 275, 276
Subtract, 217, 218, 237
Subtraction, 191
System Variables
    APPINT, 119, 120
    DELOBJ, 193
    DISPSILH, 195, 198, 199, 201
    FACETRES, 195, 197, 200,
        201, 290
    PROJMODE, 115, 116
    ISOLINES, 195, 196, 201
    SPLFRAME, 156, 163
    SURFTAB1, 167, 169, 171, 173,
        174, 179
    SURFTAB2, 167, 169, 179
    SURFTYPE, 164, 166, 186
    SURFU, 164, 166, 186
    SURFV, 164, 166, 186
    UCSFOLLOW, 44, 45
SWAPVP, 56, 111

Thickness, 61, 62, 397
Tools, 59
    Coordinate Systems, 67
        Absolute, 27, 67
        Cylindrical, 67
        Polar, 27, 67
        Relative, 27, 67
        Spherical, 67
    Elevation, 60, 80, 82
    Geometric Calculator, 68
    grid/snap, 71
    Object snaps, 71, 119
    ortho mode, 71
    Point filters, 64
    Thickness, 61, 62
Toolbars, 367, 382-386, 390, 392,
    394, 397, 399-403
    3Dtools, 401, 402
    3D Viewpoints Preset, 16
    Custom 3D tools, 117
    Draw, 182
    Modify, 123, 138, 144, 223
    Object Properties, 227
    Pan, 42
    Point filters, 66
    Properties, 157
    Render, 147, 152, 334, 362
    Solids, 214, 232, 263
    Solid_edit, 223, 402, 403
    Solidvars, 200, 400

T

TABSURF, 171, 173, 183
Tessellation lines, 195, 197
Texture map, 348

Standard, 42, 49, 53
Surfaces, 151, 155, 159, 171, 174,
 178, 181
 Surfvars, 168, 399
 UCS, 42
 View, 52, 53
 VPOINT, 17
 Zoom, 49
TRIM, 115, 116

U

UCSFOLLOW, 44, 45, 97, 101,
 102, 113
UCSICON, 2, 3, 38
Union, 201, 217, 218, 239
Units, 788
User Coordinate System (UCS), 2,
 35, 36, 39, 40, 41, 60, 71, 77, 97,
 98, 100, 113, 142, 368, 370, 392
 The 3point option, 75
 The ? option, 79
 The Object option, 76
 The Origin option, 72
 The Prev option, 79
 The Restore, Save, and Del
  options, 79
 The View option, 77
 The <World> option, 80

The X option, Y option, and
 Z option, 77
The Zaxis option, 73

V

Video card, 303
VIEW, 34
Views, 2, 371
VIEWPORTS, 54, 373, 374
VPOINT, 1, 7, 17, 33, 34
 The VPOINT Rotate option, 7,
  16, 17, 19, 20, 74
 The VPOINT Tripod option, 10
 The VPOINT Vector option, 8
 Presets, 14
VPORTS, 34, 54, 58, 390

W

Wildcards, 80
Windows 3.x, 303
Windows 95, 304
Wireframe drawing commands, 80
 The 3D polyline, 80, 82, 109
World Coordinate System (WCS),
 4, 60, 119
WYSIWYG, 22

X

XLINE, 103
XY plane, 2, 4

Z

ZOOM, 2, 48, 49, 52, 102
ZOOMALL, 91, 102, 111

About the Disk

To use the companion disk for 3D AutoCAD, create a subdirectory on your hard disk called 3DWORLD, then add the directory path to your AutoCAD support directory line in the Preferences dialogue box. All the companion disk files are contained in a self-extracting archive called 3DWORLD.EXE. Copy the file into the directory you created and run it to expand the files. You will also need to designate the 3DPROTO drawing supplied on the disk as the default prototype drawing for your work sessions.